MY SERMON NOTES

MY SERMON NOTES

CHARLES H. SPURGEON

VOLUME 3
MATTHEW TO ACTS

BAKER BOOK HOUSE
Grand Rapids, Michigan 49506

First published in 1884

First reprinted 1981 by
Baker Book House Company

FOUR-VOLUME SET
ISBN: 0-8010-8201-3

Eleventh printing, April 1993

Printed in the United States of America

PREFACE

THIS is the third portion of "My Sermon Notes," and it consists of Notes of Sermons preached by me on Sabbath and Thursday evenings. I trust it will be helpful to men who are greatly occupied, and are therefore sorely pressed for subjects of discourse. One more selection of outlines—upon certain texts which range from Romans to Revelation—will complete the series. This last part I hope to prepare for publication before this year has quite run out. I might have taken longer time over the rest of the work ; but as the sale of the former volumes indicates a want, I feel bound to supply it as speedily as I can. "The night cometh, when no man can work."

I hope and believe that these Notes will not be of much use to persons who fail to think for themselves. For such talkers I have no sort of compassion. My outlines are meant to be aids to preparation, and nothing more. The theory that they will induce men to be idle is not supported by facts. Concerning this, information of the most reliable kind is forthcoming. Those who have valued them, and turned them to account, have almost always used them in the manner which I proposed to them : they have cut them up into several sermons, of have taken the raw material and rearranged it after their own fashion, and so have made it as good as new. In several instances brethren who have been necessarily occupied in visitation and other pastoral work have found great assistance from these summaries, and have been able on the Lord's-day to give their people a fair measure of spiritual food, by working out at full length the thoughts suggested. Knowing what it is to be hardly pressed myself, and remembering my great gratitude when a friend has suggested a theme and a line of thought, I am now happy in rendering to others a service which I have so often needed myself.

Mr. PAGE, of Chelsea, has again helped me in the somewhat difficult task of appending illustrations to the outlines. We have brought forth "things new and old." In this age of Cyclopædias it is hard to find anything which has not been used in some form or other ; but yet I hope that, to a fair extent, there is real freshness about these selections. At any rate, most of the quotations and anecdotes are new *to me*. The very oldest will be novel in some places, and to some hearers.

In all these outlines evangelical truth is set forth as clearly as I am able to do it. This will injure my work in the estimation of those whose admiration I do not covet; but this will cause me no alarm, for the weight of their censure is not great. My conviction is, that the lovers of the Old Gospel are far more numerous than the cold other-gospellers suspect, and that the orthodox are increasing every day. The mania of "advanced thought" has nearly had its day, and a sorry day it has proved to many. The will-o'-the-wisp has flitted on and on towards the pestilent swamps of Socinianism. At one time the pretended goddess was resplendent in fine apparel, but the foolish creature has danced itself threadbare : its tattered garments of pretentious knowledge no longer conceal its deformity.

Better days are coming for the lovers of the eternal verities. For a season we seemed to be surrounded by a torrent of unbelief; but the waters are assuaging, and the mountains of truth lift their peaks above the flood. Whatever the times may be, there shall be no doubt as to where the writer of these outlines took up his standing in the hour of controversy. I know nothing but the doctrines of grace, the teaching of the cross, the gospel of salvation ; and I write only that these things may be the more widely published. If those who believe these truths will honour me by using my Notes, I shall rejoice, and shall trust that the blessing of God will go with their discourses. It is no small pleasure to be helping brethren in the faith to sow beside all waters the living seed of the Word of God.

While all around us workers are being taken to their reward, it becomes us to be doubly diligent in our Lord's service. Let us all use such ability as we have. One can preach sermons without aid from books ; another can fill up a frame-work, though he cannot construct one for himself; a third can only read a discourse : let no man so envy his fellow's gift as to neglect his own; but let each one do what he can, and look up for a blessing.

To God I commend these baskets of fragments which remained after the multitudes were fed : the Master's example has encouraged me to "take up" what else had been forgotten.

WESTWOOD,
March, 1886

C. H. Spurgeon

CONTENTS

CXXX

𝔐𝔞𝔱𝔱𝔥𝔢𝔴 𝔦𝔳. 3 —" 𝔍𝔣 𝔱𝔥𝔬𝔲 𝔟𝔢 𝔱𝔥𝔢 𝔖𝔬𝔫 𝔬𝔣 𝔊𝔬𝔡."

There is no sin in being tempted; for the perfect Jesus " was in all points tempted like as we are : " Heb. iv. 15.

Temptation does not necessitate sinning; for of Jesus, when tempted, we read,—" yet without sin."

Not even the worst forms of it involve sin : for Jesus endured without sin the subtlest of temptations, from the evil one himself.

It may be needful for us to be tempted—

> For test. Sincerity, faith, love, patience, are thus put to proof.
> For growth. Temptation develops and increases our graces.
> For usefulness. We become able to comfort and warn others.
> For victory. How glorious to overcome the arch-enemy !
> For God's glory. He vanquishes Satan by feeble men.

Solitude will not prevent temptation.

> It may even aid it. Jesus was tempted in the wilderness.
> Nor will fasting and prayer always keep off the tempter; for these had been fully used by our Lord.

Satan knows how to write prefaces: our text is one.

> He began the whole series of his temptations by a doubt cast upon our Lord's Sonship, and a crafty quotation from Scripture.
> He caught up the echo of the Father's word at our Lord's baptism, and began tempting where heavenly witness ended.
> He knew how to discharge a double-shotted temptation, and at once to suggest doubt and rebellion : this was such—" If thou be the Son of God, command " &c.

I. THE TEMPTER ASSAILS WITH AN " IF."

1. Not with point-blank denial. That would be too startling. Doubt serves the Satanic purpose better than heresy.

2. He grafts his " if " on a holy thing. He makes the doubt look like holy anxiety concerning divine Sonship.

3. He ifs a plain Scripture. " Thou art my Son " : Ps. ii. 7.

4. He ifs a former manifestation. At his baptism God said, "This is my beloved Son." Satan contradicts our spiritual experience.

5. He ifs a whole life. From the first Jesus had been about his Father's business; yet after thirty years his Sonship is questioned.

6. He ifs inner consciousness. Our Lord knew that he was the Father's Son ; but the evil one is daring.

7. He ifs a perfect character. Well may he question us, whose faults are so many.

II. THE TEMPTER AIMS THE "IF" AT A VITAL PART.

1. At our sonship.
   In our Lord's case he attacks his human and divine Sonship.
   In our case he would make us doubt our regeneration.

2. At our childlike spirit. He tempts us to cater for ourselves.
   "Command that these stones be made bread."

3. At our Father's honour. He tempts us to doubt our Father's providence, and to blame him for letting us hunger.

4. At our comfort and strength as members of the heavenly family.
   By robbing us of our sonship, he would leave us orphans, and consequently naked, poor, and miserable.
   Thus he would have us hindered in prayer. How could we say, "Our Father" if we doubted our sonship? Matthew vi. 9.
   Thus he would destroy patience. How can we say, "Father, thy will be done," if we are not his sons? Luke xxii. 42.
   Thus he would lay us open to the next shot, whatever that might be. Doubt of sonship leaves us naked to the enemy.

III. THE TEMPTER SUPPORTS THAT "IF" WITH CIRCUMSTANCES.

1. You are alone. Would a Father desert his Child?

2. You are in a desert. Is this the place for God's Heir?

3. You are with the wild beasts. Wretched company for a Son of God!

4. You are an hungered. How can a loving Father let his perfect Son hunger?

Put all these together, and the tempter's question comes home with awful force to one who is hungry, and alone.

When we see others thus tried, do we think them brethren? Do we not question their sonship, as Job's friends questioned him? What wonder if we question ourselves!

IV. WHEN OVERCOME, THE TEMPTER'S "IF" IS HELPFUL.

1. As coming from Satan, it is a certificate of our true descent.
   He only questions *truth :* therefore we are true sons.
   He only leads *sons* to doubt their sonship ; therefore we are sons

2. As overcome, it may be a quietus to the enemy for years.

It takes the sting out of man's questionings and suspicions; for if we have answered the devil himself we do not fear men.

It puts a sweetness into all future enjoyment of OUR FATHER.

3. As past, it is usually the prelude to angels coming and ministering to us, as in our Lord's case. No calm is so deep as that which follows a great storm. Mark iv. 39.

Friend, are you in such relation to God that it would be worth Satan's while to raise this question with you?

Those who are not heirs of God are heirs of wrath.

SELECTIONS

What force there is often in a single monosyllable! What force, for instance, in the monosyllable " If," with which this artful address begins ! It was employed by Satan, for the purpose of insinuating into the Saviour's mind a doubt of his being in reality the special object of his Father's care, and it was pronounced by him, as we may well suppose, with a cunning and malignant emphasis. How different is the use which Jesus makes of this word "if" in those lessons of Divine instruction and heavenly consolation, which he so frequently delivered to his disciples when he was on earth ! He always employed it to inspire confidence; never to excite distrust. Take a single instance of this :—" If God so clothe the grass of the field, which to-day is, and to-morrow is cast into the oven, shall he not much more clothe you, O ye of little faith ? " What a contrast between this divine remonstrance and the malicious insinuation of the great enemy of God and man !

Daniel Bagot.

God had but one Son without corruption, but he had none without temptation. Such is Satan's enmity to the Father, that the nearer and dearer any child is to him, the more will Satan trouble him, and vex him with temptations. None so well-beloved as Christ; none so much tempted as he.—*Thomas Brooks.*

Satan doth not come to Christ thus, "Thou art not the Son of God"; or, " That voice which gave thee that testimony was a lie or a delusion." No, he proceeds by questioning, which might seem to grant that he was the Son of God, yet withal might possibly beget a doubt in his mind.—*Richard Gilpin.*

Oh, this word "*if*"! Oh, that I could tear it out of my heart ! O thou poison of all my pleasures ! Thou cold icy hand, that touchest me so often, and freezest me with the touch ! "*If! If!*"—*Robert Robinson.*

CXXXI

Matthew iv. 19 —*"And he saith unto them, Follow me, and I will make you fishers of men."*

Conversion is most fully displayed when it leads converts to seek the conversion of others : we most truly follow Christ when we become fishers of men.

The great question is not so much what we are naturally, as what Jesus makes us by his grace : whoever we may be of ourselves, we can, by following Jesus, be made useful in his kingdom.

Our desire should be to be men-catchers ; and the way to attain to that sacred art is to be ourselves thoroughly captured by the great Head of the College of Fishermen. When Jesus draws *us* we shall draw men.

I. SOMETHING TO BE DONE BY US. " Follow me."

1. We must be separated to him, that we may pursue his object.
   We cannot follow him unless we leave others. Matthew vi. 24.
   We must belong to him, that his design may be our design.

2. We must abide with him, that we may catch his spirit.
   The closer our communion with Christ, the greater our power with souls. Near following means full fellowship.

3. We must obey him, that we may learn his method.
   Teach what he taught. Matthew xxviii. 20.
   Teach as he taught. Matthew xi. 29 ; 1 Thessalonians ii. 7.
   Teach such as he taught, namely, the poor, the base, children, etc.

4. We must believe him, that we may believe true doctrine.
   Christ's own teaching catches men ; let us repeat it.
   Faith in Jesus on our part is a great force to beget faith.

5. We must copy his life, that we may win his blessing from God ; for God blesses those who are like his Son.

II. SOMETHING TO BE DONE BY HIM. "I will make you."

Our following Jesus secures our education for soul-winning.

1. By our following Jesus he works conviction and conversion in men ; he uses our example as a means to this end.

2. By our discipleship the Lord makes us fit to be used.
   True soul-winners are not self-made, but Christ-made.
   The making of men-catchers is a high form of creation.

3. By our personal experience in following Jesus he instructs us till we become proficient in the holy art of soul-winning.

12

4. By inward monitions he guides us what, when, and where to speak. These must be followed up carefully if we would win men.
5. By his Spirit he qualifies us to reach men. The Spirit comes to us by our keeping close to Christ.
6. By his secret working on men's hearts he speeds us in our work. He makes us true fishers by inclining men to enter the gospel net.

III. A FIGURE INSTRUCTING US. "Fishers of men." The man who saves souls is like a fisher upon the sea.
1. A fisher is dependent and trustful.
2. He is diligent and persevering.
3. He is intelligent and watchful.
4. He is laborious and self-denying.
5. He is daring, and is not afraid to venture upon a dangerous sea.
6. He is successful. He is no fisher who never catches anything.

See the ordination of successful ministers. They are made, not born : made by God, and not by mere human training.

See how we can partake in the Lord's work, and be specimens of his workmanship : " Follow me, and I will make you."

HOOKS

I love your meetings for prayer, you cannot have too many of them: but we must work while we pray, and pray while we work. I would rather see a man, who has been saved from the gulf below, casting life-lines to others struggling in the maelström of death, than on his knees on that rock thanking God for his own deliverance ; because I believe God will accept action for others as the highest possible expression of gratitude that a saved soul can offer.—*Thomas Guthrie.*

Ministers are fishers. A busy profession, a toilsome calling, no idle man's occupation, as the vulgar conceive it, nor needless trade, taken up at last to pick a living out of. Let God's fishermen busy themselves as they must, sometimes in preparing, sometimes in mending, sometimes in casting abroad, sometimes in drawing in the net, that they may " separate the precious from the vile," etc. (Jeremiah xv. 19, Matthew xiii. 48); and no man shall have just cause to twit them with idleness, or to say they have an easy life.—*John Trapp.*

The minister is a fisherman. As such he must fit himself for his employment. If some fish will bite only by day, he must fish by day if others will bite only by moonlight, he must fish for them by moonlight —*Richard Cecil.*

13

I watched an old man trout-fishing the other day, pulling them out one after another briskly. "You manage it cleverly, old friend," I said : "I have passed a good many below who don't seem to be doing anything." The old man lifted himself up, and stuck his rod in the ground. "Well, you see, Sir, there be three rules for trout-fishing, and 'tis no good trying if you don't mind them. The first is, Keep *yourself* out of sight ; and the second is, Keep yourself farther out of sight; and the third is, Keep yourself farther still out of sight. Then you'll do it." "Good for catching men, too," thought I.—*Mark Guy Pearse.*

> Lord, speak to me, that I may speak
> In living echoes of thy tone :
> As thou hast sought, so let me seek
> Thy erring children, lost and lone.
>
> O lead me, Lord, that I may lead
> The wandering and the wayward feet ;
> O feed me, Lord, that I may feed
> Thy hungering ones with manna sweet.
>
> O strengthen me, that while I stand
> Firm on the Rock, and strong in thee,
> I may stretch out a loving hand
> To wrestlers with the troubled sea.
>
> O teach me, Lord, that I may teach
> The precious things thou dost impart ;
> And wing my words, that they may reach
> The hidden depths of many a heart.
>
> *F. R. Havergal.*

The best training for a soul-saving minister is precisely that which he would follow if his sole object were to develop the character of Christ in himself. The better the man, the more powerful will his preaching become. As he grows like Jesus, he will preach like Jesus. Given like purity of motive, tenderness of heart, and clearness of faith, and you will have like force of utterance. The direct road to success in saving souls is to become like the Saviour. The imitation of Christ is the true art of sacred rhetoric.—*C. H. S.*

Mr. Jesse relates that certain fish give preference to bait that has been perfumed. When the prince of evil goes forth in quest of victims, there does not need much allurement added to the common temptations of life to make them effective. Fishers of men, however, do well to employ all the skill they can to suit the minds and tastes of those whom they seek to gain.—*G. McMichael.*

CXXXII

Matthew vii. 21—23 —"Not every one that saith unto me, Lord, Lord, shall enter into the kingdom of heaven; but he that doeth the will of my Father which is in heaven.

"Many will say to me in that day, Lord, Lord, have we not prophesied in thy name? and in thy name have cast out devils? and in thy name done many wonderful works?

"And then will I profess unto them, I never knew you: depart from me, ye that work iniquity."

One of the best tests of everything is how it will appear in the moment of death, in the morning of resurrection, and at the day of judgment. Our Lord gives us a picture of persons as they will appear "in that day."

Riches, honours, pleasures, successes, self-congratulations, etc., should all be set in the light of "that day."

This test should especially be applied to all religious professions and exercises; for "that day" will try these things as with fire.

The persons here depicted in judgment-light were not gross and open sinners; but externally they were excellent.

I. THEY WENT A LONG WAY IN RELIGION.

1. They made an open profession. They said, "Lord, Lord."
2. They undertook Christian service, and that of a high class: they habitually prophesied and worked miracles.
3. They had obtained remarkable success.
   Devils had owned their power.
4. They were noted for their practical energy.
   They had done *many* wonders: they were active in many ways.
   They had done wonders. Astonished everybody.
5. They were diligently orthodox.
   They did everything in the name of Christ. The words "Thy name" are mentioned three times.

II. THEY KEPT IT UP A LONG WHILE.

1. They were not silenced by men.
   No one discovered their falsehood, or detected their inconsistency.

2. They were not openly disowned by the Lord himself during life.

3. They were not made a laughing-stock by being left to use the holy name without result. Acts xix. 13—17.
Devils were cast out.

4. They expected to enter the Kingdom, and they clung to that false hope to the last.
They dared to say, " Lord, Lord," to Christ himself, at the last.

III. THEY WERE FATALLY MISTAKEN.

1. Their tongue was belied by their hand. They said, " Lord, Lord," but did not do the will of the Father.

2. They used the name which is named by disciples, but did not possess the nature of obedient servants. Luke vi. 46.

3. They prophesied, but did not pray.

4. They cast out devils, but the devil was not cast out of them.

5. They attended to marvels, but not to essentials.

6. They wrought wonders, but were also workers of iniquity.

IV. THEY FOUND IT OUT IN A TERRIBLE WAY.

They had the information from the mouth of him whom they called Lord. Here let us carefully notice—

1. The solemnity of what he said. " I never knew you." He had been omitted from their religion. What an oversight !

2. The terror of what it implied : they must depart from all hope, and continue for ever to depart.

3. The awful truth of what he said. They were utter strangers to his heart. He had not chosen them, nor communed with them, nor approved them, nor cared for them.

4. The solemn fixedness of what he said. His sentence would never be recalled, altered, or ended. It stood, " depart from me."

Brethren, the Lord cannot say to some of us that he does not know us, for he has often heard our voices, and answered our requests.
He has known us—
In repentance, seeking mercy, and receiving it.
In gratitude, blessing his gracious name.
In adversity, looking for his aid, and enjoying it.
In reproach, owning his cause under ridicule.
In difficulty, seeking help and safety under his wing.
In love, enjoying happy fellowship with him.
In these and many other ways he knows us.

Professors, does Jesus know you? The church knows you, the school knows you, the world knows you; does Jesus know you?

Come unto him, ye strangers, and find eternal life in him.

WARNINGS

In many simple works God is more seen than in wonderful works. The Pharisee at heaven's gate says, "Lord, I have done many wonderful works in thy name"; but, alas! has he ever made the Lord's name wonderful?—*T. T. Lynch.*

Pollok describes the hypocritical professor as—

> "The man that stole the livery of heaven
> To serve the devil in."

I knew you well enough for "black sheep," or, rather, for reprobate goats: I knew you for hirelings and hypocrites, but I never knew you with a special knowledge of love, delight, and complacency. I never acknowledged, approved, and accepted of your persons and performances. See Psalm i. 6; Romans xi. 2.—*John Trapp.*

Not "I once knew you, but cannot own you now"; but "I *never* knew you;—as real penitents, suppliants for pardon, humble believers, true followers."—*E. R. Conder.*

Note our Lord's open confession before men and angels, and specially to the men themselves—"I never knew you." I knew about you; I knew that you professed great things; but you had no acquaintance with me; and whatever you knew about me, you did not know *me.* I was not of your company, and did not know you. Had he once known them, he would not have forgotten them.

Those who accept his invitation, "Come unto me," shall never hear him say, "Depart from me." Workers of iniquity may now come to the Saviour for mercy; but if they set up a hope of their own, and ignore the Saviour, he will bid them depart to endure the rigours of his justice. Is it not striking that preachers, casters-out of devils, and doers of wonders, may yet be workers of iniquity? They may work miracles in Christ's name, and yet have neither part nor lot in him.—*C. H. S.*

"Depart *from me,*"—a fearful sentence, a terrible separation. "From me," saith Christ, that made myself man for your sakes, that offered my blood for your redemption. "From me," that invited you to mercy, and you would not accept it. "From me," that purchased a kingdom of glory for such as believed on me, and have resolved to honour their heads with crowns of eternal joy. "Depart from me:" from my friendship, my fellowship, my paradise, my presence, my heaven.

Thomas Adams.

CXXXIII

𝕸atthew biii. 7 —" 𝕬nb 𝕵esus saith unto him, 𝕴 will come anb heal him."

𝕷uke bii. 7 —" 𝕾ay in a worb, anb my serbant shall be healeb."

The centurion who cared for the religious welfare of the people, and built them a synagogue, had also a heart of compassion for the sick. It is well when public generosity is sustained by domestic kindness.

This servant was his boy, and perhaps his slave; but he was dear to him. A good master makes a good servant.

It is well when all ranks are united in sympathy: captain and page are here united in affection.

The master showed his affection by seeking help. Heart and hand should go together. Let us not love in word only.

It is well that the followers of Jesus should be ready to help all sick folk; and that healing should be still associated with prayer to Jesus.

Mark the growingly manifest faith of the centurion, and the growing manifestation of Jesus.

> Centurion sends elders with request to "come and heal." Jesus will come and heal
> Centurion comes himself asking for "a word." Jesus gives the word, and the deed is done.

We see in this passage a miracle in the physical world, and are thereby taught what our Lord Jesus can do in the spiritual world.

Let us imitate the centurion in seeking to Jesus about others.

We learn from the narrative—

I. THE PERFECT READINESS OF CHRIST.

1. He did not debate with the elders of the Jews, and show the weakness of their plea,—" He was worthy ": Luke vii. 4, 5.

2. He cheerfully granted their request, although it was needless for him to come. "Then Jesus went with them ": Luke vii. 6.

3. He did not raise a question about the change which the centurion proposed, although he was already on the road. Luke vii. 6.

4. He did not suspect the good man's motive, as some might have done. He read his heart, and saw his true humility.

5. He did not demur to the comparison of himself to a petty officer Our Lord is never captious; but takes our meaning.

6. He promptly accepted the prayer and the faith of the centurion, gave the boon, and gave it as desired.

Our Lord's love to sinners, his forgetfulness of self, his willingness to please us, and his eagerness to fulfil his own mission, should encourage us in prayer to him for ourselves and others.

II. THE CONSCIOUS ABILITY OF CHRIST.

1. He is not puzzled with the case. It was singular for the servant to be at once paralyzed and tormented; but whatever the disease may be, the Lord says, "I will come and heal him."

2. He is not put in doubt by the extreme danger of the servant. No, he will come to him, though he hears that he is stricken down, and is utterly prostrate.

3. He speaks of healing as a matter of course.
   His coming will ensure the cure: "come and heal."

4. He treats the method of procedure as of no consequence.
   He will come or he will not come, but will "say in a word"; yet the result will be the same.

5. He wonders more at the centurion's faith than at the cure.

Omnipotent grace moves with majestic ease.
We are worried and fretted, but the Lord is not.
Let us thus be encouraged to hope.

III. THE ABIDING METHOD OF CHRIST.

He is accustomed to heal by his Word through faith. Signs and wonders are temporary, and answer a purpose for an occasion; but both faith and the Word of the Lord are matters for all time.

Our Lord did not in the case before us put in a personal appearance, but spake, and it was done; and this he does in our own day.

1. This is coming back to the original form of working in creation.
   It is apparently a greater miracle than working by visible presence; at any rate, the means are less seen.

2. This method suits true humility. We do not demand signs and wonders; the Word is enough for us. Luke vii. 7.

3. This pleases great faith; for the Word is faith's chosen manifestation of God. It rejoices more in the Word than in all things visible. Psalm cxix. 162.

4. This is perfectly reasonable. Should not a word of command from God be enough? Mark the centurion's reasoning. Matt. viii. 9.

5. This is sure to succeed. Who can resist the divine fiat? In our own case, all we need is a word from the Lord.

6. This must be confidently relied on for others. Let us use the Word, and pray the Lord to make it his own word.

Henceforth, let us go forward in his name, relying upon his Word!

INSERTIONS

Had the centurion's roof been heaven itself, it could not have been worthy to be come under of him whose word was almighty, and who was the Almighty Word of his Father. Such is Christ confessed to be by him that says, "only say the word." None but a divine power is unlimited : neither hath faith any other bounds than God himself. There needs no footing to remove mountains, or devils, but a word. Do but say the word, O Saviour, my sin shall be remitted, my soul shall be healed, my body shall be raised from dust, and both soul and body shall be glorified.—*Bishop Hall.*

"I have been informed," says Hervey, "that when the Elector of Hanover was declared by the Parliament of Great Britain successor to the vacant throne, several persons of distinction waited upon his Highness, to make timely application for valuable preferments. Several requests of this nature were granted, and confirmed by a kind of promissory note. One gentleman solicited the Mastership of the Rolls. Being indulged in his desire, he was offered the same confirmation which had been vouchsafed to other successful petitioners ; upon which he seemed to be overcome by grateful confusion and surprise, and begged that he might not put the royal donor to such unnecessary trouble, protesting that he looked upon His Highness's word as the best ratification of his suit. With this compliment the Elector was not a little pleased. 'This gentleman,' he said, 'treats me like a king ; and, whoever is disappointed, he shall certainly be gratified.'"

Our Lord can cure either by coming or by speaking. Let us not dictate to him the way in which he shall bless us. If we were permitted a choice, we ought not to select that method which makes most show, but that in which there is least to be seen and heard, yet most to be admired. Comparatively, signs and wonders show less of him than his bare Word, which he has magnified above all his name. Marvels dazzle, but the Word enlightens. That faith which sees least sees most, and that which hath no eyes at all for the visible hath a thousand eyes for the invisible. Lord, come in thy glory, and bless me, if such be thy will; but if thou wilt stay where thou art, and bless me only through thy will and Word, I will be as well content, and even more so if this method the more honours thee !—*C. H. S.*

CXXXIV

Matthew ix. 9 —"*And as Jesus passed forth from thence, he saw a man, named Matthew, sitting at the receipt of custom: and he saith unto him, Follow me. And he arose, and followed him.*"

Matthew is here writing about himself. Note his modesty in the expression—"a man, named Matthew," and in his omission of the fact that the feast mentioned in verse 10 was held in his own house.

The story is placed immediately after a miracle, as if to hint that Matthew's conversion was a miracle.

There are points of similarity between the miracle and the conversion.

Matthew was spiritually palsied by his sins, and his money-making; hence he needed the divine command, "Arise, and walk."

There may be points of likeness also between Matthew's personal story and our own. These may be profitably considered.

I. His call seemed accidental and unlikely.

Jesus had often been at Capernaum, which he had selected to be "his own city"; and yet Matthew remained unsaved. Was it likely that he would now be called? Had not his day of grace closed?

Jesus was about other business; for we read, "as Jesus passed forth from thence." Would he now be likely to call Matthew?

Jesus left many other persons uncalled; was it not highly probable that the tax-gatherer would be passed by?

Yet Jesus called to himself this "man, named Matthew," while many another man had no such special call.

"He saw a man, named Matthew," for he foresaw him.

He knew him, for he foreknew him.

In all which there is a parallel between Matthew and ourselves.

II. His call was altogether unthought of and unsought.

1. He was in a degrading business. None but the lowest of the Jews would care to gather taxes for the Roman conqueror. His discipleship would bring no honour to the Lord Jesus.

2. He was in an ensnaring business. The publicans usually made a personal profit by extorting more than was due. He was not paying away, but sitting "at the receipt of custom; and this is a pleasing exercise." Money is bird-lime to the soul.

3. He would not have dared to follow Jesus even if he had wished to do so. He felt himself to be too unworthy.

21

4. He would have been repulsed by the other disciples had he proposed to come without the Lord's open invitation.

5. He made no sign in the direction of Jesus. No prayer was offered by him, nor wish expressed towards better things.

The call was of pure grace, as it is written, "I am found of them that sought me not."

III. HIS CALL WAS GIVEN BY THE LORD, WITH FULL KNOWLEDGE OF HIM.

Jesus " saw a man, named Matthew," and called him.

1. He saw all the evil that had been in him, and was yet there.

2. He saw his adaptation for holy service, as a recorder and penman.

3. He saw all that he meant to make of him.

4. He saw in him his chosen, his redeemed, his convert, his disciple, his apostle, his biographer.

The Lord calls as he pleases, but he sees what he is doing. Sovereignty is not blind ; but acts with boundless wisdom.

IV. HIS CALL WAS GRACIOUSLY CONDESCENDING.

The Lord called " a man, named Matthew,"—that was his best.

He was a publican—that may not have been his worst.

He allowed such a sinner to be his personal attendant ; yea, called him to that honour, saying, " Follow *me*."

He allowed him to do this immediately, without putting him into quarantine. He was to follow the Lord there and then.

V. HIS CALL WAS SUBLIMELY SIMPLE.

1. Few were the words : " Follow me."
   It is very tersely recorded, " He saw. . he saith. . he arose."

2. Clear was the direction : " Follow me."

3. Personal was the address : " He saith *unto him*."

4. Royal was the command : " He saith."

VI. HIS CALL WAS IMMEDIATELY EFFECTUAL.

1. Matthew followed at once. " He arose, and followed him."

2. He followed spiritually as well as literally. He became a sincere, devout, earnest, intelligent disciple.

3. He followed wholly : bringing his voice and his pen with him.

4. He followed growingly, more and more.

5. He followed ever after, never deserting his Leader.

What a call was this! None could have given it but the Lord.

VII. His call was a door of hope for others.

1. His salvation encouraged other publicans to come to Jesus.
2. His open house gave opportunity to his friends to hear Jesus.
3. His personal ministry brought others to the Saviour.
4. His written gospel has convinced many, and will always do so.

Are *you* up to your neck in business? Are you "sitting at the receipt of custom?" Yet may a call come to you at once. It does come.

Hear it attentively, rise earnestly, and respond immediately.

Good Words

God often calls men in strange places. Not in the house of prayer, not under the preaching of the Word ; but when all these things have been absent, and all surrounding circumstances have seemed most adverse to the work of grace, that grace has put forth its power. The tavern, the theatre, the ball-room, the gaming-house, the race-course, and other similar haunts of worldliness and sin, have sometimes been the scenes of God's converting grace. As an old writer says : " Our calling is uncertain in respect of place, for God calls some from their ships, and some from their shops ; some from under the hedges, and others from the market; so that, if a man can but make out unto his own soul that he is certainly called, the time when and the place where matter little."

How I now loved those words that spake of a Christian's calling! As when the Lord said to one, " Follow me " ; and to another, " Come after me." Oh! thought I, that he would say so to me : how gladly would I run after him ! I could seldom read of any that Christ did call, but I presently wished, " Would I had been in their clothes! Would I had been born Peter, or John !" I often thought, " Would I had heard him when he called *them*, how would I have cried, 'O Lord, call me also !'" But I feared he would not call me.—*John Bunyan.*

We read in classic story how the lyre of Orpheus enchanted with its music, not only the wild beasts, but the very trees and rocks upon Olympus, so that they moved from their places to follow him; so Christ, our heavenly Orpheus, with the music of his gracious speech, draws after him those less susceptible to benign influences than beasts and trees and stones, even poor, hardened, senseless, sinful souls. Let him but strike his golden harp, and whisper in thy heart, "Come, follow me," and thou, like another Matthew, shalt be won.

CXXXV

Matthew ix. 36 —"He was moved with compassion on them."

The expression is very strong ($\dot{\epsilon}\sigma\pi\lambda\alpha\gamma\chi\nu\dot{\iota}\sigma\theta\eta$.) All that was within him was stirred by the sight which he beheld. He was full of emotion, and showed it in his whole person.

His yearning compassions gathered around ($\pi\epsilon\rho\dot{\iota}$) the people.

> Exhibit the picture of Jesus under strong emotion.
> This is a portrait of him as he appeared on many occasions.
> Indeed, the words before us might sum up his entire life.

Let us behold his compassion as manifested in—

I. THE GREAT TRANSACTIONS OF HIS LIFE.

1. The Eternal Covenant, in its conception, arranging, provisions, &c., is full of compassion to men.
2. The Incarnation of our Lord shows matchless compassion.
3. His living in the flesh among men declares it.
4. His bearing the death penalty is the highest fruit of it.
5. His intercession for sinners proves its continuance.

This is a wide subject. In every act of his grace the Lord of love manifests tender pity to men.

II. THE SPECIAL INSTANCES RECORDED BY THE EVANGELISTS.

1. In Matthew xv. 32, we see a fainting crowd, hungry, &c.
   A crowd is a sad sight : a crowd, when faint, is far more so.
   Such crowds are perishing in our cities to-day.
2. In Matthew xiv. 14, the sick are most prominent in the throng.
   Jesus lived in a vast hospital, himself suffering, as well as healing, the diseases of men.
   None can tell how deep is his pity for suffering humanity.
3. In the case mentioned in the text he saw an ignorant, neglected, perishing crowd.
   The sorrows, dangers, and sins of spiritual ignorance are great.
   The Lord Jesus is the Shepherd of the unshepherded.
4. In Matt. xx. 34, we see the blind. Jesus pities spiritual blindness.
   Dwell upon the interesting details of the two blind men.
5. In Mark i. 41, we see the leper. Christ pities sin-polluted men.
   Jesus compassionated the man who said " If thou wilt, thou canst."

6. In Mark v. 19, we have the demoniac.   Jesus pities tempted souls. The man out of whom he cast a legion of devils was to be dreaded, but the Lord gave him nothing but compassion. He pities rather than blames those sore vexed by the devil.
7. In Luke vii. 13, we meet with the widow of Nain.   The bereaved, the widow and fatherless are specially near to the heart of Jesus.

These instances should encourage similar cases to hope in our Lord.

III. THE FORESIGHTS OF COMPASSION.

Knowing our ignorance, needs, sorrows, the Lord Jesus has provided beforehand for our wants—

1. The Bible for our guidance and comfort.
2. The minister to speak as man to man, tenderly, experimentally.
3. The Holy Spirit to comfort us, and help our infirmity, in prayer, etc.
4. The mercy-seat as our constant resort.
5. The promises to be our perpetual food.
6. The ordinances to help our memories, and make truth vivid to us.

The whole system reveals a most compassionate Saviour.

IV. OUR PERSONAL RECOLLECTIONS PROVE THIS COMPASSION.

Let us remember how tenderly he dealt with us.

1. He tempered our convictions with intervals of hope.
2. He ended them ere they drove us to despair.
3. He has moderated our afflictions, and sustained us under them.
4. He has taught us, as we have been able to bear it.   "I have many things to say unto you, but ye cannot bear them now."
5. He has put us to graduated tasks.
6. He has returned to us in love after our backslidings.

Let us trust in this divine mercifulness for ourselves.
Let us commend it to those around us.
Let us imitate it in dealing compassionately with our fellows.

TOUCHES FOR THE PORTRAIT

The literal translation is—"All his bowels were agitated, and trembled with sympathy and compassion."   The ancients believed the bowels to be the seat of sympathy, or mercy.   The Greek word used here to denote compassion is the most expressive that human language is capable of employing, insomuch that our version utterly fails to convey the vastness and fulness of the meaning of the original.—*Dr. Cumming.*

Compare the impression produced upon Xerxes by the sight of his enormous army. "His heart swelled within him at the sight of such a vast assemblage of human beings ; but his feelings of pride and pleasure soon gave way to sadness, and he burst into tears at the reflection that in a hundred years not one of them would be alive."

How a tender-hearted mother would plead with a judge for her child ready to be condemned! Oh, how would her bowels work ; how would her tears trickle down ; what weeping rhetoric would she use to the judge for mercy! Thus the Lord Jesus is full of sympathy and tenderness (Heb. ii. 17), that he might be a merciful High Priest. Though he hath left his passion, yet not his compassion. An ordinary lawyer is not affected with the cause he pleads, nor doth he care which way it goes ; profit makes him plead, not affection. But Christ intercedes feelingly ; and that which makes him intercede with affection is, it is his own cause which he pleads in the cause of his people.—*Thomas Watson.*

"Five hundred millions of souls," exclaimed a missionary (many years ago), "are represented as being unenlightened ! I cannot, if I would, give up the idea of being a missionary, while I reflect upon this vast number of my fellow-sinners, who are perishing for lack of knowledge. 'Five hundred millions' intrudes itself upon my mind wherever I go, and however I am employed. When I go to bed, it is the last thing that recurs to my memory ; if I awake in the night, it is to meditate on it alone; and in the morning it is generally the first thing that occupies my thoughts."

We may suppose that there was nothing in the external appearance of these multitudes which, to the common eye, would indicate their sad condition. We may suppose that they were "well-fed and well-clad", and that their hearts, under the influence of numbers, as is generally the case, were buoyant with pleasurable excitement ; that good humour sunned their countenances, and enlivened their talk, and that—both to themselves, and to the ordinary spectator—they were a happy folk. But he, who seeth not as man seeth, looked down through the superficial stream of pleasurable excitement which now flowed and sparkled, and saw—What ? Intellect enslaved, reason blinded, moral faculties benumbed, souls 'faint " and lost,—"*scattered abroad as sheep having no shepherd.*"—*David Thomas.*

CXXXVI

Matthew x. 27 —"What I tell you in darkness, that speak ye in light: and what ye hear in the ear, that preach ye upon the housetops."

Usefulness is the great desire of our souls if we are disciples of Jesus.

We believe that it will most surely be attained by our making known the gospel. We have full faith in "the foolishness of preaching."

We feel that we have need to receive that gospel personally from the Lord himself, or we shall not know it so as to use it aright.

We must not run till we are prepared. This verse describes, and by implication promises, the needful preparation of heart. Our Lord will speak in our ear : he will commune with us in solitude.

I. AN INVALUABLE PRIVILEGE. The disciple is associated very nearly with his Lord, and received into closest fellowship with him.

We see before us three important matters.

1. We are permitted to realize our Lord's presence with us personally.

He is still on speaking terms with us : still is he our Companion in the night, our Friend in solitude.

2. We are enabled to feel his word as spoken to us.

Immediately : "*I* tell *you*." Personal contact.

Forcefully : "in the ear." Not as thundered from Sinai, but as whispered by "a still, small voice." Still, very effectually.

3. We are privileged to receive such communications again and again :

"I tell you . . ye hear."

We need precept upon precept, line upon line.

Our Lord is willing to manifest himself to his own day by day.

We shall be wise to make occasions for hearing his voice in solitude, meditation, prayer, communion, &c.

We shall do well to use occasions of the Lord's own making such as the Sabbath, sickness, the night-watches, etc.

We need for a thousand reasons this private tuition, this personal communication with our Commander-in-chief.

II. A PREPARATORY PROCESS. We do not rightly perceive what we have to make known till Jesus personally imparts his holy teaching to our inmost hearts.

We see by reason of personal contact with our Lord—

1. Truth in its personality; living, acting, feeling; for he is "the way, the truth, and the life." Truth is no theory or phantom in Christ. Substantial truth is spoken by him.

2. Truth in its purity is found in him, in his written teaching, and in that which he speaks to the heart. Truth from man is mixed and adulterated; from Jesus it is unalloyed.

3. Truth in its proportions; he teaches all truth, in its true relations. Christ is no caricaturist, partisan, or politician.

4. Truth in its power. It comes strikingly, persuasively, convincingly, omnipotently from him. It quickens, and sustains.

5. Truth in its spirit. His words are spirit, life, love.

6. Truth in its certainty. "Verily, verily," is his motto.

7. Truth in its joyfulness. He speaks delight unto the soul. The truth in Jesus is glad tidings.

See the advantage of studying in Christ's College.

III. THE CONSEQUENT PROCLAMATION. What Jesus has told us alone in the dark we are to tell out openly in the light.

Courting publicity, we are to preach "upon the housetops."

What is this message which we have heard in the ear?

We bear our willing witness that—

1. There is peace in the blood of Jesus.

2. There is sanctifying power in his Holy Spirit.

3. There is rest in faith in our Lord and God.

4. There is safety in conformity to our great Exemplar.

5. There is joy in nearness to Jesus our Lord.

As we hear more we will tell more.

Oh, that men would receive our earnest testimony!

Will not you receive it who hear us at this present hour?

PRIVATE PENCILLINGS

Claus Hames, one of the most useful preachers in Germany, once met a friend to whom he told how many times daily he was obliged to speak. His friend presently asked, "But, Friend Hames, if thou hast so much to say, when art thou still? And when does the Spirit of God speak to thee?" That simple question so impressed Hames that he resolved from that time to devote a portion of each day to retirement and silent study.

"How is it?" said a Christian man to his companion, as they were both returning from hearing the saintly Bramwell, "How is it that Brother Bramwell always tells us so much that is new?" The companion answered, "Brother Bramwell lives so near the gates of heaven that he hears a great many things which the rest of us do not get near enough to hear."—*J. H. Hitchens.*

Of a certain preacher it was said: "He preaches as if Jesus Christ were at his side. Don't you see how every now and then he turns around as if he were saying: 'Lord Jesus, what shall I say next?'"

> Take my lips, and let them be
> Filled with messages from thee.
> > *F. R. Havergal.*

> Then sorrow touched by thee grows light,
> With more than rapture's ray;
> As darkness shows us worlds of light
> We never saw by day.
> > *Thomas Moore.*

Men learn in suffering what they teach in song.

Possessors of divine truth are eager to spread it. "For," as Carlyle says, "if new-got gold is said to burn the pockets till it be cast forth into circulation; much more may new-found truth."

A servant was desired by his master to carry a present of fish to a friend, and to do it as quickly as possible. In all haste the man seized a basket, and set out; but when he reached his journey's end he became a laughing-stock, for he had forgotten the fish: his basket was empty. Teacher! Preacher! let not the like happen to thee.

Often in the South of France have I needed to have a fire lighted; but I have found little or no comfort from it when my wish has been granted. The dwellers in that mild region build their fire-places so badly that all the heat goes up the chimney. No matter how big the blaze, the hearth only seems to warm itself. Thus many professors of our holy faith would seem to get grace, and light, and pious feeling for themselves only: their heat goes up their own chimney. What is told them in the dark they keep in the dark, and that which is spoken in their ear never blesses any other ear.— *C. H. S.*

CXXXVII

Matthew x. 30 —"But the very hairs of your head are all numbered."

How considerate of our fears is the Lord Jesus! He knew that his people would be persecuted, and he sought to cheer them.

In how sweet and homely a way he puts things! He deigns to speak about the hairs of our head. Here is a proverb, simple in words, but sublime in sense.

We think we see four things in this sentence.

I. FORE-ORDINATION. The text may be read, "have all been numbered." It is of the past as well as of the present.
1. Its extent. Predestination extends to everything.
   All the man; his being as a whole is foreknown. "In thy book all my members were written": Ps. cxxxix. 16.
   All that concerns him is foreknown; even to his hair, which may be shorn from him without damage to life or health.
   All that he does; even the least and most casual thought, or act.
   All that he undergoes. This may affect his hair so as to change its colour; but every hair blanched with sorrow is numbered.
2. Its source. The counting is done by the Lord.
3. Its lessons. Jesus mentions this fore-ordination for a purpose.
   To make us brave under trial.
   To teach us to be submissive.
   To help us to be hopeful.
   To induce us to be joyful.
4. Its influence. It ennobles us to be thus minutely predestinated. If God arranges even our hairs, we are honoured indeed.
To be the subject of a divine purpose of grace is glorious.

II. KNOWLEDGE. We are known so well as to have our hairs counted. Concerning this divine knowledge let us note—
1. Its character.
   Minute. "The very hairs of your head."
   Complete. The whole man, spirit, soul, and body, is thus most assuredly well known to the Omniscient Lord.
   Pre-eminent. God knows us better than we know ourselves, or than others know us; for neither we nor they have numbered the hairs of our head.

30

Tender. Thus a mother values each hair of her darling's head.

Sympathetic. God enters into those trials, those years, and those sicknesses which are registered in a man's hair.

Constant. Not a hair falls from our head without God.

2. Its lessons.

Concerning consecration, we are taught that our least precious parts are the Lord's, and are included in the royal inventory. Let us not use even our hair for vanity.

Concerning prayer. Our heavenly Father knoweth what things we have need of. We do not pray to inform him of our case.

Concerning our circumstances. These are before the divine mind, be they little or great. Since trifling matters like our hairs are catalogued by Providence, we are assured that greater concerns are before the Father's eye.

III. VALUATION. The hairs of our head are counted because valued.

These were poor saints who were thus highly esteemed.

The numbering mentioned in the text suggests several questions.

If each hair is valued, what must their heads be worth?

What must their bodies be worth?

What must their souls be worth?

What must they have cost the Lord, their Redeemer?

How can it be thought that he will lose one of them?

Ought we not greatly to esteem them?

Is it not our duty, our honour, our joy to seek after such of them as are not yet called by grace?

IV. PRESERVATION. The hairs of their head are all numbered, because they are to be preserved from all evil.

1. From the smallest real loss' we are secured by promise. "There shall not a hair of your head perish": Luke xxi. 18.

2. From persecution we shall be rescued. "Fear not them": Matt. x. 28.

3. From accident. Nothing can harm us unless the Lord permits.

4. From necessity. You shall not die of hunger, or thirst, or nakedness. God will keep each hair of your head.

5. From sickness. It shall sanctify rather than injure you.

6. From death. In death we are not losers, but infinite gainers.

Resurrection will restore the whole man.

Let us for ourselves trust, and not be afraid.

Let us set a high value upon souls, and feel an earnest love for them.

"*Hairs*"—of which ye yourselves are heedless. Who cares for the hairs once dragged out by a comb? A hair is a proverbial expression for an utter trifle.—*John Albert Bengel.*

If God numbers their hairs, much more does he number their heads, and take care of their lives, their comforts, their souls. This intimates that God takes more care of them than they do of themselves. They who are solicitous to number their money, and goods, and cattle, yet were never careful to number their hairs, which fall, and are lost, and they never miss them : but God numbers the hairs of his people, and not a hair of their head shall perish : Luke xxi. 18. Not the least hurt shall be done them, but upon a valuable consideration : so precious to God are his saints, and their lives and deaths !—*Matthew Henry.*

> There are who sigh that no fond heart is theirs,
>   None loves them best—Oh ! vain and selfish sigh !
> Out of the bosom of His love He spares—
>   The Father spares the Son, for thee to die :
> For thee He died—for thee He lives again :
> O'er thee He watches in His boundless reign.
>
> Thou art as much His care, as if beside
>   Nor man nor angel lived in Heaven or earth :
> Thus sunbeams pour alike their glorious tide
>   To light up worlds, or wake an insect's mirth :
> They shine and shine with unexhausted store—
> Thou art thy Saviour's darling—seek no more.
>
> *John Keble.*

An Italian martyr, in the sixteenth century, was most cruelly treated in the prisons of the Inquisition. His brother, who with great difficulty obtained an interview with him, was deeply affected by the sight of his sufferings. "My brother," said the prisoner, "if you are a Christian, why do you distress yourself thus ? Do you not know that a leaf cannot fall to the ground without the will of God ? Comfort yourself in Christ Jesus, for the present troubles are not to be compared with the glory to come."

> If pestilence stalk through the land, ye say "This is God's doing" ;
> Is it not also his doing when an aphis creepeth on a rosebud ?—
> It an avalanche roll from its Alp, ye tremble at the will of Providence ;
> Is not that will concerned when the sear leaves fall from the poplar ?
>
> *Martin F. Tupper.*

CXXXVIII

Matthew x. 38 —"**He that taketh not his cross, and followeth after me, is not worthy of me.**"

Before his crucifixion, our Lord has a foresight of it, and does not hesitate to realize himself as bearing his cross.

With equal prescience he foresees each true disciple receiving and taking up his own personal cross. He sees none exempted.

Picture to the mind's eye a procession led by the cross-bearing Jesus, and made up of his cross-bearing train. This is not a pageant, but a real march of suffering. It reaches through all time.

The chief requirement of a disciple is to follow Jesus in all things, in cross-bearing as in all else.

Cross-bearing is trying, laborious, sorrowful, humiliating.

Cross-bearing is inevitable to the follower of Jesus. We are bound to take up our cross or give up all idea of being Christians.

Let us obediently enquire—

I. WHAT IS MY PECULIAR CROSS ? " He that taketh not *his* cross."

1. It may be the giving up of certain pleasures or indulgences.
2. It may be the endurance of reproach and unkindness, or remaining in poverty and obscurity for the good of others.
3. It may be the suffering of losses and persecutions, for Christ's sake.
4. It certainly means the consecrating of all to Jesus: the bowing of my whole self beneath the blessed burden of service with which he honours me.
5. It also includes the endurance of my heavenly Father's will with patience, acquiescence, and thanksgiving.

My cross is well, wisely, kindly, and surely chosen for me by my Lord. It is only meet that I should be made like my Lord in bearing it.

II. WHAT AM I TO DO WITH IT ? " Taketh . . . . followeth after me."

1. I am deliberately to take it up.

Not to choose a cross, or pine after another form of trial.

Not to make a cross, by petulance and obstinacy.

Not to murmur at the cross appointed me.

Not to despise it, by callous stoicism, or wilful neglect of duty.

Not to faint under it, fall beneath it, or run from it.

2. I am boldly to face it. It is only a wooden cross after all.

3. I am patiently to endure it, for I have only to carry it a little way.

4. I am cheerfully to resign myself to it, for my Lord appoints it.

5. I am obediently to follow Christ with it. What an honour and a comfort to be treading in his steps! This is the essential point.

It is not enough to bear a cross, we must bear it after Jesus.

I ought to be thankful that I have only to bear it, and that it does not bear me. It is a royal burden, a sanctified burden, a sanctifying burden, a burden which gives communion with Christ.

III. What should encourage me?

1. Necessity: I cannot be a disciple without cross-bearing.

2. Society: better men than I have carried it.

3. Love: Jesus bore a far heavier cross than mine.

4. Faith: grace will be given equal to the weight of the cross.

5. Hope: good to myself will result from my bearing this load.

6. Zeal: Jesus will be honoured by my patient endurance.

7. Experience: I shall yet find pleasure in it, for it will produce in me much blessing. The cross is a fruitful tree.

8. Expectation: glory will be the reward of it. No cross, no crown.

Let not the ungodly fancy that theirs is a better lot: the Psalmist says, "many sorrows shall be to the wicked."

Let not the righteous dread the cross, for it will not crush them: it may be painted with iron colours by our fears, but it is not made of that heavy metal; we can bear it, and we will bear it right joyously.

Nails

When Alexander the Great marched through Persia, his way was stopped with ice and snow, insomuch that his soldiers, being tired out with hard marches, were discouraged, and would have gone no further, which he perceiving, dismounted his horse, and went on foot through the midst of them all, making himself a way with a pickaxe; whereat they all being ashamed, first his friends, then the captains of his army, and, last of all, the common soldiers, followed him. So should all men follow Christ their Saviour, by that rough and unpleasant way of the cross that he hath traversed before them. He having drunk unto them in the cup of his passion, they are to pledge him when occasion is offered; he having left them an example of his suffering, they are to follow him in the selfsame steps of sorrow.—*John Spencer.*

The cross is easier to him who takes it up than to him who drags it along.—*J. E. Vaux.*

We are bid to *take*, not to make our cross. God in his providence will provide one for us. And we are bid to *take it up;* we hear nothing of laying it down. Our troubles and our lives live and die together.

W. Gurnall.

> Must Jesus bear the cross alone,
> And all the church go free?
> No, there's a cross for every one,
> And there's a cross for me.

"No man," said Flavel, " hath a velvet cross."

As an old Yorkshire working-man, a friend of mine, said, "Ah ! it is blessed work cross-bearing when it's tied on with love."—*Newman Hall.*

Welcome the cross of Christ, and bear it triumphantly ; but see that it be indeed *Christ's* cross, and not *thine own.— Wilcox.*

Christ's cross is the sweetest burden that ever I bore ; it is such a burden as wings are to a bird, or sails to a ship, to carry me forward to my harbour.—*Samuel Rutherford.*

Whatever the path is, Christ is there, and to be with him is joy enough for any creature, whether man or angel. He does not send us to walk in a dreary, desolate road. He does not say, " Go ye," pointing to a lonely way in which he is not to be found ; he says, " Come after me," so that we need not take a single step where his footprints cannot be seen, and where his presence may not still be found. If the sharp flints cut our feet, they have wounded his before. If the darkness gathers thickly here and there, it was a denser gloom that surrounded him. If ofttimes we must stand and fight, it was through fiercer conflicts that he passed. If the cross is heavy to our shoulder, it is light when compared with the one he bore. "Christ leads me," said Baxter, "through no darker room than he went through before." If the road were a thousand times rougher than it is, it would be well worth while to walk in it for the sake of walking with Christ there. Following Jesus means fellowship with Jesus, and the joy of that fellowship cannot be told.—*F.*

CXXXIX

Matthew xi. 28-30 —"**Come unto me, all ye that labour and are heavy laden, and I will give you rest.**

"**Take my yoke upon you, and learn of me; for I am meek and lowly in heart: and ye shall find rest unto your souls.**

"**For my yoke is easy, and my burden is light.**"

Jesus had first taught the solemn truth of *human responsibility* (verses 20-24), and afterwards he had joyfully proclaimed in prayer the doctrine of *election :* now he turns to give a free and full invitation to those who are needing rest. These three things are quite consistent, and should be found in all Christian preaching.

Remember who he is who thus invites men to come to him.

The Son of the Highest, the revealer of God *then* and *now ;* he bids men draw near to himself without fear, and rest in such nearness.

The Saviour ever living, having once died, is waiting to receive and save all who will come to him ; and such he will bless with rest.

In our Lord's gracious invitation you note—

I. A CHARACTER WHICH DESCRIBES YOU.

    1. Labouring, "all ye that labour," in whatever form.

        In the service of formal religion, in the attempt to keep the law, or in any other way of self-justification.

        In the service of self to get gain, honour, ease, etc.

        In the service of the world to discover, invent, legislate, etc.

        In the service of Satan, lust, drink, infidelity, etc.

    2. Laden. All who are "heavy laden" are called.

        Laden heavily because weary, vexed, disappointed, despairing.

        Laden with sin, guilt, dread, remorse, fear of death.

        Laden with care, anxiety, greed, ambition, etc.

        Laden with sorrow, poverty, oppression, slander, etc.

        Laden with doubt, temptation, conflict, inner faintness, etc.

II. A BLESSING WHICH INVITES YOU.

    1. Rest to be given. "I will give you rest."

        To the conscience, by atonement and pardon.

        To the mind, by infallible instruction and establishment.

        To the heart a rest for love. Jesus fills and contents the heart.

        To the energies, by giving an object worth attaining.

        To the apprehensions, assuring that all things work for good.

2. Rest to be found. "Ye shall find rest unto your souls."

This is rest upon rest, deepening, settling.

This is rest which comes of conquered passion, desire, etc.

This is rest which comes of being fully consecrated to the Lord.

How such rest would cheer you, strengthen you, save you!

How it would counteract the labours and the loads!

III. A DIRECTION TO GUIDE YOU.

1. "*Come* unto me."

Come to a person, to Jesus, the living Saviour and Example.

Come at once, Jesus is ready now. Are you?

Come *all* who labour and are loaded. None will be refused.

Come laden, with your burdens on your hearts, and "I will give you rest." Come as you are. Come by faith.

2. "*Take* my yoke upon you."

Be obedient to my command.

Be willing to be conformed to me in service and burden-bearing.

Be submissive to the afflictions which I may lay upon you.

3. "*Learn* of me."

You do not know; but must be content to learn.

You must not cavil; but have a mind to learn.

You must learn by heart, and copy my meekness and lowliness.

IV. AN ARGUMENT TO PERSUADE YOU.

You wish to be like your Lord in restfulness and service; then come and learn of him, and remember that he is—

1. A lowly Teacher: bearing with failure, repeating his lessons, assisting the disciple, restoring the fallen.

2. Laying no heavy burden. "My yoke is easy," etc.

3. Giving rest by the burden which he causes you to bear: "Take my yoke . . . . and ye shall find rest."

MAGNETS

The immediate occasion of the invitation, with its deep earnestness of pity and sympathy, was found, I doubt not, in the outward appearance of the crowd actually surrounding Jesus. Probably by this time it was about sunset. After a day of exhausting toil for our Saviour himself; the workman from the field, the busy trader, the fisher with his nets, the slave with his burden, the rich man with his heavier burden of care, the grey-haired sinner stooping under the weight of years, and inly burdened with remorse and fear;—these, and such as these, met the Saviour's eye, which read their hearts; but in them he saw represented our toiling, suffering world, and uttered a voice of invitation meant to reach, and destined yet to reach, all mankind. *"I will give you rest."* Rest for the burdened conscience, in pardon ; for the unquiet intellect, in truth ; for the aching thirsty heart, in divine love ; for the care-fretted spirit, in God's providence and promises ; for the weary with sorrow and suffering, in the present foretaste, and shortly in the actual enjoyment of "his rest."—*E. R. Conder.*

"Come," saith Christ, "and I will give you rest." I will not *show* you rest, nor barely *tell* you of rest, but I will *give* you rest. I am faithfulness itself, and cannot lie, I *will* give you rest. I that have the greatest power to give it, the greatest will to give it, the greatest right to give it, come, laden sinners, and *I* will give you rest. Rest is the most desirable good, the most suitable good, and to you the greatest good. Come, saith Christ, that is, believe in me, and I will give you rest ; I will give you peace with God, and peace with conscience : I will turn your storm into an everlasting calm ; I will give you such rest, that the world can neither give to you nor take from you.—*Thomas Brooks.*

Lord, thou madest us for thyself, and we can find no rest till we find rest in thee !—*Augustine.*

A poor English girl, in Miss Leigh's home in Paris, ill in body and hopeless in spirit, was greatly affected by hearing some children singing "I heard the voice of Jesus say." When they came to the words, "weary, and worn, and sad," she moaned, "That's me ! That's me ! What did he do ? Fill it up, fill it up ! " She never rested until she had heard the whole of the hymn which tells how Jesus gives rest to such. By-and-by she asked, "Is that true ? " On being answered, "Yes," she asked, "Have you come to Jesus ? Has he given you rest ? " "He has." Raising herself, she asked, " Do you mind my coming very close to you ? May be it would be easier to go to Jesus with one who has been before than to go to him alone." So saying, she nestled her head on the shoulder of her who watched, and clutching her as one in the agony of death, she murmured, " Now, try and take me with you to Jesus."—*The Sunday at Home.*

There are many heads resting on Christ's bosom, but there's room for yours there.—*Samuel Rutherford.*

CXL

𝔐𝔞𝔱𝔱𝔥𝔢𝔴 𝔵𝔦. 28 —" 𝕮𝔬𝔪𝔢 𝔲𝔫𝔱𝔬 𝔪𝔢, 𝔞𝔩𝔩 𝔶𝔢 𝔱𝔥𝔞𝔱 𝔩𝔞𝔟𝔬𝔲𝔯 𝔞𝔫𝔡 𝔞𝔯𝔢 𝔥𝔢𝔞𝔳𝔶 𝔩𝔞𝔡𝔢𝔫, 𝔞𝔫𝔡 𝕴 𝔴𝔦𝔩𝔩 𝔤𝔦𝔳𝔢 𝔶𝔬𝔲 𝔯𝔢𝔰𝔱."

This text is often preached from, but never too often, since the sorrows with which it deals always abound, and the remedy is always effective.

This time we purpose to view it from our Lord's side.

He entreats the weary to come to him. He beseeches them to learn of him. He not only receives those who come, but begs them to come. What is this desire which burns in his bosom? And whence comes it?

Let us carefully consider—

J Who is he?

1. One who has been rejected, yet he cries "Come unto me."
2. One whose rejection involves us in fearful guilt, yet he is ready to forgive, and to bestow rest upon us if we come.
3. One who knows his Father's purpose, but fears not to give a pressing invitation to all who labour and are heavy laden.
4. One who has all power to receive such as come, and to give rest to them all. This is no vain invitation saying more than it means.
5. One who as the Son of God is infinitely blessed, and yet finds new joy in giving rest to poor restless men.

II. Whom does he call, and why?

1. Labourers, with more than they can do: disquieted, unhappy. These he calls to himself that he may give them rest, and cause them to find rest.
2. Heavy laden ones, with more than they can bear: oppressed, sorrowful, ready to die.
3. The poor and illiterate who need to be taught.
4. The spiritually burdened, who much need a helping hand, and can only find it in him.

III. What causes his desire for them?

Not his own need of them.

Not their personal worthiness.

Nor aught that they are or can ever be. But,—

1. He has a love to our race. "My delights were with the sons of men": Prov. viii. 31. He would have these resting with himself.
2. He is himself a man, and knows the needs of men.
3. He has done so much to buy us rest that he would fain give it to us.

4. He delights to do more and more for us: it is his joy to give good things to men.

5. He knows what our ruin will be unless we find rest in him.

6. He knows what our bliss will be if we come unto him.

IV. How then shall we treat this call?

1. It is very earnest, let us heed it.

2. It is very simple, let the poorest seize upon it.

3. It exactly suits us. Does it not suit you?

4. It is very gracious, let us accept it.

ECHOES

The most condescending affections that ever he discovered, the most gracious invitations that ever he made, were at those times when he had a sense of his glory in a particular manner, to show his intention in his possessing it. When he spake of all things delivered to him by his Father, an invitation to men to come unto him is the use he makes of it: Matt. xi. 27, 28. If this be the use he makes of his glory, to invite us, it should be the use we should make of the thoughts of it, to accept his proffer. A nation should run to him because he is glorified.

Stephen Charnock.

"Come unto me," is the invitation of this Blessed One, so intensely human, though so gloriously divine, "Unto me," in whose arms little children were embraced, on whose bosom a frail mortal lay: "unto me," who hungered, thirsted, fainted, sorrowed, wept, and yet whose love, and grief, and pains, and tears, wore the expression of emotions felt in the mighty heart of God.—*Caird.*

> Lord, I have invited all,
> And I shall
> Still invite, still call to thee:
> For it seems but just and right
> In my sight,
> Where is all, there all should be.
>
> *George Herbert.*

It runs thus—you to me, and I to you. Here is a double communion set up. This is all to our advantage, and to the display of our Lord's great graciousness. We come, and therein he obtains the company of a beggar, a leper, a patient, a repulsive rebel: this is no gain to anything in him except his pity. But surely he expects something of us to reward him for receiving us? By no means. We are to come to him, not that we may give him something, but that he may give everything to us. What a Lord is this!

CXLI

Matthew xiv. 31 —" And immediately Jesus stretched forth his hand, and caught him, and said unto him, O thou of little faith, wherefore didst thou doubt ? "

Our Lord did not question the doubter till he had saved the sinker.

His rebukes are always timely.

The question was not only well deserved as a rebuke, but it was specially instructive, and no doubt it proved useful in after years.

When the grace of faith is really present, doubt has to answer for itself, and to die if it cannot defend itself.

Oh, that it may die in us at once !

We will put the question of our text to the two great classes of men.

I. WHEREFORE DOST THOU DOUBT, O CHRISTIAN ?

   1. *Let us mention some supposably valid reasons.*

      Can you quote past experience of broken promises ?

      Is the present evil beyond the power of Omnipotence ?

      Are the promises abolished ? Are the purposes of grace annulled ?

      Has God himself changed ? Is his mercy clean gone for ever ?

   None of these supposable reasons have any existence.

   2. *Let us hear your actual reasons ; if you dare state them.*

      My sense of guilt is peculiarly deep and clear.

      My inbred sin has risen upon me with terrible fury.

      My failures justify despair when viewed by the side of other men's attainments, and my own obligations.

      My trials are so peculiar, so fierce, so long, so varied.

      My heart fails me. I can bear up no longer.

      My fears predict greater evils still, and threaten ultimate ruin.

   Many such insufficient reasonings becloud the mind ; and it may be wisdom to look them in the face, and so dissipate them.

   3. *Let us view these reasonings from other standpoints.*

      How would you have viewed them when first you believed ?

      How did you view former trials when they came in your way ; and how do you view them now that you have overcome them ?

      What do you think of your trials when you are lying in Jesus bosom—assured of his love ?

41

How do you speak of them when you are instructing others ?

How will they appear to you when you get to heaven ?

Jesus is now near you. How can you take such gloomy views of things in his presence ?

4. *Shall we hint at the true reasons of your doubting ?*

You were self-confident, and that confidence has failed you.

You looked too much to things seen by the light of sense ; and now that it is dark, you are in consequence troubled.

You took your eye off from your Lord.

Perhaps you neglected prayer, watching, repentance, etc.

When you find out the real reason of your doubt, cry for pardon, and seek to the Holy Spirit to restore faith, and set you right.

II. Wherefore dost thou doubt, o sinner ?

The Lord's hand is stretched out to save sinking sinners.

Do not distrust the power of Jesus to save *you* from sinking.

1. *Let us suppose good reasons for your doubting.*

Have others believed and perished ?

Have you yourself tried faith in Jesus, and found it vain ?

Has the blood of Jesus lost its power ?

Has the Holy Spirit ceased to comfort, enlighten, renew ?

Is the gospel abrogated ? Is God's mercy clean gone for ever ?

None of these can be answered in the affirmative.

2. *Let us hear your apparent reasons.*

Your sins are great, numerous, aggravated, and singular.

You cannot think that salvation is for you.

You have refused the gospel call so long.

Your heart is so dreadfully hard and unfeeling.

None of these are sufficient reasons for doubting Almighty love.

3. *Let us learn the way to deal with such unreasonable doubting.*

Repent of it, for it dishonours the power and promise of the Father, the blood of Jesus, and the grace of the Holy Spirit.

End it, by simply believing what is so surely true.

Run as far as possible the other way. Believe up to the hilt.

In every case, let us be sure that to believe God is sanctified common-sense, and to doubt him is an extravagance of folly.

42

Mr. Haslam has reported a conversation between two poor aged Christians to the following effect: " Oh ! " said the husband, who was evidently the weaker vessel, " I've got so little faith, I do get these 'ere doubts so much." " Yes," added the wife, " and ye keeps them, Peter, and brings them to me."

Though the providence of God may be exceedingly dark, the language of faith is, " The Lord is ready to save." If you look into your past experience, you will find that God has done great things for you. Is it not true that nine-tenths of all the difficulty you have anticipated have never come to pass at all? I have great sympathy with Billy Bray, whose wife said to him, when he came home, having given all his money away, " I never saw such a man in my life. Thee'lt go and look after other people's wives and children, and help them, and thee own wife and children may starve." Billy, with great force, said, " Well, woman, thee'st never starved yet;" and that was the fact, for there she stood, a living witness to his word.—*Henry Varley.*

Good old Mr. Crisp, who had been President of the Baptist College at Bristol for fifty years, was towards the end of his life fearful that his faith would fail. Being reminded of the passage, " He that spared not his own Son, but delivered him up for us all, how shall he not with him also freely give us all things ? " he said, after repeating and dwelling on the last words, " No, it would be wrong to doubt ; I cannot, I dare not, I will not doubt ! "—*S. A. Swaine, in " Faithful Men."*

When darkness long has veiled my mind,
  And smiling day once more appears,
Then, my Redeemer ! then I find
  The folly of my doubts and fears.

I chide my unbelieving heart ;
  And blush that I should ever be
Thus prone to act so base a part,
  Or harbour one hard thought of thee.

Cowper.

Certain persons think that doubting is a needful part of Christian experience, but it is by no means the case. A child may have a deep experience of its father's love, and yet it may never have known a doubt of him. All the experience of a Christian is not Christian experience. If many Christians are despondent, it is no reason why I must be : it is rather a reason why I should watch against it. What if many sheep suffer from the fly ; am I to be anxious to have my fleece fly-blown in order to be like them? Never doubt the Lord till you have cause for it ; and then you will never doubt him as long as you live.

CXLII

Matthew xx. 3, 4 —"And he went out about the third hour, and saw others standing idle in the market-place,

"And said unto them; Go ye also into the vineyard, and whatsoever is right I will give you. And they went their way."

The reason for employing these people must have been gracious.

Surely the good man could have waited till the next morning; but he charitably chose to employ the needy ones at once. He did not need labourers, but the poor men needed their pennies.

Certainly it is sovereign grace alone which leads the Lord God to engage such sorry labourers as we are.

Let us enquire—

I. How may the Lord be said to go out?

    1. Inasmuch as the impulse of grace comes first in every case, and none go into the vineyard till he calls them.

    2. Inasmuch as there are times of revival, when the Lord goes forth by the power of his Spirit, and many are brought in.

    3. Inasmuch as there are times of personal visitation with most men when they are specially moved to holy things.

II. What is the hour here mentioned?

It represents the period between 25 and 35 years of age, or thereabouts.

    1. The dew of youth's earliest and best morning hour is gone.

    2. Habits of idleness have been formed by standing in the market-place so long. It is harder to begin at the third hour than at the first. Loiterers are usually spoiled by their loafing ways.

    3. Satan is ready with temptation to lure them to his service.

    4. Their sun may go down suddenly, for life is uncertain. Many a day of life has closed at its third hour.

    5. Fair opportunity for work yet remains; but it will speedily pass away as the hours steal round.

    6. As yet the noblest of all work has not been commenced; for only by working for our Lord can life be made sublime.

III. What were they doing to whom he spoke? "Standing idle in the market-place."

    1. Many are altogether idling in a literal sense. They are mere loafers and *dilettanti*, with nothing to do.

2. Many are idle with laborious business—industrious triflers, wearied with toils which accomplish nothing of real worth.

3. Many are idle because of their constant indecision. Unstable as water they do not excel. James i. 6.

4. Many are idle though full of sanguine intentions ; but as yet their resolves are not carried out.

IV. WHAT WORK WOULD THE LORD HAVE THEM DO ?
He would have them work by day in his vineyard.

1. The work is such as many of the best of men enjoy.

2. The work is proper and fit for you.

3. For that work the Lord will find you tools and strength.

4. You shall work with your Lord, and so be ennobled.

5. Your work shall be growingly pleasant to you.

6. Your work shall be graciously rewarded at the last.

V. WHAT DID THEY DO IN ANSWER TO HIS CALL ? " They went their way."

May you, who are in a similar time of the day, imitate them !

1. They went at once. The parable indicates immediate service.

2. They worked with a will.

3. They never left the service, but remained till night.

4. They received the full reward at the day's end.

Let us pray the Lord to go out among our young men and women.

Let us expect to see such come into the church, and let us guide them in their work, for they come into the vineyard to labour.

Let us enquire if some will come *now*.

SPADES

Have you never thought with extreme sadness of the many men and women upon our earth whose lives are useless ? Have you never reflected upon the millions of people who waste in nothingness their thoughts, their affections, their energies, all their powers, which frivolity dissipates as the sand of the desert absorbs the water which is sent upon it from the sky ? These beings pass onward, without even asking themselves toward what end they journey, or for what reason they were placed here below.—*Eugène Bersier.*

All activity out of Christ, all labour that is not labour in his church, is in his sight a " *standing idle.*"—*Archbishop Trench.*

45

A good minister, now in heaven, once preached to his congregation a powerful sermon, founded upon the words of Christ, " Why stand ye here all the day idle ? " The sermon did good to many, among whom was a lady who went to the minister the next day, and said, " Doctor, I want a spade." We should be happy to put spades into the hands of all our idle friends. There are Sunday-school spades, Mission-room spades, Tract-distribution spades, Sick-visitation spades, &c., &c. Who will apply for them ?—*Home Evangel.*

What can I do the cause of God to aid ?
　　Can powers so weak as mine
　　Forward the great design ?
Not by young hands are mighty efforts made.

Not mighty efforts, but a willing mind,
　　Not strong, but ready hands
　　The vineyard's Lord demands ;
For every age fit labour he will find.

Come, then, in childhood, to the vineyard's gate ;
　　E'en you can dress the roots,
　　And train the tender shoots—
Then why in sloth and sin contented wait ?

To move the hardened soil, to bend and lift
　　The fallen branch, to tread
　　The winepress full and red,
These need a stronger arm, a nobler gift ;

But all can aid the work. The little child
　　May gather up some weed,
　　Or drop some fertile seed,
Or strew with flowers the path which else were dark and wild.

J. H. Clinch.

"Are you not wearying for the heavenly rest ?" said Whitefield to an old minister. " No, certainly not ! " he replied. " Why not ?" was the surprised rejoinder. " Why, my good brother," said the aged saint, " If you were to send your servant into the fields, to do a certain portion of work for you, and promised to give him rest and refreshment in the evening, what would you say if you found him languid and discontented in the middle of the day, and murmuring, ' Would to God it were evening'? Would you not bid him be up and doing, and finish his work, and then go home, and enjoy the promised rest ? Just so does God require of you and me that, instead of looking for Saturday night, we do our day's work in the day."

CXLIII

Matthew xxii. 8—10 —"Then saith he to his servants, The wedding is ready, but they which were bidden were not worthy.

"Go ye therefore into the highways, and as many as ye shall find, bid to the marriage.

"So those servants went out into the highways, and gathered together all as many as they found, both bad and good : and the wedding was furnished with guests."

The grand design of God is to make a marriage for his Son.

Our Lord Jesus has espoused his Church, and there must be a feast at the wedding. Is it not meet that it should be so ?

A feast would be a failure if none came to it, and therefore the present need is that the wedding be "furnished with guests."

I. THE FIRST INVITATION WAS A FAILURE.

This is seen in Jewish history.

Among Gentiles, those to whom the gospel invitation specially comes are, as a rule, unwilling to accept it.

Up to this hour, children of godly parents, and hearers of the word, many of them refuse the invitation for reasons of their own.

The invitation was refused—

1. Not because it involved suffering, for it was a wedding-feast to which they were bidden.

2. Nor because there were no adequate preparations,—"The wedding is ready."

3. Nor because the invitations were not delivered, or were misunderstood,—they "were bidden."

4. But because they were not fit for the high joy.
   They were not loyal to their King.
   They were not attached to his royal Son.
   They were not pleased with his noble marriage.
   They were wrapt up in self-interest.
   They were cruel to well-intentioned messengers.

5. Therefore they were punished with fire and sword.
   But this destruction was no wedding-feast for the King's Son
   This punishment was no joy to the King.

Love must reign : mercy must be glorious ; Christ must reveal his grace ; otherwise he has no joy of his union with mankind.

Therefore—

II. The commission was enlarged.

1. Disappointment must arouse activity and enterprise,—" Go ye."
2. Disappointment suggests change of sphere,—" into the highways."
3. A wide invitation is to be tried,—" as many as ye shall find, bid."
4. A keen outlook is to be kept,—" as many as ye shall find."
5. Publicity is to be courted,—" went out into the highways."
6. Small numbers,—ones and twos, are to be pressed in.

This is said to have been the result of the anger of the King.

So good is the Lord that his wrath to despisers works good for others.

III. The new mission was fulfilled.

The particulars of it will be suggestive for ourselves at this present era.

1. The former servants, who had escaped death, went out again.
2. Other servants, who had not gone at first, entered zealously into the joyful but needful service.
3. They went in many directions,—" into the highways."
4. They went out at once. Not an hour could be left unused.
5. They pointed all they met to one centre.
6. They welcomed all sorts of characters,—" as many as they found."
7. They found them willing to come. He who sent the messengers inclined the guests : none seem to have refused.

This blessed service is being carried on at this very hour.

IV. The great design was accomplished.

1. The King's bounty was displayed before the world.
2. His provision was used. Think of grace and pardon unused !
3. The happiness of men was promoted : they feasted to the full.
4. Their grateful praise was evoked. All the guests were joyful in their King as they feasted at his table.
5. The marriage was graced.
6. The slight put upon the King's Son, by the churls who refused to come, was more than removed.
7. The quality of the guests most fully displayed the wisdom, grace, and condescension of the Host.

The whole business worked for the highest glory of the King and his Son.

Amen ! So let it be among us !

The wicked, for the slight breakfast of this world, lose the Lamb's supper of glory (Rev. xix. 9); where these four things concur, that make a perfect feast :—A good time, eternity ; a good place, heaven ; a good company, the saints ; good cheer, glory.—*Thomas Adams.*

The devil does not like field-preaching ; neither do I. I love a commodious room, a soft cushion, a handsome pulpit ; but where is my zeal if I do not trample all these under foot in order to save one more soul ?—*John Wesley.*

> " Call them in "—the Jew, the Gentile ;
> Bid the stranger to the feast ;
> " Call them in "—the rich, the noble,
> From the highest to the least :
> Forth the Father runs to meet them,
> He hath all their sorrows seen ;
> Robe, and ring, and royal sandals,
> Wait the lost ones : " Call them in."
> *Sacred Songs and Solos.*

From hedges and lanes of conscious nakedness and need, the marriage-festival is furnished with guests. To the poor the gospel is preached, and the poor in spirit gladly listen, whether they are clothed in purple or in rags.— *William Arnot.*

We might do better if we went further afield. Our invitations to Christ, which fall so feebly on the ears of those who regularly hear us, would be welcomed by those to whom we never deliver them. We are fools to waste time in the shallows of our churches and chapels when the deep outside teems with waiting fishes. We need *fresh* hearers : the newer the news to any man, the more likely is he to regard it as good news. Music-hall work, out-door preaching, and house-to-house visitation have virgin soil to deal with, and there is none like it. Invite the oft-invited —certainly ; but do not forget that those who have never been invited as yet cannot have been hardened by refusals. Beggars in the highways had never been bidden to a marriage-feast before ; and so, when they were surprised with an invitation, they raised no questions, but gladly hastened to the banquet.

CXLIV

Matthew xxv. 10 —"They that were ready went in with him to the marriage: and the door was shut."

During the waiting period, the virgins seemed much alike, even as at this day one can hardly discern the false professor from the true.

When the midnight cry was heard the difference began to appear, as it will do when the Second Advent approaches.

When the Bridegroom was actually come, they were finally divided.

Let us prayerfully consider—

1. THE READY, AND THEIR ENTRANCE.

   1. What is this readiness? "They that were ready."

     It is not a fruit of nature. None are ready to enter the marriage-feast of glory while they are in an unregenerate condition.

     It must be a work of grace; since we are unable to make ourselves fit for the vision of God, and the glory of Christ is too bright for us to be naturally fit to share in it.

     It should be our daily concern. He who is ready for the marriage feast is ready to live, and ready to die—ready for anything.

     It mainly consists in a secret work wrought in us.

      In being reconciled to God by the death of his Son.

      In being regenerated, and so made meet for glory.

      In being anointed with the Spirit, and fitted for holy service.

      In being quickened into a high and holy fellowship with God.

      In being delighted with God, and so being ready to enjoy him.

     It should be our present enquiry whether we are now "ready."

     Some make no profession, never pray, nor praise.

     Others make profession, but neither love, nor trust; they have lamps, but no oil with which to keep them burning.

   2. What is this entrance? A going in unto glory to be for ever with the Lord. 1 Thess. iv. 17.

     Immediate. "They that were ready *went in*." No sooner was the Bridegroom come, than they went in. Love brooks no delays.

     Intimate. They "went in *with him*." This is the glory of heaven, and the crown of its joys, that we go into them with Jesus, who remains our constant companion therein.

     Joyous. "They went in with him *to the marriage*."

     Personal. "*They* went in": each one entered for herself.

Eternal. "The door was shut"—to shut them in for ever. "He shutteth, and no man openeth." Rev. iii. 7.

Actual. In all the marriage-festival each one of the wise virgins had a share : indeed, they enjoyed more than appears in the parable, for they were brides, as well as maids of honour.

What a world of meaning lies in that abundant entrance which will be ministered to all the faithful ! 2 Peter i. 11.

II. THE UNREADY, AND THEIR EXCLUSION.

1. What is this unreadiness ?

It was the absence of a secret essential ; but that absence was consistent with much apparent preparation.

These persons had the name and character of virgins.

They had the lamps or torches of true bridesmaids.

They were companions of the true virgins.

They acted like the true ; in their virtues and in their faults.

They awakened as the true did, startled by the same cry.

They prayed also, after a fashion,—" give us of your oil."

Yet were they never ready to enter in with the King.

They had no heart-care to be found ready, hence flaming external lamps, but no hidden internal oil.

They had no faith-foresight ; they had not provided for the probable waiting, and the late coming.

They played the fool with Christ's wedding-feast, not thinking it worth the purchase of a little oil, but going to it with torches which would inevitably go out in smoke.

They put off till night what should have been done at once.

2. What is this exclusion ?

It was universal to all who were not ready.

It was complete : " the door was shut,"—shut for those without quite as surely as for those within.

It was just ; for they were not ready, and so slighted the King.

It was final. Since the fatal news that the door was shut, no news has come that it has been opened, or that it ever will be.

What if the cry were heard at this moment, " Behold he cometh " ? As yet the door is not shut. Be ready ere it closes.

FLASHES FROM THE LAMPS

" Uncle Ned," a coloured Baptist of the South, was talking with his former master's son. " Child," said the old man solemnly, " yer talk is too highfalutin' for me ; but de Bible is plain as A B C, whar it says yer got ter 'pent and be baptizen, or yer will be damned. Ise erfeared, fact I knows, yer's not dun nuther. 'Member, honey, ther Scripture says,— 'keep yer lamp trum an' er burning, an' yer ile-can full to pour in it.'" "Now, Uncle Ned," was the evasive reply, " I hope you don't think my lamp is without oil, do you?" "Child, 'tain't even got no wick in it. Fac' is, Ise erfeared *yer ain't even got a lamp*," muttered the old negro, as he mournfully shambled off.

The poet Cowper tells us that, when under conviction of sin, he dreamed that he was walking in Westminster Abbey, waiting for prayers to begin. " Presently I heard the minister's voice, and hastened towards the choir. Just as I was upon the point of entering, the iron gate under the organ was flung in my face, with a jar that made the Abbey ring. The noise awakened me ; and a sentence of excommunication from all the churches upon earth could not have been so dreadful to me as the interpretation which I could not avoid putting upon this dream."

Have you not felt a fainting of heart, and a bitterness of spirit, when, after much preparation for an important journey, you have arrived at the appointed place, and found that the ship or train, by which you intended to travel, had gone with all who were ready at the appointed time, and left you behind ? Can you multiply finitude by infinitude ? Can you conceive the dismay which will fill your soul if you come too late to the closed door of heaven, and begin the hopeless cry, " Lord, Lord, open to us " ?—*William Arnot.*

A lady, who heard Whitefield, in Scotland, preach upon the words, " And the door was shut," being placed near two dashing young men, but at a considerable distance from the pulpit, witnessed their mirth ; and overheard one say, in a low tone, to the other, " Well, what if the door *be* shut ? Another will open." Thus they turned off the solemnity of the text. 'Mr. Whitefield had not proceeded far when he said, " It is possible there may be some careless, trifling person here to-day, who may ward off the force of this impressive subject by lightly thinking, 'What matter if the door be shut ? Another will open.'" The two young men were paralyzed, and looked at each other. Mr. Whitefield proceeded : " Yes ; another *will* open. And I will tell you what door it will be : it will be the door of the bottomless pit !—the door of hell !—the door which conceals from the eyes of angels the horrors of damnation ! "

CXLV

Matthew xxvii. 29 —"And when they had platted a crown of thorns, they put it upon his head, and a reed in his right hand : and they bowed the knee before him, and mocked him, saying, Hail, King of the Jews ! "

The shameful spectacle ! What element of scorn is lacking !

Roman soldiers mocking a supposed rival of Cæsar are sure to go to the utmost lengths in their derision.

Jesus himself is a victim so novel in his gentle weakness that they set no bounds to their scorn.

The spectacle is as cruel as it is derisive. Thorns and rough blows accentuate mockeries and scoffs.

Roman legionaries were the brutalized instruments of a race noted for its ignorance of all tenderness ; they wrought cruelties with a singular zest, being most at home in amusements of the most cruel kind.

Let us go into the Hall of the Prætorian guard, and watch with our Lord in the hour of his mockery.

I. HERE LEARN A LESSON FOR YOUR HEART.

In the Lord of glory thus made the centre of cruel scorn—

1. See what sin deserved. It is all laid on him.

Ridicule for its folly. It should be despised for its mad rebellion against the omnipotent will of the great King.

Scorn for its pretensions. How dared it propose to usurp dominion over hearts and lives which belonged alone to God ?

Shame for its audacity. It dared defy the Eternal to battle. Oh, wretched, braggart sin !

2. See how low your Saviour stooped for your sake.

He is made the Substitute for foolish, sinful man ; and is treated as such.

He is scoffed at by soldiers of the meanest grade.

He is made a puppet for men who play the fool.

3. See how your Redeemer loved you.

He bears immeasurable contempt, bears in silence, bears to the bitter end ; and all for love of his people.

4. See the grand facts behind the scorn.

He is a King in very surety. They said, "Hail, King !" and he is indeed the King whom all shall hail.

He is glorified by conquering earth's sorrow: he is crowned with thorns. What a glorious diadem! No other coronet ever betokened such a conquest.

He rules by weakness: a reed is his sceptre. What a glory to be able to reign, not by force of arms, but by patience and gentleness!

He makes men bow the knee: real homage is his; he reigns, whether men will have it so or not.

He is the true Monarch of the Jews. In him the dynasty of David endures for ever, and Israel has hope of glory.

5. See that you honour and love him in proportion to this shame and mockery.

Bernard used to say, ' The more vile Christ hath made himself *for* us, the more dear he ought to be *to* us."

Can you ever reach so great a height?

II. HERE LEARN A LESSON FOR YOUR CONSCIENCE.

1. Jesus may still be mocked.

By deriding his people. "Saul, Saul, why persecutest thou me?" Men mock the Master in the servant.

By contemning his doctrine. Many do this who affect to admire his character. This is the peculiar sin of the present age.

By resolves never fulfilled. Sinners vow, but never pay; confess faults, and cling to them. This is to insult the Lord.

By beliefs never obeyed. It is common to pretend to a belief which never affects the life, mocking great truths by acting contrary to them.

By professions never justified. May not many a church-member be guilty of putting the Lord to an open shame in this fashion?

2. If guilty of mocking him, what shall you do?

Do not despair, but confess and lament your sin.

Do not give all up for lost. Believe and live.

Do not repeat the sad offence. Repent, and quit the crime.

Do not abide in sullen silence. Honour him whom you once despised.

3. What shall you do in any case?

Crown him with love.

Sceptre him with obedience.

Bow the knee of worship.

Proclaim him King by your personal testimony.

Ye sinners, destroy the sins which grieved your Saviour!

Ye saints, defy all the contempt of the world for his sake!

Whither, O whither, dost thou stoop, O thou co-eternal Son of thine eternal Father? Whither dost thou abase thyself for me? I have sinned, and thou art punished; I have exalted myself, and thou art dejected; I have clad myself with shame, and thou art stripped; I have made myself naked, and thou art clothed with robes of dishonour; my head hath devised evil, and thine is pierced with thorns; I have smitten thee, and thou art smitten for me; I have dishonoured thee, and thou, for my sake, art scorned; thou art made the sport of men, for me that have deserved to be insulted by devils!—*Bishop Hall.*

Christ's head hath sanctified all thorns; his back, all furrows; his hands, all nails; his side, all spears; his heart, all sorrows that can ever come to any of his children.—*Samuel Clark, in "The Saint's Nosegay."*

Here we see our King receiving the best homage the world would give him. His robe was some old cloak of purple. Behold his crown, platted of thorns! His coronation is performed by a ribald soldiery. His sceptre is a reed; his homage is given by the knee of scorn; his proclamation by the mouth of ridicule. How then can we expect honour for ourselves?

Let us never despise the weak, or scoff at brethren who may appear singular, or oppress any man of woman born. Haply we may be following the act of these Prætorians, and may be insulting saints more like to Jesus than we are ourselves. To be ridiculed may give us communion with the Lord Jesus, but to ridicule others will place us in fellowship with his persecutors.—*C. H. S.*

During the last moments of a gracious lady, speech had left her; but she managed to articulate the word "Bring." Her friends, in ignorance of her meaning, offered her food, but she shook her head, and again repeated the word "Bring." They then offered her grapes, which she also declined, and, for the third time uttered the word "Bring." Thinking she desired to see some absent friends, they brought them to her: but again she shook her head; and then, by a great effort, she succeeded in completing the sentence—

> "Bring forth the royal diadem,
> And crown Him Lord of all;"

and then passed away to be with Jesus.—*Newman Hall.*

CXLVI

Matthew xxbiii. 9, 10 —"And as they went to tell his disciples, behold, Jesus met them, saying, All hail. And they came and held him by the feet, and worshipped him.

"Then said Jesus unto them, Be not afraid: go tell my brethren that they go into Galilee, and there shall they see me."

All that concerns our Lord after his resurrection is calm and happy. A French writer calls the forty days on earth, "the life of Jesus Christ in glory": truly it was glory as full as earth could then bear.

His tomb was empty, and consequently the disciples' griefs would have been over had they fully understood what that vacant grave meant.

Then was their choicest time for living fellowship with their risen Lord, and he did not fail to grant them the privilege on many memorable occasions.

Since our Lord is risen, we also may have happy communion with him.

These are days in which we may expect him to manifest himself to us spiritually, as he did for forty days to the disciples corporeally.

Let us not be satisfied unless it is often said of us, "Jesus met them."

I. IN THE WAY OF SERVICE JESUS MEETS US. "As they went to tell his disciples, behold, Jesus met them."

   1. He may come at other times, as he did to those who visited the sepulchre, to those walking out to Emmaus, to others fishing, and to the eleven assembled for mutual consolation.

   2. He is likeliest to come when we are doing his work, since—
   We are then most awake, and most able to see him.
   We are then in special need of him.
   We are then most in accord with him.

   3. But come when Jesus may, it will be a blessed visitation, worthy to be prefaced by a "Behold!" Oh, that he would come *now!*

II. WHEN JESUS MEETS US, HE HAS EVER A GOOD WORD FOR US.

   The fittest motto for resurrection fellowship is "All hail!"

   1. A word of salutation. He is not ashamed to call us brethren, and welcome us with "All hail!"

   2. A word of benediction. He wishes us well, and expresses his hearty, sacred desire by the words "All hail!"

   3. A word of gratulation. He was glad to see these women, he gave them glad tidings, he bade them be glad, he made them glad, he was glad with them, saying, "All hail!"

56

4. A word of pacification.   He afterwards said, " Be not afraid " ; but this was virtually contained in his " All hail ! "   His presence can never mean us harm ; it ever works us health.

III. WHEN JESUS MEETS US, IT BECOMES US TO AROUSE OURSELVES.
We ought at such times to be like the disciples, who were—

1. All alive with hopeful energy. "They came." In eager haste they drew near to him. What life it would put into preachers and hearers if the Lord Jesus would manifestly appear unto them ! Dulness flees when Jesus is seen.

2. All aglow with happy excitement. They "held him by the feet,"—hardly knowing what they did, but enraptured with the sight of him.

3. All ardent with reverent love. They "worshipped him." What heartiness they threw into that lowly adoration !

4. All amazed at his glory. They were prostrate, and began to fear.

5. All afraid lest they should lose their bliss. They grasped him, and held him by the feet.

IV. FROM SUCH A MEETING WE SHOULD GO ON A FURTHER ERRAND.

1. We must not plead spiritual absorption as an excuse for inactivity, but we must " go " at our Lord's bidding.

2. We must seek the good of others because of their relation to our Lord. He says, " tell *my brethren*."

3. We must communicate what our Lord has imparted,—" go tell."

4. We must encourage our brethren by the assurance that joy similar to ours awaits them,—"there shall *they* see me." Thus shall we best realize and retain the choice benefits of intercourse with the Lord. Not only for ourselves, but mainly for the benefit of others, are we to behold our Lord.

Let us go to holy work hoping to meet Jesus as we go.
Let us go to more holy work when we have met him.
Let us labour to "abide in him ", looking, for his promised appearing and exhorting others to do the same.

It is said that a venturesome diplomatist once asked the Emperor Nicholas who was the most distinguished of His Majesty's subjects. According to report, the Czar replied that the most distinguished Russian was he whomsoever the Emperor honoured by speaking to him. Royal vanity dictated that reply, but we speak " words of truth and soberness " when we say that the most distinguished of men is he whom the Lord of hosts honours by admitting to communion with himself. " Speak, Lord ; for thy servant heareth."

> In vain thou strugglest to get free,
> I never will unloose my hold ;
> Art thou the Man that died for me ?
> The secret of Thy love unfold.
> Wrestling, I will not let thee go,
> Till I Thy name, Thy nature know.
>
> *Charles Wesley.*

There is a striking legend illustrating the blessedness of performing our duty at whatever cost to our own inclination. A monk had seen a beautiful vision of our Saviour, and in silent bliss he was gazing upon it. The hour arrived at which it was his duty to feed the poor at the convent-gate. He would fain have lingered in his cell to enjoy the vision ; but, under a sense of duty, he tore himself away from it to perform his humble service. When he returned, he found the blessed vision still waiting for him, and heard a voice, saying, " Hadst thou staid, I would have gone. As thou hast gone, I have remained."

It is a blessed thing to go forth with the Master's message after having seen him ; it is delightful to meet him on the way when we are going to tell his disciples ; and it is inexpressibly pleasant to find him in the assembly bearing witness with us. To go *from* the Lord, *for* the Lord, *with* the Lord, is such an agreeable combination that it cannot be described, but must be personally experienced. The Lord Jesus is by no means niggardly in his converse with his people : he meets us as often as we are fit to be met, and oftener ; and he uses such familiarities as could never have been expected had they not been already enjoyed. Who would have dreamed of his saying " All hail ! " if he had not himself selected the term ?—*C. H. S.*

A good theme might be found in the words of the message recorded in our text. Jesus prepares his messengers by saying " Be not afraid." Those who bear tidings for him should be calm and happy. He calls his disciples by a sweet name "my brethren " ; invites them to meet him ; appoints a well-known trysting-place ; and promises to be there. Whatever else they had begun to do, they must make this their chief business, to be at Galilee to commune with him, to put themselves at his disposal, and to receive his commission.—*C. H. S.*

CXLVII

Mark ib. 24 —"And he said unto them, Take heed what ye hear : with what measure ye mete, it shall be measured to you : and unto you that hear shall more be given."

In these days we have many instructions as to preaching ; but our Lord principally gave directions as to hearing. The art of attention is as difficult as that of homiletics.

The text may be viewed as a note of *discrimination*. Hear the truth, and the truth only. Be not indifferent as to your spiritual meat, but use discernment. 1 John iv. 1 ; Job xii. 11.

We shall use it as a note of *arousing*. When you do hear the truth, give it such attention as it deserves. Give good heed to it.

I. HERE IS A PRECEPT. "Take heed what ye hear."

The previous verse is—" If any man have ears to hear, let him hear ; " that is—use your ears well, and to the best purpose.

1. Hear with discrimination, shunning false doctrine. John x. 5.
2. Hear with attention ; really and earnestly hearing. Matt. xiii. 23.
3. Hear for yourself, with personal application. 1 Sam. iii. 9.
4. Hear retentively, endeavouring to remember the truth.
5. Hear desiringly, praying that the Word may be blessed to you.
6. Hear practically, obeying the exhortation which has come to you.

This hearing is to be given, not to a favourite set of doctrines, but to the whole of the Word of God. Ps. cxix. 128.

II. HERE IS A PROVERB. "With what measure ye mete, it shall be measured to you."

In proportion as you give yourself to hearing, you shall gain by hearing.

This is practically illustrated in the result of preaching.

1. Those who have no interest in the Word find it uninteresting.
2. Those who desire to find fault find faults enough.
3. Those who seek solid truth learn it from any faithful ministry.
4. Those who hunger find food.
5. Those who bring faith receive assurance.
6. Those who come joyfully are made glad.

But no man finds blessing by hearing error.

Nor by careless, forgetful, cavilling hearing of the truth.

III. Here is a promise. " Unto you that hear shall more be given.'
You that hear shall have—

1. More desire to hear.
2. More understanding of what you hear.
3. More convincement of the truth of what you hear.
4. More personal possession of the blessings of which you hear.
5. More delight while hearing the glorious gospel.
6. More practical benefit therefrom.

God giveth more to those who value what they have.

For practical application let us say—

Hear.   It is your wisdom to know what God says.
Hear well.   God's teaching deserves the deepest attention.
               It will repay the best consideration.
Hear often. Waste no Sabbath, nor any one of its services.
               Use week-day lectures and prayer-meetings.
Hear better. You will grow the holier thereby.
               You will find heavenly joy by hearing with faith.

HEAR ! HEAR !

What care I to see a man run after a sermon if he cozens and cheats as soon as he comes home ?—*John Selden.*

A heart-memory is better than a mere head-memory. It were better to carry away a little of the life of God in our souls than if we were able to repeat every word of every sermon we ever heard.—*De Sales.*

Ebenezer Blackwell was a rich banker, a zealous Methodist, and a great friend of the Wesleys. " Are you going to hear Mr. Wesley preach ? " said one to Mr. Blackwell. " No," he answered, " I am going to hear God ; I listen to him, whoever preaches ; otherwise I lose all my labour."

Once-a-day-hearers, represented by a Perthshire landlord, were pithily rebuked by Mr. Walker, the minister of Muthill. The landowner, meeting the minister on Monday, explained to him that he had not been hearing him at the second service on the previous day, as he could not *digest* more than one sermon. " I rather think," said Mr. Walker, " the appetite is at fault rather than the digestion."

Alas, the place of hearing is the place of sleeping with many a fine professor ! I have often observed that those that keep shops can briskly attend upon a twopenny customer, but when they come themselves to God's market, they spend their time too much in letting their thoughts wander from God's commandments, or in a nasty, drowsy way. The head, also, and hearts of most hearers, are to the Word as the sieve is to water : they can hold no sermons, remember no texts, bring home no proofs, produce none of the sermon to the edification and profit of others.—*John Bunyan.*

Some can be content to hear all pleasant things, as the promises and mercies of God ; but judgments and reproofs, threats and checks, these they cannot brook ; like unto those who, in medicine, care only for a pleasant smell or appearance in the remedy, as pills rolled in gold, but have no regard for the efficacy of the physic. Some can willingly hear that which concerns other men and their sins, their lives and manners, but nothing touching themselves or their own sins ; as men can willingly abide to hear of other men's deaths, but cannot abide to think of their own.—*Richard Stock.*

If verse 23 exhorts us to hear, verse 24 exhorts us to look to that which we do hear, and use it rightly. " Take heed what ye hear," means " Look after it as you would look after money that you have received." Learning a truth is not the end, but the beginning. After it is learnt, it is to be applied, kept, obeyed. And it would appear from the next sentence that, unless it is shared with others, we can neither get it nor keep it for ourselves. " With what measure ye mete, [understand, ' mete out your light,'] it shall be measured unto you : and more shall be given unto you." *(Revised Version.)* To learn the truth of God you need to listen, but you need to tell it to another as well. The meaning of this passage is brought out in the words of the old Rabbi : " Much have I learnt from my tutors ; more from my companions ; but most of all from my pupils." The more light you give another, the more you get yourself. You get a better grip of truth by pondering it with the wish to impart it. The love, which imparts what you have, opens your heart to receive something still higher. It is true, not only in regard to money, but to knowledge, and all power of help, that, " There is that scattereth, and yet increaseth ; and there is that withholdeth more than is meet, but it tendeth to poverty." He is a dull teacher that does not learn by all he teaches. Rejoice in your work ; it is worth doing well, for it is the best way of learning.—*Richard Glover.*

CXLVIII

Mark b. 6 —"But when he saw Jesus afar off, he ran and worshipped him."

Luke xb. 20 —"But when he was yet a great way off, his father saw him, and had compassion, and ran, and fell on his neck, and kissed him."

These two texts have a measure of apparent likeness : the man runs to Jesus from afar, and the Father runs to the prodigal from afar.

They do, however, as much illustrate the difference as the likeness of our action towards the Lord, and the Lord's action towards us.

From the two together a blended lesson may be learned.

I. THE SINNER'S PLACE. "Afar off." Jesus is afar off in the sinner's apprehension, and the sinner is in very deed far off from God.

   1. As to character. What a difference between the demoniac and the Lord Jesus : between the prodigal son and the great Father !

   2. As to knowledge. The demoniac knew Jesus, but knew little of his love. The prodigal knew little of his Father's great heart.

   3. As to hope. The man possessed of a devil had no hope of recovery, or but a faint one, and that hope the demons tried to extinguish. The prodigal only hoped to be received as a hired servant : he felt that his sins had put him far away from the true position of a son.

   4. As to possession. The demoniac had no hold upon the Saviour ; on the contrary, he cried, "What have I to do with thee ?" The prodigal thought he had lost all claim to his Father, and therefore said, "I am no more worthy to be called thy son."

Immeasurable is the distance between God and a sinner : it is wide as the gulf between sin and holiness, death and life, hell and heaven.

II. THE SINNER'S PRIVILEGE. "He saw Jesus."

This much you, who are most under Satan's influence, are able to see concerning Jesus : you know that—

   1. There is such a Person. He is God and man, the Saviour.

   2. He has done great things.

   3. He is able to cast out the powers of evil.

   4. He may cast them out from you, and deliver you.

III. THE SINNER'S WISEST COURSE. " He ran and worshipped him."

The demoniac was all in confusion, for he was under contending influences : his own spirit and the evil spirit strove together.

He ran towards Jesus, and worshipped him ; and yet in the same breath he cried, " What have I to do with thee ? " Thus are sinners tossed about.

But it is the sinner's wisest course to run to Jesus, for—

1. He is the Son of the Most High God. John i. 34.

2. He is the great enemy of our enemy, the devil. Heb. ii. 14.

3. He is abundantly able to drive out a legion of devils.

4. He can cause us to be clothed, and in our right mind.

5. He permits us even now to draw near and worship him.

It was the prodigal's wisdom to hasten to his Father.

Like arguments may be easily found in his case.

IV. THE SECRET OF HOPE FOR SINNERS. " His Father saw him "

1. The returning sinner was seen from afar by omniscience.

2. He was recognized as a son is known by his Father.

3. He was understood, beloved, and accepted by his Father.

This is the basis of hope for lost ones : not so much what *they* can see, as the fact that the Lord of love and grace sees them in all their sin and misery.

V. THE ACTION OF THE SINNER'S FATHER. He "ran, and fell on his neck, and kissed him."

1. Here was great tenderness,—"his Father saw him, and had compassion."

2. Here was great swiftness,—" and ran."

3. Here was great condescension,—he " ran, and fell on his neck."

4. Here were great love and mercy,—" and kissed him."

The Father's running made an end of the son's fears, and brought swift realization of joyful acceptance.

Let us run to our Saviour, and our Father.

Let us rejoice that our Saviour and our Father run to meet *us*.

RUNNING COMMENTS

A needle will move towards a magnet when once a magnet has moved near to it. Our heart manifests a sweet willingness towards salvation and holiness when the great and glorious good-will of the Lord operates upon it. It is ours to run to Jesus as if all the running were ours ; but the secret truth is that the Lord runs towards us, and this is the very heart of the business.—*C. H. S.*

The mother, as she sits in her house, hears a little one shriek, and knows the voice, and cries out, " Oh ! 'tis my child ! " Away she throws all she hath in her hands, and runs to her babe. Thus God takes the alarm of his children's cry. "I heard Ephraim bemoaning himself," saith the Lord ; his cry pierced God's ear, and his ear affected his bowels, and his bowels called up his power to the rescue of him.— *William Gurnall.*

God will pardon a repentant sinner more quickly than a mother would snatch her child out of the fire.— *Vianney.*

When either God or man is strongly moved, the pace is running. A soul in distress runs to Jesus : God in compassion runs to meet returning wanderers. A slow pace evidences an unwilling heart ; hence delay to repent is a deadly sign. With sin within thee, Christ before thee, time pressing thee, eternity awaiting thee, hell beneath thee, heaven above thee ; O sinner, thou mayest well run ! It is the pace of one hunting after the game he desires, one anxious to win a prize, one escaping the avenger of blood. He that would have heaven must run for it.— *C. H. S.*

A father, whose affluence was considerable, mourned over a reckless son, whose misconduct brought shame upon himself and his family. From home the prodigal went into another country, and for years he was lost to his relatives. A chance occurring, the sorrowing parent sent by a friend this message, should he meet his boy, " *Your father loves you still.*" The bearer long sought him in vain. At last he saw him enter a house of vice, and called him ; and there, at a late hour of evening, he delivered this message. The dissolute gambler's heart was touched. The thought that his father still loved him, and wished to forgive him, broke the spell of Satan. He abandoned his profligacy, and returned to his father. Oh, the power of such a message of inalienable love from God !— *The Preacher's Commentary.*

CXLIX

Mark b. 7 —"And cried with a loud voice, and said, What have I to do with thee, Jesus, thou Son of the most high God? I adjure thee by God, that thou torment me not."

The coming of Jesus into a place puts all into commotion.

The gospel is a great disturber of sinful peace.

Like the sun among wild beasts, owls, and bats, it creates a stir. In this case, a legion of devils began to move.

I. THE DEVIL CRIES OUT AGAINST THE INTRUSION OF CHRIST. " What have I to do with thee ? "

1. Christ's nature is so contrary to that of the devil that war is inevitable as soon as Jesus comes upon the scene.

2. There are no designs of grace for Satan, and, therefore, as he has nothing to hope for from Jesus, he dreads his coming.

3. He wishes to be let alone ; for thoughtlessness, stagnation, and despair suit his plans.

4. He knows his powerlessness against the Son of the Most High God, and has no wish to try a fall with him.

5. He dreads his doom : for Jesus will not hesitate to torment him by the sight of good done, and evil overcome.

II. MEN UNDER THE DEVIL'S INFLUENCE CRY OUT AGAINST THE INCOMING OF CHRIST BY THE GOSPEL.

1. Conscience is feared by them : they do not wish to have it disturbed, instructed, and placed in power.

2. Change is dreaded by them ; for they love sin, and its gains, and pleasures, and know that Jesus wars with these things.

3. They claim a right to be let alone : this is their idea of religious liberty. They would not be questioned either by God or man.

4. They argue that the gospel cannot bless *them.*

They expect nothing from it, for they do not know its rich benedictions, or the power of sovereign, almighty grace.

They think themselves too poor, too ignorant, too busy, too sinful, too weak, too involved, and perhaps too aged, to receive any good from the gospel.

5. They view Jesus as a tormentor, who will rob them of pleasure, sting their consciences, and drive them to obnoxious duties.

Therefore they cry out, " What have we to do with thee ? "

III. Sober men can answer these outcries.

They endeavour to answer the question,—"What have I to do with thee?" They remember a fact, and make an enquiry.

1. I have to do with him inevitably.

He has come to save, and I am responsible for accepting or refusing his grace.

I am his creature, as he is the Son of God, and he has power over me, and a right to my obedience.

I am under his rule, and he will judge me at the last day.

2. Has he to do with me graciously?

He has to do with me by the gospel which he has sent me.

He has abundantly much to do with me if he has wrought in me repentance, faith, prayer, etc.

He has everything to do with me if he has bestowed on me pardon, peace, sanctification, etc.

IV. Men saved from Satan raise an opposite cry.

According to the instance before us in the narrative—

1. They beg to sit at Jesus' feet, clothed, and in their right mind.

2. They ask to be with him always, and never to cease from personal attendance upon him.

3. They go at his bidding, and publish abroad what great things Jesus has done for them.

4. Henceforth they have nothing to do but to live for Jesus, and for him alone.

Come, ye despisers, and see yourselves as in a looking-glass!
Look until you see yourselves transformed.

Cases in point

Conversion is feared as a great danger by natural men, lest the promises put them on the pain and labour of godliness; for men do flee nothing but that which they apprehend as evil, dangerous, and so the true object of fear. Now, when Felix and Agrippa were both upon the wheel of the great Potter, I cannot say that conversion formally was begun, yet materially it was. The one trembled, and so was afraid and fled, and did put Paul away till another time. He saw the danger of grace (Acts xxiv. 25, 26), and fled from it. The other said that he was half a Christian (but it was the poorer half), and "he arose, and went aside." (Acts xxvi. 28, 30, 31.) "Their eyes they have closed; lest at any time they should see with their eyes, and hear with their ears, and should understand with their heart, and should be converted, and I should heal them." (Matt. xiii. 15.) In which words it is evident that conversion is feared as an evil.

A wretch once jested that he was once in danger to be catched, when a Puritan preacher, as he said, " was preaching with divine power, and evidence of the Spirit of God."—*Samuel Rutherford*.

It is said that Voltaire, being pressed in his last moments to acknowledge the Divinity of Christ, turned away, and said feebly, " For the love of God don't mention that Man—allow me to die in peace ! "

A number of young men were sitting together in a country store one evening, telling what they did not believe, and what they were not afraid to do. Finally, the leader in the group remarked that, so far as he was concerned, he would be willing at any time to sign away all his interest in Christ for a five-dollar bill. "What did I understand you to say ? " asked an old farmer, who happened to be in the store, and who had overheard the remark. " I said that for five dollars I would sign away all my interest in Christ, and so I will." The old farmer, who had learned to know the human heart pretty well, drew out his leathern wallet, took therefrom a five-dollar bill, and put it in the storekeeper's hand. Then calling for ink and paper, he said : "My young friend, if you will just step to the desk now, and write as I direct, the money is yours." The young man took the pen, and began : " In the presence of these witnesses, I, A—— B——, for the sum of five dollars received, do now, once for all, and for ever, sign away all my interest "—then he dropped the pen, and with a forced smile, said : "*I take it back, I was only fooling.*" That young man did not dare to sign that paper. Why ? He had an accusing conscience. He knew that there was a God. He believed in religion. He meant to be a Christian some time. And so do you, reader. Notwithstanding your apparent indifference, your trifling conduct, your boasting speech, you would not to-day for ten thousand dollars sign away, if such a thing were possible, your interest in Jesus Christ. You do not desire or expect to lose heaven.—*The Congregationalist (American)*.

CL

Mark viii. 22-25 —"And he cometh to Bethsaida; and they bring a blind man unto him, and besought him to touch him.

"And he took the blind man by the hand, and led him out of the town; and when he had spit on his eyes, and put his hands upon him, he asked him if he saw ought.

"And he looked up, and said, I see men as trees, walking.

"After that he put his hands again upon his eyes, and made him look up: and he was restored, and saw every man clearly."

Men arrive at Christ by different processes : one is found by Christ himself, another comes to him, another is borne of four, and this blind man is led. This matters little, so long as we do come to him.

The act of bringing men to Jesus is most commendable.

It proves kindly feeling.

It shows practical faith in the power of Jesus.

It is thus an act of true wisdom.

It is exceedingly acceptable to the Lord; and is sure to prove effectual when the person himself willingly comes.

In this case there was something faulty in the bringing, since there was a measure of dictation as to the method in which the Lord should operate.

I. IT IS A COMMON WEAKNESS OF FAITH TO EXPECT THE BLESSING IN A CERTAIN FIXED WAY. "They besought him to touch him."

The Lord has his usual ways, but he is not bound to them.

Yet too often we think and act as if he were so.

1. We dream that deliverance from trouble must come in one way.

2. We look for sanctification either by afflictions or by ecstasies.

3. We hope for salvation only by one form of experience.

4. We look to see others converted in one fashion of feeling only, or by some one favourite ministry.

5. We expect a revival to take the stereotyped shape.

II. WHILE OUR LORD HONOURS FAITH, HE DOES NOT DEFER TO ITS WEAKNESS.

He did not consent to work in the prescribed manner.

He touched, but no healing came; and thus he proved that the miracle was not attached to that special form of operation.

He did nothing to the blind man before their eyes; but led him out of the town. He would not indulge their observation, or curiosity.

He did not heal him instantly, as they expected.

He used a means never suggested by them—"spit on his eyes," etc.

When he did put his hands on him, he did it twice, so that, even in compliance with their wish, he vindicated his own freedom.

1. Thus he refused to foster the superstition which limited his power.

2. Thus he used a method more suited to the case.

3. Thus he gave to the people larger instruction.

4. Thus he displayed to the individual a more personal care.

The like happens in each distinct conversion : its speciality is justified in a multitude of ways.

III. While our Lord rebukes the weakness of faith, he honours faith itself.

1. The blind man had consented to be led to Jesus, and Jesus leads him further. He refuses none because their coming to him has been less their own spontaneous act than yielding to the persuasion of others.

2. His friends had asked for sight, and the Lord gave sight. If we have praying faith, he will keep pace with it.

3. The man and his friends had exhibited confidence in him, and he gave them even more than they expected. If we can confide, we shall receive.

4. The cure was perfect, and the method used displayed the completeness of it. Jesus gives perfect gifts to imperfect faith.

Faith ever honours the Lord, and therefore the Lord honours *it*.

If faith were not thus rewarded, Jesus himself would suffer dishonour.

He who has faith shall surely see; he who demands signs shall not be satisfied.

Let us for ever have done with prescribing methods to our Lord.

Jesus will surely heal those who believe in him; he knows the best method; and he is to be trusted without reserve.

Examples

This case, and that of the deaf and stammering man brought to Christ in Decapolis, have many points of resemblance. In both, those who brought the diseased to Jesus prescribed to him the mode of cure. Was it for the purpose of reproving and counteracting the prejudice which connected the cure with a certain kind of manipulation, on the part of the curer, that Jesus, in both instances, went so far out of his usual course, varying the manner of his action so singularly that, out of all his miracles of healing, these two stand distinguished by the unique mode of their performance? It is certain that, had Jesus observed one uniform method of healing, the spirit of formalism and superstition, which lies so deep in our nature, would have seized upon it, and linked it, inseparably, with the divine virtue that went out of him, confounding the channel with the blessing it conveyed. As we ponder the life of our Redeemer, dwelling particularly on those parts of it—such as his institution of the sacraments—in which food might have been furnished upon which the spirit of formalism might have fed, more and more do we admire the pains evidently taken to give to that strong tendency of our nature as little material as possible to fasten on.—*Dr. Hanna.*

Is the sick man the doctor, that he should choose the remedy?
Madame Swetchine.

John Newton's hymn is a case in point. We quote a verse or two :—

I asked the Lord that I might grow
    In faith, and love, and every grace ;
Might more of His salvation know,
    And seek, more earnestly, His face.

I hoped that in some favoured hour,
    At once He'd answer my request ;
And, by His love's constraining power,
    Subdue my sins, and give me rest.

Instead of this He made me feel
    The hidden evils of my heart,
And let the angry powers of hell
    Assault my soul in every part.

Thus did infinite wisdom answer his prayer in a way which he had never dreamed of, and yet it was the right way, as he confessed.

So apt are people, as in the case of Naaman, to settle in their own minds the method of the work of grace, that it is hard to overcome their preconceptions. I met with one young woman, before whom I set the way of salvation by faith alone. She was long in accepting, or even understanding it ; and when she did grasp it, and the joy of it filled her heart, she exclaimed, with surprise, " I never thought that people could find peace in this way." " Why not ? " I asked her, and she replied very energetically, "I always believed that one must almost go to hell to get to heaven. My father was so full of despair that they locked him up in the asylum for six munths, and then at last he got religion."—*C.H.S.*

70

CLI

Mark ix. 24 —"And straightway the father of the child cried out, and said with tears, Lord, I believe; help thou mine unbelief."

Here was a man fully aroused to anxiety, prayer, and the use of means, and yet his desire was not at once granted to him.

Even so, many are in earnest about their souls, and yet do not immediately find conscious salvation.

This drives them to yet deeper grief.

Perhaps this father's case may help them to understand their own.

His child was not cured, but even appeared to be worse than ever.

Yet the matter came to a happy issue through the power of our Lord Jesus Christ.

Let us note the case carefully, and observe—

I. The suspected difficulty.

1. The father may have thought it lay with the disciples.
   Yet alone they could never have done anything.
   Had their Lord been with th:m, they could have done everything.
   The main difficulty was not with the disciples, though it was partly there.

2. He probably thought that the case itself was well-nigh hopeless.
   The disease was—
   So fitful and mysterious.
   So terribly violent and sudden in its attacks.
   So deep-seated, and of such long continuance.
   So near to utterly destroying life.

   But, after all, it is not our own case, or the case of those for whom we plead, which presents any unusual impediment to divine power. The Lord delights to work impossibilities.

3. He half hinted that the difficulty might lie with the Master. "If thou canst do anything, have compassion on us, and help us."
   "If thou canst." Had he seen the transfiguration, he would have known the *power* and glory of the Lord.
   "Have compassion." Could he have read the Lord's heart, he would have felt sure that the Saviour's *pity* was already aroused.

Rest assured, O anxious heart, that the difficulty of your case lies alone in your want of faith !

II. THE TEARFUL DISCOVERY. "He said with tears, Lord, I believe; help thou mine unbelief."

The Lord Jesus repudiated the insinuation that there was any question as to his power, and cast the "if" back upon the father with "If thou canst believe." Then—

1. The man's little faith discovered his unbelief.

2. He was distressed and alarmed at the sight of his own unbelief.

3. He turned his thoughts and prayers in that direction. It was now not so much " Help my child," as " Help my unbelief."

4. He became deeply sensible of the sin and danger of unbelief.

Let us look in the same direction personally, and we shall see that unbelief is an alarming and criminal thing ; for it doubts—

The power of Omnipotence.
The value of the promise of God.
The efficacy of Christ's blood.
The prevalence of his plea.
The almightiness of the Spirit.
The truth of the gospel.

In fact, unbelief robs God of his glory in every way, and therefore it cannot receive a blessing from the Lord.   Heb. xi. 6.

III. THE INTELLIGENT APPEAL. " Lord, I believe; help thou mine unbelief."

In his great perplexity he cries to Jesus only.

1. On the basis of faith,—" Lord, I believe."

2. With confession of sin,—" mine unbelief."

3. To One who knows how to help in this matter,—" Lord, help."

4. To One who is himself the best remedy for unbelief,—"help thou."

Unbelief is overcome when we fly to Jesus, and consider—
The majesty of his divine nature.
The tenderness of his humanity.
The graciousness of his offices.
The grandeur of his atonement.
The glorious object of his work.

Come to Jesus with any case, and in every case.

Come with your little faith and with your great unbelief, for in this matter also he can help as none other can.

HELPS

There is no sin which may not be traced up to unbelief.—*Mason.*

"Lord, I believe," etc. This act of his, in putting forth his faith to believe as he could, was the way to believe as he would.—*Trapp.*

A young man, in the seventeenth century, being in deep distress of mind, applied to Dr. Goodwin for advice and consolation. After he had laid before him the long and black list of sins that troubled his conscience, the doctor reminded him that there was one blacker still, which he had not named. "What can that be, sir?" he despondingly asked. "The sin," replied the doctor, "I refer to is that of refusing to believe in Christ Jesus as a Saviour." The simple word banished the anxious one's guilty fears.

There was once a good woman who was well known among her circle for her simple faith, and her great calmness in the midst of many trials. Another woman, living at a distance, hearing of her, said, "I must go and see that woman, and learn the secret of her holy, happy life." She went; and accosting the woman, said, "Are you the woman with the great faith?" "No," replied she, "I am not the woman with the great faith; but I am the woman with a little faith in the great God."

> O help us, through the prayer of faith,
>   More firmly to believe ;
> For still the more Thy servant hath,
>   The more shall he receive.
> *Milman.*

A friend complained to Gotthold of the weakness of his faith, and the distress this gave him. Gotthold pointed to a vine, which had twined itself around a ploe, and was hanging loaded with beautiful clusters, and said, "Frail is that plant; but what harm is done to it by its frailty, especially as the Creator has been pleased to make it what it is? As little will it prejudice your faith that it is weak, provided only it be sincere and unfeigned. Faith is the work of God, and he bestows it in such measure as he wills and judges right. Let the measure of it which he has given you be deemed sufficient by you. Take for pole and prop the cross of the Saviour, and the Word of God; twine around these with all the power which God vouchsafes. A heart sensible of its weakness, and prostrating itself continually at the feet of the divine mercy, is more acceptable than that which presumes upon the strength of its faith, and falls into false security and pride. Can you suppose that the sinful woman, who lay and wept at the Lord's feet, was less approved than the swelling and haughty Pharisee?"—*Christian Scriver.*

CLII

Mark x. 49, 50 —"And Jesus stood still, and commanded him to be called. And they call the blind man, saying unto him, Be of good comfort, rise; he calleth thee.

"And he, casting away his garment, rose, and came to Jesus."

This man is a picture of what we would fain have every seeker of Christ to become.

In his lonely darkness, and deep poverty, he thought and became persuaded that Jesus was the Son of David.

Though he had no sight, he made good use of his hearing. If we have not all gifts, let us use those which we have.

I. HE SOUGHT THE LORD UNDER DISCOURAGEMENTS.

1. No one prompted his seeking.
2. Many opposed his attempts. "Many charged him that he should hold his peace": verse 48.
3. For a while he was unheeded by the Lord himself.
4. He was but a blind beggar, and this alone might have checked some pleaders.

Let our hearers imitate his dogged resolution.

II. HE RECEIVED ENCOURAGEMENT.

This came from our Lord's commanding him to be called.

There are several kinds of calls which come to men at the bidding of our Lord Jesus. There is the—

1. Universal call. Jesus is lifted up that all who look to him may live. John iii. 14, 15. The gospel is preached to every creature.
2. Character call. To those who labour, and are heavy-laden. Many are the gospel promises which call the sinful, the mourning, the weary to Jesus. Is. lv. 7. Matt. xi. 28. Acts ii. 38, 39.
3. Ministerial call. Given by the Lord's sent servants, and so backed by his authority. Acts xiii. 26, 38, 39 ; xvi. 31.
4. Effectual call. Sent home by the Holy Spirit. This is the calling of which we read, "whom he called, them he also justified": Rom. viii. 30.

III. BUT ENCOURAGEMENT DID NOT CONTENT HIM ; HE STILL SOUGHT JESUS.

To stop short of Jesus and healing would have been folly indeed.

1. He arose. Hopefully, resolutely, he quitted his begging posture. In order to salvation we must be on the alert, and in earnest.

2. He cast away his garment, and every hindrance. Our righteousness, our comfortable sin, our habit,—anything, everything we must quit for Christ.

3. He came to Jesus. In the darkness occasioned by his blindness, he followed the Saviour's voice.

4. He stated his case. " Lord, that I might receive my sight ! "

5. He received salvation. Jesus said unto him, " Thy faith hath made thee whole." He obtained perfect eyesight ; and in all respects he was in complete health.

IV. HAVING FOUND JESUS, HE KEPT TO HIM.

1. He used his sight to see his Lord.

2. He became his avowed disciple. See verse 52.

3. He went with Jesus on his way to the cross, and to the crown.

4. He remained a well-known disciple, whose father's name is given.

This man came out of cursed Jericho : are there not some to come from our slums and degraded districts ?

This man at best was a beggar, but the Lord Jesus did not disdain his company. He was a standing glory to the Lord, for every one would know him as the blind man whose eyes had been opened.

Let seeking souls persevere under all drawbacks. Do not mind those who would keep you back. Let none hinder you from finding Christ and salvation.

Though blind, and poor, and miserable, you shall yet see, and smile, and sing, and follow Jesus.

ENCOURAGEMENTS

"*And commanded him to be called.*" By this circumstance he administered reproof and instruction : reproof, by ordering those to help the poor man who had endeavoured to check him : instruction, by teaching us that, though he does not stand in need of our help, he will not dispense with our services ; that we are to aid each other ; that though we cannot recover our fellow-creatures, we may frequently bring them to the place and means of cure.— *William Jay.*

> Sad one, in secret, bending low,
> A dart in thy breast that the world may not know,
> Striving the favour of God to win,—
> Asking his pardon for days of sin ;
> Press on, press on, with thy earnest cry,
> "Jesus of Nazareth passeth by."

Mrs. Sigourney.

"And he, casting away his garment, rose, and came to Jesus." I remember once reading these words on a memorial tablet in a country church. Inscriptions on tombstones are often unsatisfactory, and scriptural quotations upon them most inappropriate; but this one was as suitable as it was singular. The squire of the village, a high-churchman, and an ardent sportsman, had late in life come under the influence of Christian friends, who brought him to a knowledge of the gospel; and to him the words of the Evangelist were applied. They were very suggestive. They told of pride, and worldly pursuits, and self-righteousness, of all to which the man had clung for a life-time, cast away that he might come to the Saviour. For a sinner saved in life's last hours a better epitaph could hardly have been chosen. I admired the piety that compared the rich man lying there to the poor blind beggar of the gospel story; the once highly esteemed garment of personal righteousness to the beggar's worthless robe; and that expressed the one hope and refuge of the soul in Christ by the words " he came to Jesus." It reminded me of the lines on William Carey's tomb—

> A guilty, weak, and helpless worm,
> On thy kind arms I fall;
> Be Thou my strength and righteousness.
> My Jesus and my all.

P.

Success in this world comes only to those who exhibit determination. Can we hope for salvation unless our mind is truly set upon it? Grace makes a man to be as resolved to be saved as this beggar was to get to Jesus, and gain his sight. "I must see him," said an applicant at the door of a public person. "You cannot see him," said the servant; but the man waited at the door. A friend went out to him, and said, " You cannot see the master, but I can give you an answer." "No," said the unfortunate pleader, " I will stay all night on the doorstep, but I will see the man himself. He alone will serve my turn." You do not wonder that, after many rebuffs, he ultimately gained his point: it would be an infinitely greater wonder if an importunate sinner did not obtain an audience from the Lord Jesus. If you must have grace, you shall have it. If you will not be put off, you shall not be put off. Whether things look favourable, or unfavourable, press you on till you find Jesus, and you shall find him.—*C. H. S.*

CLIII

Mark xii. 34 —"And when Jesus saw that he answered discreetly, he said unto him, Thou art not far from the kingdom of God."

The kingdom of God is set up among men.
Those who are in it are—

>Quickened with divine life. "He is not the God of the dead, but the God of the living": verse 27.
>
>Received under the reign of grace. Rom. v. 21.
>
>Obedient to the law of love. 1 John iv. 7.
>
>Favoured with divine privileges. Matt. vi. 33; Luke xii. 32.
>
>Raised to special dignities. Rev. i. 6.
>
>Indulged with peculiar happiness. Matt. xxv. 34.

Those who are outside of it are in some respects on a level.
But in other regards, some are "far off", and others "not far."
The scribe in the narrative was on the borders of the kingdom.
Of such a character we will now treat.

I. WHAT ARE ITS MARKS?

1. Truthfulness of spirit.

    This man was candid as a student of the law.
    This man was honest as a teacher of the law.
    This man was fair as a controversialist.
    A spirit of general uprightness, sincerity, and fairness, is a great moral advantage.

2. Spiritual perception. This scribe must have spoken with great discretion, or the Lord Jesus would not have taken such special notice of his reply. He saw—

    More than a Papist, who makes everything of ceremonies.
    More than a mere doctrinalist, who puts head-knowledge above heart-experience and holiness.
    More than a moralist, who forgets the love of the heart.

3. Acquaintance with the law.

    Those who see the unity, and yet the breadth and spirituality of the law's demands are in a hopeful condition.
    Still more, those who perceive that their own lives fall short of those demands, and grieve on that account.

4. Teachableness, which this man clearly exhibited, is a good sign; especially if we are willing to learn truth, although its advocate is unpopular.

5. A sense of need of Christ, which did not appear in the case ot this scribe, but is seen in many who attend the ministry.

6. A horror of wrong-doing, and of impurity of every kind.

7. A high regard for holy things, and a practical interest in them.

8. A diligent commencement of prayer, Bible-reading, meditation, regular hearing of the word, and other gracious habits.

There are other signs, but time would fail us to mention more.

Many of these appear, like blossoms on a tree, but they disappoint the hopes which they excite.

II. What are its dangers?

No man is safe till he is actually in the kingdom : the border-land is full of peril. There is the danger—

1. Lest you slip back from this hopefulness.

2. Lest you rest content to stop where you are.

3. Lest you grow proud and self-righteous.

4. Lest you proceed from being candid to become indifferent.

5. Lest you die ere the decisive step be taken.

III. What are its duties?

Though your condition is not one in which to rest, it is one which involves you in many responsibilities, since it is a condition of singular privilege.

1. Thank God for dealing so mercifully with you.

2. Admit with deep sincerity that you need supernatural help for entrance into the kingdom.

3. Tremble lest that decisive and saving step be never taken.

4. Decide at once through divine grace. Oh, for the Spirit of God to work effectually upon you !

What a pity that any should perish who are so near !

What horror to see such hopeful ones cast away !

How fatal to stop short of saving faith !

EXPOSTULATIONS

Among those who have turned out to be the most determined enemies of the gospel are many, who once were so near to conversion, that it was a wonder that they avoided it. Such persons seem ever after to take vengeance upon the holy influence which had almost proved too much for them. Hence our fear for persons under gracious impressions; for, if they do not now decide for God, they will become the more desperate in sin. That which is set in the sun, if it be not softened, will be hardened. I remember well a man, who, under the influence of an earnest revivalist, was brought to his knees, to cry for mercy, in the presence of his wife and others ; but never afterwards would he enter a place of worship, or pay attention to religious conversation. He declared that his escape was so narrow that he would never run the risk again. Alas, that one should graze the gate of heaven, and yet drive on to hell !—*C. H. S.*

Some are in the suburbs of the city of refuge. I warn you against staying there. Oh, what pity is it that any should perish at the gates of salvation for want of another step !

He that makes but one step up a stair, though he be not much nearer to the top of the house, yet he has stepped from the ground, and is delivered from the foulness and dampness of that. So, he that taketh the first step of prayer by truly crying,—" O Lord, be merciful unto me ! " though he be not established in heaven, yet he has stepped from off the world, and the miserable comforts thereof.—*Dr. Donne.*

A Christian minister says, " When, after safely circumnavigating the globe, *The Royal Charter* went to pieces in Moelfra Bay, on the coast of Wales, it was my melancholy duty to visit and seek to comfort the wife of the first officer, made by that calamity a widow. The ship had been telegraphed from Queenstown, and the lady was sitting in the parlour expecting her husband, with the table spread for his evening meal, when the messenger came to tell her he was drowned. Never can I forget the grief, so stricken and tearless, with which she wrung my hand, as she said, ' So near home, and yet lost ! ' That seemed to me the most terrible of human sorrow. But, ah ! that is nothing to the anguish which must wring the soul which is compelled to say at last, ' Once I was at the very gate of heaven, and had almost entered in, but now I am in hell ! ' "

I remember a man coming to me in great distress of soul, and his case made a deep impression upon my mind. He was a man-of-war's man, with all the frankness of a British tar, but, alas ! also, with a sailor's fondness for strong drink. As we talked and prayed together, the tears literally rained down the poor fellow's weather-beaten face, and he trembled violently. " Oh, sir," he exclaimed, " I could fight for it ! " Truly, if salvation could have been obtained by some deed of daring, he would have won it. He left me without finding peace, and the next day he went back *drunk*, to join his ship ; and I have never heard of him since.—*J. W. H.*

CLIV

Mark xiv. 32 —"And they came to a place which was named Gethsemane."

Our Lord left the table of happy fellowship, and passed over the brook Kedron, so associated with the sorrows of David. 2 Sam. xv. 23.

He then entered into the garden, named Gethsemane, not to hide himself from death, but to prepare for it by a season of special prayer.

Gethsemane was our Lord's place of secret prayer. John xviii. 1, 2.

If *he* resorted to his closet in the hour of trial, we need to do so far more.

In his solitary supplication he was oppressed with a great grief, and overwhelmed with a terrible anguish.

It was a killing change from the cheerful communion of the Supper to the lone agony of the garden.

Let us think with great solemnity of the olive-garden where the Saviour sweat as it were great drops of blood.

I. THE CHOICE OF THE SPOT—

    1. Showed his serenity of mind, and his courage.

        He goes to his usual place of secret prayer.

        He goes there though Judas knew the place.

    2. Manifested his wisdom.

        Holy memories there aided his faith.

        Deep solitude was suitable for his prayers and cries.

        Congenial gloom fitted his exceeding sorrow.

    3. Bequeathed us lessons.

        In a garden, Paradise was lost and won.

        In Gethsemane, the olive-press, our Lord himself was crushed.

        In our griefs, let us retreat to our God in secret.

        In our special prayers, let us not be ashamed to let them be known to our choicer friends, for Jesus took his disciples with him to his secret devotions in Gethsemane.

II. THE EXERCISE UPON THE SPOT.

Every item is worthy of attention and imitation.

    1. He took all due precautions for others.

        He would not have his disciples surprised, and therefore bade them watch. So should we care for others in our own extremity. The intensity of his intercourse with God did not cause him to forget one of his companions.

2. He solicited the sympathy of friends.

We may not despise this; though, like our Lord, we shall prove the feebleness of it, and cry, "Could ye not watch with me?"

3. He prayed and wrestled with God.

In lowliest posture and manner.   See verse 35.
In piteous repetition of his cry.   See verses 36 and 39.
In awful agony of spirit even to a bloody sweat.   Luke xxii. 44.
In full and true submission.   Matt. xxvi. 42, 44.

4. He again and again sought human sympathy, but made excuse for his friends when they failed him.   See verse 38.   We ought not to be soured in spirit even when we are bitterly disappointed.

5. He returned to his God, and poured out his soul in strong crying and tears, until he was heard in that he feared.   Heb. v. 7.

III. THE TRIUMPH UPON THE SPOT.

1. Behold his perfect resignation.   He struggles with "if it be possible," but conquers with "not what I will, but what thou wilt."   He is our example of patience.

2. Rejoice in his strong resolve.   He had undertaken, and would go through with it.   Luke ix. 51; xii. 50.

3. Mark the angelic service rendered.   The blood-bestained Sufferer has still all heaven at his call.   Matt. xxvi. 53.

4. Remember his majestic bearing towards his enemies.

He meets them bravely.   Matt. xxvi. 55.
He makes them fall.   John xviii. 6.
He yields himself, but not to force.   John xviii. 8.
He goes to the cross, and transforms it to a throne.

We, too, may expect our minor Gethsemane.
We shall not be there without a Friend, for he is with us.
We shall conquer by his might, and in his manner.

IN MEMORIAM

The late Rev. W. H. Krause, of Dublin, was visiting a lady in a depressed state, "weak, oh, so weak!"   She told him that she had been very much troubled in mind that day, because in meditation and prayer she had found it impossible to govern her thoughts, and kept merely going over the same things again and again.   "Well, my dear friend," was his prompt reply, "there is provision in the gospel for that too. Our Lord Jesus Christ, when *his* soul was exceeding sorrowful, even unto death, three times prayed, and spoke *the same words*."   This seasonable application of Scripture was a source of great comfort to her.

Gethsemane, the olive-press !
(And why so called let Christians guess.)
Fit name, fit place, where vengeance strove,
And griped and grappled hard with love.

Joseph Hart.

"My will, not thine, be done," turned Paradise into a desert. "Thy will, not mine, be done," turned the desert into Paradise, and made Gethsemane the gate of heaven.—*E. ae Pressensé.*

An inscription in a garden in Wales runs thus :—

" In a garden the first of our race was deceived,
In a garden the promise of grace he received,
In a garden was Jesus betrayed to his doom,
In a garden his body was laid in the tomb."

There will be no Christian but what will have a Gethsemane, but every praying Christian will find that there is no Gethsemane without its angel.—*Thomas Binney.*

The Father heard ; and angels, there,
Sustained the Son of God in prayer,
    In sad Gethsemane ;
He drank the dreadful cup of pain—
Then rose to life and joy again.

When storms of sorrow round us sweep,
And scenes of anguish make us weep ;
    To sad Gethsemane
We'll look, and see the Saviour there,
And humbly bow, like Him, in prayer.

S. F. Smith.

"*And there appeared an angel unto him from heaven, strengthening him.*"—What ! The Son of God receives help from an angel, who is but his creature ? Yes. And we learn thereby to expect help and comfort from simple persons and common things, when God pleases. All strength and comfort come from God, but he makes creatures his ministers to bring it. We should thank both them and him.—*Practical Reflections on every verse of the Holy Gospels, by a Clergyman.*

There is something in an olive-garden, on a hill-side, which makes it most suitable for prayer and meditation. The shade is solemn, the terraces divide better than distance, the ground is suitable for kneeling upon, and the surroundings are all in accord with holy thoughts. I can hardly tell why it is, but often as I have sat in an olive-garden, I have never been without the sense that it was the place and the hour of prayer.—*C. H. S.*

CLV

Mark xiv. 72 —" And when he thought thereon, he wept."

Repentance is wrought by the Spirit of God.

But he works it in us by leading us to think upon the evil of sin.

Peter could not help weeping when he remembered his grievous fault.

Let us at this time—

I. Study peter's case, and use it for our own instruction.

  1. He considered that he had denied his Lord.

     Have we never done the like ?

     This may be done in many ways.

  2. He reflected upon the excellence of the Lord whom he had denied.

  3. He remembered the position in which his Lord had placed him,— making him an apostle, and one of the first of them.

     Have we not been placed in positions of trust?

  4. He bethought him of the special intercourse which he had enjoyed. He and James and John had been most favoured. Matt. xvii. 1—13 ; xxvi. 36—46 ; Mark v. 37—43.

     Have not we known joyous fellowship with our Lord?

  5. He recollected that he had been solemnly forewarned by his Lord. Have we not sinned against light and knowledge?

  6. He recalled his own vows, pledges, and boasts. " Although all shall be offended, yet will not I ": verse 29.

     Have we not broken very earnest declarations ?

  7. He thought upon the special circumstances of his Lord when he had so wickedly denied him.

     Are there no aggravations in our case ?

  8. He revolved in his mind his repetitions of the offence, and those repetitions with added aggravations : his lie, his oath, etc.

     We ought to dwell on each item of our transgressions, that we may be brought to a more thorough repentance of them.

II. Study our own lives, and use the study for our further humiliation.

  1. Think upon our transgressions while unregenerate.

  2. Think upon our resistance of light, and conscience, and the Holy Spirit before we were overcome by divine grace.

  3. Think upon our small progress in the divine life.

  4. Think upon our backslidings and heart-wanderings.

  5. Think upon our neglect of the souls of others.

6. Think upon our little communion with our Lord.

7. Think upon the little glory we are bringing to his great name.

8. Think upon our matchless obligations to his infinite love.

Each of these meditations is calculated to make us weep.

III. Study the effect of these thoughts upon our own minds.

   1. Can we think of these things without emotion?

This is possible; for many excuse their sin on the ground of their circumstances, their constitution, their company, their trade, their fate: they even lay the blame on Satan, or some other tempter. Certain hard hearts treat the matter with supreme indifference.

This is perilous. It is to be feared that such a man is not Peter, but Judas: not a fallen saint, but a son of perdition.

   2. Are we moved by thoughts of these things?

There are other reflections which may move us far more.

Our Lord forgives us, and numbers us with his brethren.

He asks us if we love him, and he bids us feed his sheep.

Surely, when we dwell on these themes, it must be true of each of us—"When he thought thereon, he wept."

RECOLLECTIONS

Peter's recollection of what he had formerly heard was another occasion of his repentance. We do not sufficiently consider how much more we need recollection than information. We know a thousand things, but it is necessary that they should be kept alive in our hearts by a constant and vivid recollection. It is, therefore, extremely absurd and childish for people to say, "You tell me nothing but what I know." I answer, you forget many things; and, therefore, it is necessary that line should be upon line, and precept upon precept. Peter, himself, afterwards said, in his Epistles, "I will not be negligent to put you always in remembrance of these things, though ye know them." We are prone to forget what we do know; whereas we should consider that, whatever good thing we know is only so far good to us as it is remembered to purpose.—*Richard Cecil.*

Peter falls dreadfully, but by repentance rises sweetly; a look of love from Christ melts him into tears. He knew that repentance was the key to the kingdom of grace. At once his faith was so great that he leaped, as it were, into a sea of waters to come to Christ; so now his repentance was so great that he leaped, as it were, into a sea of tears, for that he had gone from Christ. Some say that, after his sad fall, he was ever and anon weeping, and that his face was even furrowed with continual tears. He had no sooner taken in poison but he vomited it up again, ere it got to the vitals ; he had no sooner handled this serpent but he turned it into a rod, to scourge his soul with remorse for sinning against such clear light, and strong love, and sweet discoveries of the heart of Christ to him.

Clement notes that Peter so repented that, all his life after, every night when he heard the cock crow, he would fall upon his knees, and, weeping bitterly, would beg pardon for his sin. Ah ! souls, you can easily sin as the saints, but can you repent with the saints ? Many can sin with David and Peter, who cannot repent with David and Peter, and so must perish for ever.—*Thomas Brooks.*

Cowper describes the time when he reflected on the necessity of repentance. " I knew that many persons had spoken of shedding tears for sin ; but when I asked myself, whether the time would ever come, when I should weep for mine, it seemed to me that a stone might sooner do it. . . . Not knowing that Christ was exalted to give repentance, I despaired of ever attaining it." A friend came to his bed-side, and declared to him the gospel. He insisted on the all-atoning efficacy of the blood of Jesus, and his righteousness for our justification. " While I heard this part of his discourse, and the Scriptures on which he founded it, my heart began to burn within me ; my soul was pierced with a sense of my bitter ingratitude to so merciful a Saviour ; and those tears, which I thought impossible, burst forth freely."—*Cowper's "Memoirs of his Early Life."*

Nothing will make the faces of God's children more fair than for them to wash themselves every morning in their tears.—*Samuel Clark.*

The old Greeks thought that memory must be a source of torture in the next world, so they interposed between the two worlds the waters of Lethe, the river of forgetfulness ; but believers in Christ want no river of oblivion on the borders of Elysium. Calvary is on this side, and that is enough.—*Alexander Maclaren.*

CLVI

Mark xvi. 10 —"And she went and told them that had been with him, as they mourned and wept."

Mark is graphic : he paints an interior like a Dutch artist.

We see a choice company,—"them that had been with him."

We know many of the individuals, and are interested to note what they are doing, and how they bear their bereavement.

We see—

I. A SORROWING ASSEMBLY. "As they mourned and wept."

What a scene ! We behold a common mourning, abundantly expressed by tears and lamentations.

They mourned—

1. Because they had believed in Jesus, and loved him ; and therefore they were concerned at what had happened.
2. Because they felt their great loss in losing him.
3. Because they had seen his sufferings and death.
4. Because they remembered their ill-conduct towards **him.**
5. Because their hopes concerning him were disappointed.
6. Because they were utterly bewildered as to what was now to be done, seeing their Leader was gone.

In considering the death of Jesus, there is just cause for mourning.

Let us intelligently mourn for him, since our sins occasioned his woes and death.

II. A CONSOLING MESSENGER. Mary Magdalene came and told them that Jesus had risen, and had appeared unto her.

Concerning this ministry, we note—

1. She was one of themselves. The witnesses to our Lord's resurrection were such as his disciples, and, indeed, all the world, might safely trust. They were not strangers, but individuals well known to those who heard them.
2. She came with the best of news. She declared that Jesus was indeed risen. The resurrection of our divine Lord —
   Removes the cause of our sorrow.
   Assures us of the help of a living Redeemer. John xiv. 19.
   Secures our own personal resurrection. 1 Cor. xv. 23.
   Brings us personal justification. Rom. iv. 25.
3. She was not believed.
   Unbelief is apt to become chronic : they had not believed the Lord when he foretold his own resurrection, and so they do not believe an eye-witness who reported it.

Unbelief is cruelly unjust : they made Mary Magdalene a liar, and yet all of them esteemed her.

III. A REASSURING REFLECTION.

1. We are not the only persons who have mourned an absent Lord.
2. We are not the only messengers who have been rejected.
3. We are sure beyond all doubt of the resurrection of Christ.
   The evidence is more abundant than that which testifies to any other great historical event.
   The apostles so believed it as to die as witnesses of it.
   They were very slow to be convinced, and therefore that which forced *them* to believe should have the like effect upon the most careful of *us*.
4. We have thus the most ample reason for joy concerning our Lord.

Let us not think too mournfully of our Lord's passion.

Let us not be too mournful about anything, now that we know that we have a living Saviour for our Friend.

MEMORANDA

In the famous picture-gallery of Bologna, there is a striking picture by Domenichino, representing an angel standing beside the empty cross, from which the body of Christ has just been removed.   He holds in his hand the crown of thorns, that had just fallen from the august Sufferer's brow ; and the expression that passes over his face, as he feels with his finger the sharpness of one of the protruding thorns, is full of meaning. It is a look of wonder and surprise.   To the pure, unstained, immortal nature of the angel, all that suffering is a profound mystery.   The death of Christ was equally a mystery to his disciples.—*Hugh Macmillan.*

A sorrow is none the less sharp because it is founded upon a mistake. Jacob mourned very bitterly for Joseph, though his darling was not torn in pieces, but on the way to be lord over all Egypt.   Yet while there is of necessity so much well-founded sorrow in the world, it is a pity that one unnecessary pang should be endured, and endured by those who have the best possible grounds for joy.   The case in the text before us is a typical one.   Thousands are at this day mourning and weeping who ought to be rejoicing.   Oh, the mass of needless grief !   Unbelief works for the father of lies in this matter, and works misery out of falsehood among those who are not in truth children of sadness, but heirs of light and joy.   Rise, faith, and with thy light chase away this darkness !   And if even thou must have thy lamp trimmed by a humble Mary, do not despise her kindly aid.

CLVII

Luke v. 26 —"We have seen strange things to-day."

The world is aweary, and longs for something novel.

The greatest stranger in the world is Jesus; and, alas, he is the least seen, and the least spoken of by the most of men!

If men would come and watch him, they would see strange things.

His person, his life, his death, his teaching, are full of strange things.

What he is now doing has as much as ever the element of strangeness and wonder about it.

I. MARK THE STRANGE THINGS OF THAT PARTICULAR DAY.

1. Power present to heal doctors! Verse 17.
2. Faith reaching down to the Lord from above! Verse 19.
3. Jesus pardoning sin with a word. Verse 20.
4. Jesus practising thought-reading. Verse 22.
5. Jesus making a man carry the bed which had carried him. Verse 25.

II. MARK THE STRANGE THINGS OF CHRIST'S DAY.

1. The Maker of men born among men. The Infinite an infant.
2. The Lord of all serving all.
3. The Just One accused, condemned, and sacrificed for sin.
4. The Crucified rising from the dead.
5. Death slain by the dying of the Lord.

These are but incidents in a life which is all strange and marvellous.

III. MARK THE STRANGE THINGS SEEN BY BELIEVERS IN THEIR DAY WITHIN THEMSELVES AND OTHERS.

1. A self-condemned sinner justified by faith.
2. A natural heart renewed by grace.
3. A soul preserved in spiritual life amid killing evils, like the bush which burned with fire and was not consumed.
4. Evil made to work for good by providential wisdom.
5. Strength made perfect in weakness.
6. The Holy Ghost dwelling in a believer.
7. Heaven enjoyed on earth.

These are a small number out of a host of strange things.

Life never grows stale to a companion of Jesus.

Do you find it becoming so, and are you a believer?

Seek the conversion of your family, and your neighbourhood.

Seek to know more of Jesus at work among men.

This will cause you to see stranger and stranger things, till you see the strangest of all with Christ in glory.

WONDERS

Wonder at the work of God is natural, justifiable, commendable. He is a God of wonders. It is right to say of the Lord's doing, " It is marvellous in our eyes." We are to talk of all his wondrous works ; but this must be in the spirit of devout admiration, not in the spirit of suspicion and doubt. A holy, grateful wonder should be indulged to the full; but a cold, sceptical wonder should be resisted as a suggestion from Satan. Faith accounts all things possible with God ; it is unbelief that incredulously marvels at the work of his hand.

Guthrie, of Fenwick, a Scotch minister, once visited a dying woman. He found her anxious about her state, but very ignorant. His explanation of the gospel was joyfully received by her, and soon after she died. On his return home, Guthrie said, " I have seen a strange thing to-day— a woman whom I found in a state of nature, I saw in a state of grace, and left in a state of glory."

In a manuscript by an old Scotch minister, in the early part of the last century, there is a remarkable account of the conversion of Lord Jeddart, who had been famous for his recklessness in sin, and of the astonishment it caused among Christian people. A little after his conversion, and before the thing was known, he came to the Lord's table. He sat next a lady who had her hands over her face, and did not see him till he delivered the cup out of his hand. When she saw that it was Lord Jeddart, who had been so renowned for sin, she fell a-trembling terribly for very amazement that such a man should be there. He noticed it, and said, "Madam, be not troubled : the grace of God is free ! " This calmed the lady ; but when we consider what sort of man Lord Jeddart had been, we can account for her surprise.

When I get to heaven, I shall see three wonders there :—the first wonder will be to see many people there whom I did not expect to see ; the second wonder will be to miss many people whom I did expect to see ; and the third and greatest wonder of all will be to find myself there.— *John Newton.*

> Wonders of grace to God belong,
> Repeat His mercies in your song.
>
> *Dr. Watts.*

CLVIII
Luke vii. 38 —"At his feet."

Orientals are demonstrative, and in their devotions they pay greater attention to bodily posture than we do. Let us be the more careful of the posture of our souls.

It is interesting to consider our posture towards our Lord.

He bears us on his heart (Solomon's Song viii. 6), in his bosom (Is. xl. 11), in his hand (Is. xlix. 2, li. 16), on his shoulders (Luke xv. 5). But yet " at his feet " is our most usual place.

I. IT IS A BECOMING POSTURE.

The posture is admirable for many reasons.

1. As he is divine, let us pay him lowliest reverence.
2. As we are sinful, let us make humble confession.
3. As he is Lord, let us make full submission.
4. As he is All in All, let us manifest immovable dependence.
5. As he is infinitely wise, let us wait his appointed time.

The best are at his feet joyfully, bowing before him.

The worst *must* come there, whether they will or no.

II. IT IS A HELPFUL POSTURE.

1. For a weeping penitent (Luke vii. 38).
   Our humility will help penitence.
   Our lowly submission will bring assurance.
   Our full obeisance will prepare for service.

2. For a resting convert (Luke viii. 35).
   In such a position devils are driven out, and no longer rule us.
   In such a position they are kept off, and cannot return.
   In such a position we give the best proof of being in our right mind.

3. For a pleading intercessor (Luke viii. 41).
   We plead best when we are lowliest.
   We may be rulers of the synagogue, but when our heart is breaking we find most hope "at his feet."

4. For a willing learner (Luke x. 39). Mary "at his feet" showed—
   A lowly sense of personal ignorance.
   A believing acceptance of the Lord's teaching.
   A hopeful uplooking to him.

5. For a grateful worshipper (Luke xvii. 16).
   So the healed leper expressed his thanks.
   So angels adore, giving him thanks, while bending low.
   So would our hearts bow in unutterable gratitude.

6. For a saint beholding his Lord's glory (Rev. i. 17).

Overwhelmed, humbled, overjoyed, exhausted with excess of ecstasy.

Come, then, and submit to Jesus, and bow at his feet.

He is so worthy : pay him all reverence.

He has received from you so much despite : kiss his feet.

He will so freely forgive : this may well cause you to bow in the dust before him.

He will give you such joy : in fact, no joy excels that of full submission to his blessed sway.

III. IT IS A SAFE POSTURE.

1. Jesus will not refuse us that position, for it is one which we ought to occupy.

2. Jesus will not spurn the humbly submissive, who in self-despair cast themselves before him.

3. Jesus will not suffer any to harm those who seek refuge at his feet.

4. Jesus will not deny us the eternal privilege of abiding there.

Let this be our continual posture —" at his feet."

Sorrowing or rejoicing ; hoping or fearing ;
Suffering or working ; teaching or learning ;
In secret or in public ; in life and in death.

"Oh, that I might for ever sit
With Mary at the Master's feet."

CLIPPINGS

In order that the mats or carpets, which are hallowed by domestic prayer, may not be rendered unclean by any pollution of the streets, each guest, as he enters a house in Syria or Palestine, takes off his sandals, and leaves them at the door. He then proceeds to his place at the table. In ancient times, as we find throughout the Old Testament, it was the custom of the Jews to eat their meals sitting cross-legged—as is still common throughout the East—in front of a tray placed on a low stool, on which is set the dish containing the heap of food, from which all help themselves in common. But this custom, though it has been resumed for centuries, appears to have been abandoned by the Jews in the period succeeding the captivity. Whether they had borrowed the recumbent posture at meals from the Persians, or not, it is certain, from the expressions employed, that, in the time of our Lord, the Jews, like the Greeks and Romans, reclined at banquets, upon couches placed round tables of much the same height as those now in use. We shall see, hereafter, that even the Passover was eaten in this attitude. The beautiful, and profoundly moving incident, which occurred in Simon's house, can only be understood by remembering that, as the guests lay on the couches which surrounded the tables, their feet would be turned towards any spectators who were standing outside the circle of bidden guests.—*Archdeacon Farrar.*

Artabanus, one of the military officers of the Athenians, was applied to by a certain great man, who told him that he desired an audience of the king. He was answered that, before it was granted, he must prostrate himself before him, for it was a custom of the country for the king to admit no one to his presence who would not worship him. That which was an arrogant assumption in an earthly king is a proper condition of our approach to the King of kings. Humility is the foundation of our intercourse with him. We must bow before his throne. No sinner who is too proud to yield obedience to this law may expect any favours from his hands.—*Handbook of Illustration.*

When the Danish missionaries, stationed at Malabar, set some of their converts to translate a catechism, in which it was asserted that believers become the sons of God, one of the translators was so startled that he suddenly laid down his pen, and exclaimed, "It is too much. Let me rather render it, 'They shall be permitted to kiss his feet.'"—*G. S. Bowes.*

The Rev. Mr. Young was, one stormy day, visiting one of his people, an old man, who lived in great poverty, in a lonely cottage, a few miles from Jedburgh. He found him sitting with the Bible open on his knees, but in outward circumstances of great discomfort, the snow drifting through the roof, and under the door, and scarcely any fire on the hearth. "What are you about to-day, John?" was Mr. Young's question on entering. "Ah! sir," said the happy saint, "I'm sitting under his shadow, wi' great delight."—*The Christian Treasury.*

The end of all Christian preaching is to cast the sinner trembling at the feet of mercy.—*Vinet.*

> Low at Thy feet my soul would lie,
> Here safety dwells, and peace divine;
> Still let me live beneath Thine eye,
> For life, eternal life, is Thine.
> *Anne Steele.*

CLIX

Luke bii. 42—" Tell me, therefore, which of them will love him most ? "

It is right for us to desire to be among the most loving servants of the Lord Jesus. It would be an interesting question concerning a company just joining the church,—"Which of them will love him most ?"

How can we reach this point ? How can we love him most ?

We would love him as did the penitent who washed his feet with tears : whence shall come such eminence of love ?

The passage before us may help us to a conclusion on that point.

I. WE MUST FIRST BE SAVED IN THE SAME MANNER AS OTHERS.

The road to eminence in love is just the plain way of salvation, which all who are in Christ must travel. There is no new gospel of the higher life, and there need be no singularity of dress, abode, or vow, in order to attain the greatest heights of love.

1. All are in debt ; we must heartily own this to be our own case.

2. None have anything to pay ; we must confess this, without reserve, as being our own personal condition.

3. The loving Lord forgives in each case : personally we have exceeding great need of such remission. We must feel this.

4. In each case he forgives frankly, or without any consideration or compensation : it must be so with us. We must accept free grace and undeserved favour.

5 Out of this arises love. By a sense of free grace we begin to love our Lord ; and in the same way we go on to love him more.

The more clear our sense of sinnership, and the more conscious our obligation to free grace, the more likely are we to love much.

II. WE MUST AIM AT A DEEP SENSE OF SIN.

1. It was the *consciousness* of great indebtedness which created the great love in the penitent woman. Not her sin, but the consciousness of it, was the basis of her loving character.

2. Where sin has been open and loud, there ought to be this specially humbling consciousness ; for it would be an evidence of untruthfulness if it were not manifest. 1 Cor. xv. 9.

3. Yet is it frequently found in the most moral, and it abounds in saints of high degree. In fact, these are the persons who are most capable of feeling the evil of sin, and the greatness of the love which pardons it. 1 John i. 8.

93

4. It is to be cultivated. The more we bewail sin the better, and **we** must aim at great tenderness of heart in reference to it.

In order to cultivate it we must seek to get—

A clearer view of the law's requirements. Luke x. 26, 27.

A fuller idea of God's excellences, especially of his holiness. Job xlii. 5, 6.

A sharper sense of sin's tendencies in ourselves, towards God, and towards men ; and also a more overwhelming conviction of its dreadful punishment. Rom. vii. 13 ; Ps. li. 3, 4 ; John v. 28, 29.

A deeper consciousness of the love of God to us. 1 John iii. 1, 2.

A keener valuation of the cost of redemption. 1 Peter i. 18, 19.

A surer persuasion of the perfection of our pardon will also help to show the baseness of our sin. Ezek. xvi. 62, 63.

By these means, and all others, we must endeavour to keep our conscience active, that our heart may be sensitive.

III. THIS WILL LEAD TO A HIGHLY LOVING CARRIAGE TOWARDS OUR LORD.

We shall so love him as to behave like the penitent in the narrative.

1. We shall desire to be near him, even at his feet.

2. We shall make bold confession, and shall do this at all risks ; honouring him before gainsayers, and doing so though it may cause others to make unkind remarks.

3. We shall show deep humility, delighting even to wash his feet.

4. We shall exhibit thorough contrition, beholding him with tears.

5. We shall render earnest service ; doing all that lies in our power for Jesus, even as this woman did.

6. We shall make total consecration of all that we have : our tears, our eyes, our choicest gifts, our hearts, ourselves, etc.

Thus shall we reach the goal we desire.

A company of those who "love him most", dwelling in any place, would give a tone to the society around them.

We have enough of head-workers ; now for heart-lovers.

Why should we not aim to be among the closest followers of our Lord, loving most, and living specially consecrated lives ?

EXPERIMENTAL REMARKS

A spiritual experience which is thoroughly flavoured with a deep and bitter sense of sin is of great value to him that hath had it. It is terrible in the drinking, but it is most wholesome in the bowels, and in the whole of the after-life. Possibly much of the flimsy piety of the day arises from the ease with which men reach to peace and joy in these evangelistic days. We would not judge modern converts, but we certainly prefer that form of spiritual exercise which leads the soul by the way of Weeping-cross, and makes it see its blackness before it assures it that it is "clean every whit." Too many think lightly of sin, and therefore lightly of a Saviour. He who has stood before his God, convicted, and condemned, with the rope about his neck, is the man to weep for joy when he is pardoned, to hate the evil which has been forgiven him, and to live to the honour of the Redeemer by whose blood he has been cleansed.

Many of the most eminent of the saints were, before conversion, ringleaders in sin : instances will suggest themselves to all readers of church history. We naturally expect that a remarkable conversion should show itself by special fruits ; we very properly doubt it if it does not. A virulent rebel, when he returns to his Lord, is bound to be valiant as well as loyal ; for he remembers that he not only owes fealty to his Lord by nature, but he owes that life a second time to his Prince's clemency. Those who were once far gone in sin ought always to be found in the thick of the battle against sin. Bold blasphemers ought to be enthusiasts for the honour of their Lord when they are washed from their iniquities. As they say reclaimed poachers make the best game-keepers, so should the greatest sinners be the raw material out of which the Lord's transforming grace shall create great saints.

The Christian mentions a reminiscence of that saintly man, Mr. Pennefather. One day a member of his household knocked at the door of his study, and when at length it was opened, the good man was in tears. Being anxiously asked the cause, he replied, " My sins ! my sins ! " The sensitiveness of that holy soul, its quickened estimate of sin, its reverent conception of God's righteousness, which the tearful exclamation manifested, commend his memory to our love and veneration. All who knew him loved him as a living manifestation of the seven beatitudes.

I have heard say that the depth of a Scotch loch corresponds with the height of the surrounding mountains. So deep thy sense of obligation for pardoned sin, so high thy love to him who has forgiven thee.—*C.H.S.*

Love to the Saviour rises in the heart of a saved man in proportion to the sense which he entertains of his own sinfulness on the one hand, and of the mercy of God on the other. Thus the height of a saint's love to the Lord is as the depths of his own humility : as this root strikes down unseen into the ground, that blossoming branch rises higher in the sky —*William Arnot.*

95

CLX

Luke biii. 40 —"And it came to pass, that, when Jesus was returned, the people gladly received him: for they were all waiting for him."

Jesus went to those who refused him in the land of Gadara; and there he saved one, to show the freeness and sovereignty of his grace.

He then quitted the inhospitable country, to show that he forces himself on none. Wisdom abandons those who refuse her counsels. Prov. i. 24. Those whom the Lord has chosen shall be willing in the day of his power. Ps. cx. 3.

In the Revised Version we read, " The multitude welcomed him."

When Jesus is waited for and welcomed, he delights to come.

He is not waited for by all in our congregations ; so that we may ask the question of our present hearers—Do you welcome Christ? Let it be answered by each one this day.

I. A BEAUTIFUL SIGHT. "They were all waiting for him."

This waiting may be seen in several different forms.

1. A gathered congregation, waiting in the place where prayer is wont to be made. Want of punctuality, and irregular attendance, often show that Jesus is not waited for.

2. A praying company, an earnest church, looking for revival, and prepared to co-operate in labour for it. Some churches do not wait for the Lord's presence, and would not be ready for him if he were to come.

3. A seeking sinner, sighing for mercy, searching the Scriptures, hearing the Word, enquiring of Christians, constantly praying, and thus "waiting for him."

4. A departing saint, longing for home : saying, like Jacob, "I have waited for thy salvation, O Lord" : Gen. xlix. 18.

5. An instructed church, looking for the Second Advent. Rev. xxii. 17.

It is good for the eyes to behold such sights.

II. A SURE ARRIVAL. " Jesus was returned."

We are quite sure that our Lord will graciously appear to those who are " all waiting for him ", since—

1. His Spirit is there already, making them wait. Romans viii. 23.

2. His heart is there, in sympathy with them, longing to bless them.

3. His work is there. He has brought them into that waiting

96

condition, and now he has found a sphere wherein to display his grace to saints and sinners.

4. His promise is there, "Lo, I am with you alway": Matt. xxviii. 20.

5. His custom is to be there. His delights are still with the sons of men. Proverbs viii. 31.

What countless blessings his coming will bring!

III. A HEARTY WELCOME. "The people gladly received him."

1. Their fears made him welcome.

They feared lest he might have gone for ever from them. Ps. lxxvii. 7.

2. Their hopes made him welcome.

They trusted that now their sick would be cured, and their dead would be raised.

3. Their prayers made him welcome.

Those who pray that Jesus may come are glad when he comes.

4. Their faith made him welcome.

Jairus now looked to have his child healed. See verse 41.

5. Their love made him welcome.

When our heart is with him, we rejoice in his appearing.

6. Their care for others made him welcome.

Jesus never disappoints those who wait for him.

Jesus never refuses those who welcome him.

Jesus is near us now: will you not open the doors of your hearts to receive him? Rev. iii. 20.

HEARTY WELCOME

A congregation cannot be said to welcome the Lord Jesus unless they are all there, which requires *punctuality;* unless they have come with design to meet him, which implies prayerful *expectancy;* unless they are ready to hear from him, which involves *attention;* and unless they are resolved to accept his teaching, which demands *obedience.*

When the inhabitants of Mentone desired a visit from the Prince of Savoy, they made a way for him over the mountains. Hills were tunnelled, and valleys bridged, that the beloved sovereign might receive the welcome of his subjects. If we would really welcome the Lord Jesus, we must make a road for him by abasing our pride, elevating our thoughts, removing our evil habits, and preparing our hearts. Never did a soul cast up a highway for the Lord, and then fail to enjoy his company.—*C.H.S.*

97

CLXI

Luke x. 39 —"And she had a sister called Mary, which also sat at Jesus' feet, and heard his word."

The family at Bethany was highly favoured by being permitted to entertain our Lord so often.

They all appreciated the privilege, but Mary made the wisest use of it.

Martha sought to serve the Lord with her very best.

Mary was full of love to Jesus, as we know by her anointing him, and therefore she also would serve him with her very best.

She did so by attending to his words.

She was a wise and saintly woman, and our Lord commended her chosen method of service.

It will be safe, therefore, for us to follow her example.

Let us learn from the woman who sat as a learner at the feet of our Lord, and thus taught us to choose the good part.

Here we see—

I. LOVE AT LEISURE. " Which also sat at Jesus' feet."

When the evening comes on, and all the members of the family are around the fireside, then love rests and communes, forgetting all care, happily at home, oblivious of the outside world, and of time itself.

Like Mary—

We would feel ourselves quite at home with Jesus our Lord.

We would be free from worldly care—leaving all with Jesus.

We would even be free from the care of his service, the battle for his Kingdom, and the burden of the souls committed to our charge.

We would sweetly enjoy the happy leisure which he provides for us, as we muse upon the rest-giving themes which he reveals so clearly, and makes so true to us—

His work for us, finished, accepted, abidingly effectual, and perpetually overflowing with priceless blessings.

His great gifts received, which are greater than those to come.

All other needful and promised benedictions of grace, sure to come in due season. Rom. viii. 32.

All our future, for time and for eternity, safe in his dear hands.

Let us, without fear, enjoy leisure with Jesus—leisure, but not laziness :—leisure to love, to learn, to commune, to copy.

Leisure in a home where others are cumbered. See verses 40-42.

Leisure to sit, and to sit in the most delightful of all places.

98

II. LOVE IN LOWLINESS. "At Jesus' feet."

In this lowliness let each one personally copy Mary.

Say unto yourself, " I choose the feet of Jesus to be my place."

Let me be—

Not a busy housewife and manager, which any one may be, and yet be graceless; but—

1. A penitent, which is an acknowledgment of my unworthiness.

2. A disciple, which is a confession of my ignorance.

3. A receiver, which is an admission of my emptiness.

This posture befits me when I think of what I was, what I am, what I must be, what my Lord is, and what he is to me.

Let me bless his condescending love, which permits me this bliss.

III. LOVE LISTENING. "And heard his word."

She could not have heard if she had not been at leisure to *sit*, nor if she had not been lowly, and chosen to sit *at his feet*.

Be it ours to hear that love-word which says, " Hearken, O daughter, and consider ": Ps. xlv. 10.

Listening to what Jesus says in his Word, in his creation, in his providence, and by his Spirit in our soul.

Listening to the tones and accents with which he emphasizes and sweetens all that he says.

Listening to himself. Studying *him*, reading his very heart.

Listening, and not obtruding our own self-formed thoughts, notions, reasonings, questionings, desires, and prejudices.

Listening, and forgetting the observations and unbeliefs of others.

Listening, and bidding all cares lie still, that they may no more disturb the reverent silence of the heart.

How sweet ! How instructive ! How truly " the good part " !

IV. LOVE IN POSSESSION.

She had obtained her Lord, his love, his presence, his word, his fellowship, and she sat there *in full enjoyment* to delight her soul with that which she had so joyfully lighted upon.

She had in this one thing supplied her soul's necessity, and so she sat down *in perfect satisfaction*.

She had her Lord's promise that she should not be robbed of it, and she sat down *in full assurance*, to be happy in her possession

Her Lord's promise assured her that she should not lose the good part, which she had chosen,—

By a cold word from her Lord.

By the angry expostulation of her sister.

By any future affliction, or temptation, or occupation.

Nor even by death itself.

Now, then, she rests *in resolute constancy:* she has reached her *ultimatum:* she will go no further than her Lord and his word.

Oh, to be more with Jesus! This is true life.

Oh, to hear Jesus more! This is true service.

Oh, to love Jesus more! This is true treasure.

Oh, to abide with Jesus, and never dream of going beyond him! This is true wisdom.

QUIET MORSELS

Behold Mary, all reverence, all attention, all composure, feeding on the doctrine of eternal life—she "sat at Jesus feet." She wisely and zealously improved the opportunity given her for the good of her soul. "This is my summer, my harvest: let me redeem the time."—*Jay.*

Mary sitteth to hear the word, as Christ used to sit when he preached the word (Matthew v., Luke xiv., John viii.); to show that the word is to be preached and heard with a quiet mind. In a still night, every voice is heard, and when the body is quiet, the mind most commonly is quiet also. . . . When our minds are quiet, we are fit to deal with heavenly matters; therefore the doctors conferred sitting in the temple, and God delighteth to deal with us when we are most in private; he appeared to Abraham sitting in the door of his tent. (Gen. xviii.) The Holy Ghost came down upon the Apostles, and filled all the house where they were sitting. (Acts ii.) The eunuch, sitting in his chariot, was called and converted by Philip's preaching. (Acts viii.)—*Henry Smith.*

Whether shall we praise more, Mary's humility, or her docility? I do not see her take a stool and sit by him, or a chair and sit above him; but, as desiring to show her heart was as low as her knees, she sits at his feet. She was lowly set, and richly warmed with his heavenly beams. The greater submission, the more grace. If there be one hollow in the valley lower than another, thither the waters gather.—*Bishop Hall.*

Dr. Chalmers' complained: "I am hustled out of my spirituality."

At the feet of Jesus, list'ning to His word;
Learning wisdom's lesson from her loving Lord;
Mary, led by heav'nly grace,
Chose the meek disciple's place.
At the feet of Jesus is the place for me;
There a humble learner would I choose to be,
Sacred Songs and Solos.

Luke xv. 4—6 —"What man of you, having an hundred sheep, if he lose one of them, doth not leave the ninety and nine in the wilderness, and go after that which is lost, until he find it?

"And when he hath found it, he layeth it on his shoulders, rejoicing.

"And when he cometh home, he calleth together his friends and neighbours, saying unto them, Rejoice with me; for I have found my sheep which was lost."

The love of Jesus is not mere sentiment; it is active and energetic.

It is prevenient love, going after sheep that have no notion of returning to the fold from which they have wandered.

It is engrossing, making him leave all else: making one lost one to be of more present importance than ninety and nine.

It sets him upon resolute, determined, persevering search.

Let us behold our great Shepherd —

I. IN THE SEARCH. "Until he find it."

Mark him well, as, with his eyes, and heart, and all his faculties, he goes "after that which is lost."

1. No rejoicing is on his countenance. He is anxious for the lost.

2. No hesitation is in his mind. Despite the roughness of the way, or the length of the time, or the darkness of the night, he still pursues his lost one.

3. No anger is in his heart. The many wanderings of the sheep cost him dear, but he counts them as nothing, so that he may but find it.

4. No pausing because of weariness. Love makes him forget himself, and causes him to renew his strength.

5. No giving up the search. His varied non-successes do not compel him to return defeated.

Such must our searches after others be.

We must labour after each soul until we find it.

II. AT THE CAPTURE. "When he hath found it."

Mark the Shepherd when the sheep is at last within reach.

1. Wanderer held. How firm the grip! How hearty! How entire!

2. Weight borne. No chiding, smiting, driving; but a lift, a self-loading, an easing of the wanderer.

3. Distance travelled. Every step is for the Shepherd.

He must tread painfully all that length of road over which the sheep had wandered so wantonly.

The sheep is carried back with no suffering on its own part.

4. Shepherd rejoicing to bear the burden.

The sheep is so dear that its weight is a load of love.

The Shepherd is so good that he finds joy in his own toil.

5. Sheep rejoicing, too. Surely it is glad to be found of the Shepherd, and so to have its wanderings ended, its weariness rested, its distance removed, its perfect restoration secured.

III. IN THE HOME-BRINGING. "When he cometh home."

Mark well the end of the Shepherd's toil and care : he does not end his care till he has brought the stray one " home."

1. Heaven is home to Christ.

2. Jesus must carry us all the way there.

3. The Shepherd's mission for lost souls is known in glory, and watched with holy sympathy : in this all heavenly ones are " his friends and neighbours."

4. Jesus loves others to rejoice with him over the accomplishment of his design. "He calleth together his friends." See how they crowd around him ! What a meeting !

5. Repentance is also regarded as our being brought home. See verse 7. " I have found " refers to the repenting sinner, and it is a finding which secures salvation, or angels would not rejoice over it.

6. One sinner can make all heaven glad. See verses 7 and 10.

Let us learn a lesson from each of the three pictures which we have looked upon—

Of perseverance till souls are saved.

Of patience with souls who are newly found.

Of encouragement in expectation of the gathering into glory of those for whom we labour on behalf of Jesus.

SHEEP-TRACKS

One evening in 1861, as General Garibaldi was going home, he met a Sardinian shepherd lamenting the loss of a lamb out of his flock. Garibaldi at once turned to his staff, and announced his intention of scouring the mountain in search of the lamb. A grand expedition was organized. Lanterns were brought, and old officers of many a campaign started off, full of zeal, to hunt the fugitive. But no lamb was found, and the soldiers were ordered to their beds. The next morning, Garibaldi's attendant found him in bed, fast asleep. He was surprised at this, for the General was always up before anybody else. The attendant went off softly, and returned in half-an-hour. Garibaldi still slept. After another delay, the attendant awoke him. The General rubbed his eyes, and so did his attendant, when he saw the old warrior take from under the covering the lost lamb, and bid him convey it to the shepherd. The General had kept up the search through the night, until he had found it. Even so doth the Good Shepherd go in search of his lost sheep until he finds them.—*The Preachers' Monthly.*

Christ a Shepherd.—He is the Good Shepherd that laid down his life for the sheep (John x. 11); the Great Shepherd that was brought again from the dead (Heb. xiii. 20); the Chief Shepherd who shall appear again (1 Peter v. 4); the Shepherd and Bishop of souls (1 Peter ii. 25); he is the Shepherd of the sheep, who gathers the lambs with his arm, and carries them in his bosom (John x., Isaiah xl. 11); the Shepherd of Israel (Ezekiel xxxiv. 23); Jehovah's Shepherd (Zechariah xiii. 7).—*John Bate.*

Why doth he not drive the sheep before him, especially seeing it was lively enough to lose itself? First, because, though it had wildness more than enough to go astray, it had not wisdom enough to go right. Secondly, because probably the silly sheep had tired itself with wandering. "The people shall weary themselves for very vanity" (Hab. ii. 13). Therefore the kind Shepherd brings it home on his own shoulders.—*Thomas Fuller.*

Yam Sing, on his examination for membership on experience before the Baptist Church, San Francisco, in response to the question, "How did you find Jesus?" answered, "I no find Jesus at all; he find me." He passed.

A little boy, in a Chinese Christian family at Amoy, wishing to make a profession of religion, was told that he was too young to be received into the church. He replied, "Jesus has promised to carry the lambs in his bosom. I am only a little boy; it will be easier for Jesus to carry me."—*The Sunday-School Teacher.*

CLXIII

Luke xix. 5 —"And when Jesus came to the place, he looked up, and saw him, and said unto him, Zacchæus, make haste, and come down; for to-day I must abide at thy house."

Our Saviour for the first time invited himself to a man's house.

Thus he proved the freeness and authority of his grace. "I am found of them that sought me not": Isaiah lxv. 1.

We ought rather to invite him to our houses.

We should at least cheerfully accept his offer to come to us.

Perhaps at this hour he presses himself upon us.

Yet we may feel ourselves quite as unlikely to entertain our Lord as Zacchæus seemed to be. He was a man—

> In a despised calling—a publican, or tax-collector.
> In bad odour with respectable folk.
> Rich, with the suspicion of getting his wealth wrongly.
> Eccentric, for else he had hardly climbed a tree.
> Excommunicated because of his becoming a Roman tax-gatherer.
> Not at all the choice of society in any respect.

To such a man Jesus came; and he may come to us even if we are similarly tabooed by our neighbours, and are therefore disposed to fear that he will pass us by.

I. LET US CONSIDER THE NECESSITY WHICH PRESSED UPON THE SAVIOUR TO ABIDE IN THE HOUSE OF ZACCHÆUS.

He felt an urgent need of—

1. A sinner who needed and would accept his mercy.
2. A person who would illustrate the sovereignty of his choice.
3. A character whose renewal would magnify his grace.
4. A host who would entertain him with hearty hospitality.
5. A case which would advertise his gospel. Verses 9 and 10.

There was a necessity of predestination which rendered it true, "To-day I must abide at thy house."

There was a necessity of love in the Redeemer's gracious heart.

There was also a necessity in order to the blessing of others through Zacchæus.

II. LET US ENQUIRE WHETHER SUCH A NECESSITY EXISTS IN REFERENCE TO OURSELVES.

We can ascertain this by answering the following questions, which are suggested by the behaviour of Zacchæus to our Lord :—

1. Will we receive him this day? "He made haste."

2 Will we receive him heartily? "Received him joyfully."

3. Will we receive him whatever others say? "They all murmured."

4. Will we receive him as Lord? "He said, Behold, Lord."

5. Will we receive him so as to place our substance under the control of his laws? Verse 8.

If these things be so, Jesus must abide with us.

He cannot fail to come where he will have such a welcome.

III. LET US FULLY UNDERSTAND WHAT THAT NECESSITY INVOLVES.

If the Lord Jesus comes to abide in our house—

1. We must be ready to face objections at home.

2. We must get rid of all in our house which would be objectionable to him. Perhaps there is much there which he would never tolerate.

3. We must admit none who would grieve our heavenly Guest. His friendship must end our friendship with the world.

4. We must let him rule the house and ourselves, without rival or reserve, henceforth and for ever.

5. We must let him use us and ours as instruments for the further spread of his kingdom.

Why should we not to-day receive our Lord?

There is no reason why we must not.

There are many reasons why we must do so at once.

Lord, issue thine own mandate, and say, "I must."

NOTEWORTHY PASSAGES

Had our Saviour said no more but "Zacchæus, come down," the poor man would have thought himself taxed for his boldness and curiosity: it were better to be unknown than noted for misbehaviour. But how the next words comfort him: "For to-day I must abide at thy house"! What a sweet familiarity was here! as if Christ had been many years acquainted with Zacchæus, whom he now first saw. Contrary to custom the host is invited by the guest, and called to an unexpected entertainment. Well did our Saviour hear Zacchæus' heart inviting him, though his mouth did not: desires are the language of the spirit, and are heard by him that is the God of spirits.—*Bishop Hall.*

Now, Christ begins to call Zacchæus from the tree to be converted, as God called Adam from among the trees of the garden to be judged: Genesis iii. 8, 9. Before, Zacchæus was too low, and therefore was fain to climb; but now he is too high, and therefore he must come down — *Henry Smith.*

CLXIV

Luke xxii. 19, 20 —"And he took bread, and gave thanks, and brake it, and gave unto them, saying, This is my body which is given for you: this do in remembrance of me.

"Likewise also the cup after supper, saying, This cup is the new testament in my blood, which is shed for you."

Here we have full directions for observing the Lord's Supper.

You see what it was, and how it was done.

The directions are plain, clear, definite.

It will not be right to do something else; we must "this do."

Nor this for another purpose; but "this do in remembrance of me."

This command raises a previous question:—Do you know him? He who does not know him cannot remember him.

This being premised, let us observe that—

I. The main object of the supper is a personal memorial.

"In remembrance *of me.*" We are to remember not so much his doctrines, or precepts, as his person.

Remember the Lord Jesus at this Supper—

1. As the trust of your hearts.
2. As the object of your gratitude.
3. As the Lord of your conduct.
4. As the joy of your lives.
5. As the Representative of your persons.
6. As the Rewarder of your hopes.

Remember what he was, what he is, what he will be.

Remember him with heartiness, concentration of thought, realizing vividness, and deep emotion.

II. The memorial itself is striking.

1. Simple, and therefore like himself, who is transparent and unpretentious truth. Only bread broken, and wine poured out.
2. Frequent,—"as oft as ye drink it," and so pointing to our constant need. He intended the Supper to be often enjoyed.
3. Universal, and so showing the need of all. "Drink ye all of it." In every land, all his people are to eat and drink at this table.
4. His death is the best memory of himself, and it is by showing forth *his death* that we remember *him.*

5. His covenant relation is a great aid to memory; hence he speaks of— "The new covenant in my blood." We do not forget Adam, our first covenant-head; nor can we forget our second Adam.

6. Our *receiving* him is the best method of keeping him in memory; therefore we eat and drink in this ordinance.

No better memorial could have been ordained.

III. THE OBJECT AIMED AT IS ITSELF INVITING.

Since we are invited to come to the holy Supper that we may remember our Lord, we may safely infer that—

1. We may come to it, though we have forgotten him often and sadly. In fact, this will be a reason for coming.

2. We may come, though others may be forgetful of him. We come not to judge *them*, but to remember him ourselves.

3. We may come, though weak for aught else but the memory of his goodness.

4. It will be sweet, cheering, sanctifying, quickening, to remember him; therefore let us not fail to come.

Let us at the sacred table quit all other themes.

Let us not burden ourselves with regrets, resolves, &c.

Let us muse wholly and alone on him whose flesh is meat indeed, whose blood is drink indeed: John vi. 55.

TESTIMONIES

Our Lord Jesus has his own memorials of us, even as he has given us a memorial of himself. The prints of the nails constitute forget-me-nots of a peculiarly personal and abiding kind : " Behold, I have graven thee upon the palms of my hands " : Isaiah xlix. 16. By these marks he sees what he has already suffered, and he pledges himself to do nothing apart from those sufferings, for his hands, with which he works, are pierced. Since he thus bears in his hands the marks of his passion, let us bear them on our hearts.

Frequently to me the Supper has been much better than a sermon. It has the same teaching-power, but it is more vivid. The Lord is known of us in the breaking of bread, though our eyes have been holden during his discourse. I can see a good meaning in the saying of Henry III., of France, when he preferred the Sacrament to a sermon: " I had rather see my Friend than hear him talked about." I love to hear my Lord talked about, for so I often see him, and I see him in no other way in the Supper than in a sermon ; but sometimes, when my eye is weak with weeping, or dim with dust, that double glass of the bread and wine suits me best.—*C. H. S.*

107

"This do in remembrance of me."—1. This command implies a knowledge of himself. To remember, we must first know. It is no use saying to a man born blind, " Remember the sunshine." 2. It reveals the love of Christ. Why should he care about our remembering him? Dying voices have said to some of us, " Think of me sometimes ; don't forget me." It is the very nature of love to want to be remembered. 3. It implies a tendency to forget. God never founds a needless institution. It is a sin that we do not remember Christ more. We should thankfully use every help to memory.—*Outline of an Address by Dr. Stanford.*

At school we used certain books called " Aids to Memory." I am sure they rather perplexed than assisted me. Their utility was equivalent to that of a bundle of staves under a traveller's arm : true, he might use them one by one to walk with, but in the meantime he carried a host of others which he would never need. But our Saviour was wiser than all our teachers, and his remembrancers are true and real aids to memory. His love-tokens have an unmistakable language, and they sweetly win our attention.—*C. H. S.*

If a friend gives us a ring at his death, we wear it to keep up the memory of our friend ; much more, then, ought we to keep up the memorial of Christ's death in the sacrament.—*Thomas Watson.*

In mem'ry of Thy cross and shame, (1 Cor. xi. 23-26,)
I take this Supper in Thy name ;
This juice of grape, and flour of wheat,
My outward man doth drink and eat.
Oh, may my inward man be fed
With better wine and better bread !
May Thy rich flesh and precious blood
Supply my spirit's daily food ! (John vi. 54.)
I thank Thee, Lord, Thou diedst for me :
Oh, may I live and die to Thee ! (Rom. xiv. 7-10.)

A. A. Rees.

CLXV

Luke xxii. 27 —"**I am among you as he that serveth.**"

Singular fact with regard to the apostles. They were at the same time troubled with two questions : "Which of them should be accounted the greatest?" and "Which of them should betray his Master?"

Where humility should have abounded ambition intruded.

Of the evil of self-seeking our Lord would cure the apostles.

The remedy which he used was his own conduct. John xiii. 12-17.

If he made himself least, they must not strive to be greatest.

May this example be blessed to us also !

Let us attentively note—

I. OUR LORD'S POSITION. "I am among you as he that serveth."

1. In the world our Lord was not one of the cultured few on whom others wait. He was a working-man, and in spirit he was *servus servorum*, servant of servants. Mark x. 45.

2. In the circle of his own disciples he was one that served. Where he was most Master he was most servant.

   He was like a shepherd, servant to the sheep.

   He was like a nurse, servant to a child.

3. In the celebration of the Supper, our Lord was specially among them "as he that serveth," for he washed his disciples' feet.

4. In the whole course of his life, Jesus on earth ever took the place of the servant, or slave.

   His ear was bored by his entering into covenant. "Mine ears hast thou digged, or pierced " : Ps. xl. 6 (*Margin*) ; Ex. xxi. 6.

   His office was announced at his coming, "Lo, I come to do thy will !" Ps. xl. 7 ; Heb. x. 5-9.

   His nature was fitted for service : he "took upon him the form of a servant " : Phil. ii. 7.

   He assumed the lowest place among men. Ps. xxii. 6 ; Is. liii. 3.

   He cared for others, and not for himself. "The Son of man came not to be served but to serve " : Mark x. 45.

   He laid aside his own will. John iv. 34 ; vi. 38.

   He bore patiently all manner of hardness. 1 Peter ii. 23.

II. THE WONDER OF IT—That he should be a servant among his own servants.

The marvel of it was rendered the greater—

1. As he was Lord of all by nature and essence. Col. i. 15-19.

2. As he was superior in wisdom, holiness, power, and in every other way, to the very best of them. Matt. viii. 26, 27 ; John xiv. 9.

3. As he was so greatly their Benefactor. John xv. 16.

4. As they were such poor creatures, and so unworthy to be served. How could it be that they suffered themselves to be served of him? How could it be that he endured to serve them?

III. THE EXPLANATION OF IT.

We must look for this to his own nature.

1. He is so infinitely great. Heb. i. 2-4.

2. He is so immeasurably full of love. John xv. 9; 1 John iii. 16.

Because of these two things he condescended so marvellously.

IV. THE IMITATION OF IT.

Let us copy our Lord—

1. In cheerfully choosing to fulfil the most lowly offices.

2. In manifesting great lowliness of spirit, and humility of bearing. Eph. iv. 1-3; Phil. ii. 3; 1 Peter v. 5.

3. In laying ourselves out for the good of others. Let self-sacrifice be the rule of our existence. 2 Cor. xii. 15.

4. In gladly bearing injustice rather than break the peace, avenge ourselves, or grieve others. 1 Peter ii. 19, 20; iii. 14.

5. In selecting that place in which we receive least, and give most;— choosing to wait at table rather than to sit at meat.

Does not the text rebuke our pride?

Does it not arouse our adoring love?

Does it not lead us to gird up our loins to serve the brethren?

CONCERNING SERVICE

When the son of Gamaliel was married, Rabbis Eliezer, Joshuah, and Zadig were invited to the marriage-feast. Gamaliel, though one of the most distinguished men among the Israelites, himself waited on his guests, and pouring out a cup of wine, handed it to Eliezer, who politely refused it. Gamaliel then handed it to Joshuah. The latter accepted it. " How is this, friend Joshuah?" said Eliezer, "shall we sit and permit so great a man to wait on us?" "Why not?" replied Joshuah, "a man even greater than he did so long before him. Was not our father Abraham a very great man? Yet even he waited upon his guests, as it is written, ' *and he* (Abraham) *stood by them whilst they were eating.*' Perhaps you may think he did so because he knew them to be angels; no such thing. He supposed them to be Arabian travellers, else he would neither have offered them water to wash their feet, nor viands to allay their hunger. Why, then, shall we prevent our kind host from imitating so excellent an example?" "I know," exclaimed Rabbi Zadig, "a Being still greater than Abraham, who doth the same. "Indeed," continued he, "how long shall we be engaged in reciting the praises of created beings, and neglect the glory of the Creator? Even he, blessed be his name, causes the winds to blow, the clouds to accumulate, and the rain to descend! He fertilizes the earth, and daily prepares a magnificent table for his creatures. Why, then, shall we hinder our kind host, Gamaliel, from following so glorious an example?"—*Hebrew Tales.*

An old woman in Glencroe, visited by William McGavin, was found seated in bed, which, contrary to usual experience in the district, was scrupulously clean.

"You are an old servant of Christ, I understand," said he.

"Servant of Christ!" she responded, "Na, na; I'm naething pit a puir sinner. It's nine-and-forty years syne he pegan tae serve me."

"Serve you; how?"

"Dae ye no ken that?" she replied. "In the hoose o' Christ the Maister serves a' the guests. Did he no' himsel' say, 'I'm amang ye as ane that serveth'? When he brocht me hame tae himsel' he then pegan tae serve me, an' he ha' served me ere syne. Nane ere compleened o' Christ pein' a pad servant!"

"Well, but I hope you are a servant for all that. In the state of glory his servants serve him; and what is perfected there must begin here."

"That's a' fery true. I ken that I'm under his authority, pit somehoo I dinna like tae think much aboot servin' Christ. It gi'es me nae comfort."—*The Sword and the Trowel.*

Why is it that so many professed Christians "feel above" undertaking humble work for God and humanity? We have heard of a minister of Christ complaining that his station was "beneath his talents"! As if the soul of a beggar were beneath the genius of a Paul! Some are unwilling to enter a mission-school, or to distribute tracts through a poor district, strangely forgetting that their divine Master was himself a missionary. Have such never learned that the towel wherewith Jesus wiped his disciples' feet outshone the purple that wrapped Cæsar's limbs? Do they not know that the post of honour is the post of service? "My seat in the Sunday-school is higher than my seat in the Senate," said an eminent Christian statesman.—*Dr. Cuyler.*

CLXVI

Luke xxiii. 34 —"Then said Jesus, Father, forgive them ; for they know not what they do."

Let us go to Calvary to learn how we may be forgiven ;
And then let us linger there to learn how we may forgive.
There shall we see what sin is, as it murders the Lord of love ;
And see also how almighty mercy prevailed against it.

As we behold our Lord nailed to the cross, and hear his first words upon the tree, let us watch, and learn, and love.

I. WE SEE THE LOVE OF JESUS ENDURING—

To the closing act of human malice.
To the utmost endurance of shame. Phil. ii. 8 ; Heb. xii. 2.
To the extreme limit of personal suffering. Psalm xxii. 1-18.

We see not alone patience that bears without complaint, but love that labours to bestow benefits upon its enemies.

II. WE SEE THAT LOVE REVEALING ITSELF.

Love can use no better instrument than prayer.
Love, when in a death-agony, still prays.
Love thus brings heaven to the succour of those for whom it cares.
Love thus, to the highest, blesses its object.

To this present our Lord Jesus continues to bless the people of his choice by continually interceding for them. Rom. viii. 34 ; Heb. vii. 25. This is his daily prayer for us.

III. WE SEE FOR WHAT THAT LOVE PRAYS.

Forgiveness is the first, chief, and basis blessing.
Forgiveness from the Father can even go so far as to pardon the murder of his Son.
Forgiveness is the great petition of our Lord's sacrifice.

Love admits that pardon is needed, and it shudders at the thought of what must come to the guilty if pardon be not given.

IV. WE SEE HOW THE LOVING JESUS PRAYS.

For his wanton murderers in the very act.
For their full and immediate forgiveness.
For no other reason except their ignorance ; and this plea grace alone could suggest or accept.

Are there any so guilty that Jesus would refuse to intercede for them ?

112

V. We see how his prayer both warns and woos.

It warns, for it suggests that there is a limit to the possibility of pardon. Men may so sin that there shall remain no plea of ignorance; nay, no plea whatever.

It woos, for it proves that if there be a plea, Jesus will find it.

Come and trust your case in his hands; he will draw out his own brief, and invent his own arguments of love.

VI. We see how he instructs from the cross.

He teaches us to put the best construction on the deeds of our fellow-men, and to discover mitigating circumstances when they work us grievous ill.

He teaches us to forgive the utmost wrong. Mark xi. 25.

He teaches us to pray for others to our last breath. Acts vii. 59, 60.

That glorious appeal to the divine Fatherhood, once made by the Lord Jesus, still prevails for us.

Let the chief of sinners come unto God with the music of "Father, forgive them," sounding in their ears.

Commendations and Recommendations

It is well to suppose ignorance when we suffer wrong. A cruel letter came to me in my illness, but I hoped the writer did not know how depressed I was; a gossip repeated a silly slander, but I always believed that she thought it was the truth; an individual intentionally grossly insulted me, but I mistook it for a rough jest. In every case I have found it to my own comfort to believe that there must have been a mistake; besides, it makes it much easier to remove any unpleasant feeling if all along you have treated it as an error of judgment, or a blunder, occasioned by want of better information.—*C. H. S.*

There is something in this plea that at first confounds me, and that makes me ask with reverence in what sense Christ used it. Surely ignorance is not the gospel plea. Ignorance gives no man a claim on God . . . We are not to say, "Being justified by ignorance, we have peace with God." . . . . Ignorance is not innocence, it is often a sin; and one sin is no salvation from another.

The ignorance of Christ's enemies of what is involved in their capital crime brings them within the pale of mercy, and allows their pardon to be a possibility—a possibility on the ground which his cross supplies. Perhaps no mere men really know what they do in repudiating Christ. Satan knew what he did, and nothing has been said in our hearing of any gospel for him; but human sinners cannot fully know; and their

ignorance, though it does not make sin sinless, leaves it pardonable.—
Charles Stanford.

O Saviour, thou couldst not but be heard! Those, who out of ignorance and simplicity thus persecuted thee, find the happy issue of
thine intercession. Now I see whence it was that three thousand souls
were converted soon after, at one sermon. It was not Peter's speech, it
was thy prayer, that was thus effectual. Now they have grace to know
and confess whence they have both forgiveness and salvation, and can
recompense their blasphemies with thanksgiving. What sin is there,
Lord, whereof I can despair of the remission? Or what offence can I
be unwilling to remit, when thou prayest for the forgiveness of thy
murderers and blasphemers?—*Bishop Hall.*

> To do him any wrong was to beget
> A kindness from him; for his heart was rich,
> Of such fine mould, that if you sow'd therein
> The seed of Hate, it blossomed Charity.

It was a mark of true moral grandeur in the character of Phocion,
that, as he was about to be put to death, when one asked him whether
he had any commands to leave for his son, he exclaimed, "Yes, by all
means, tell him from me to forget the ill-treatment I have received from
the Athenians." Such a spirit of forgiveness, if it became a heathen,
will much more become a disciple of the gentle and loving Christ, who,
in his dying hour, prayed, "Father, forgive them; for they know not
what they do." No one has a right to claim the Christian spirit who
refuses to forgive a foe, and even cement his forgiveness by some act of
self-denying love.

A great boy in a school was so abusive to the younger ones, that the
teacher took the vote of the school whether he should be expelled. All
the small boys voted to expel him except one, who was scarcely five years
old. Yet he knew very well that the bad boy would continue to abuse
him. "Why, then, did you vote for him to stay?" said the teacher.
"Because, if he is expelled, perhaps he will not learn any more about
God, and so he will become still more wicked." "Do you forgive him,
then?" said the teacher. "Yes," said he, "father and mother forgive
me when I do wrong; God forgives me too; and I must do the same."—
The Biblical Treasury.

CLXVII

Luke xxiv. 36 —"And as they thus spake, Jesus himself stood in the midst of them, and saith unto them, Peace be unto you."

From what a man has been it is usually safe to infer what he is.

This is eminently the case with our Lord Jesus, since he is unchangeable. What he was to his disciples in the days of his flesh, he will be to his followers at this present hour.

We gather that he loves to reveal himself to his saints when they are assembled on the Sabbath-day, for he did so when on earth.

Let us consider the visit described in the text.

Uninvited, unexpected, undeserved, but most welcome was that visit.

Jesus stood in the centre to be near to them all, and that he might assume the place which a leader should take among his followers.

I. WHEN HE APPEARED.

1. When they had been acting unworthily by fleeing from him at his betrayal, and deserting him at his trial.

2. When they were unprepared, and unbelieving, doubting his express promise, and refusing the testimony of his messengers.

3. When they greatly needed his presence, for they were like sheep without a shepherd.

4. When they were exercising the little life they had by coming together in loving assembly. So far they were doing well, and acting in a way which was likely to bring blessing.

5. When they were lamenting his absence, and thus proving their desire after him. This is an admirable means of gaining his presence

6. When certain among them were testifying concerning him.

Are not *we* in a similar condition?

May we not hopefully look for our Lord's manifestation of himself?

II. WHAT HE SAID. " Peace be unto you."

1. It was a benediction : he wished them peace.

2. It was a declaration : they were at peace with God.

3. It was a fiat : he inspired them with peace.

4. It was an absolution : he blotted out all offences which might have spoiled their peace.

The Lord by his Holy Spirit can calm our perturbed minds, relieve of all care, discharge from all sin, deliver from all spiritual conflict, and give to each one of us immediate and perfect peace.

115

III. What came of his appearing.

1. He banished their doubts. Even Thomas had to shake off his obstinate unbelief.
2. He revealed and sealed his love upon their hearts by showing them his hands and his feet.
3. He refreshed their memories. " These are the words which I spake unto you " : verse 44.
4. He opened their understandings : verse 45.
5. He showed them their position. " Ye are witnesses of these things " : verse 48.
6. He filled them with joy. John xx. 20.

Has the Lord come into our midst during this service ?

Has he breathed into our souls a special peace ?

If so, let us wait a while, and further enjoy his company, and praise his condescending love.

If we do not feel that we have been thus favoured, let us tarry behind, and further seek his face.

A special meeting for praise and prayer will be held during the next half-hour. O Lord Jesus, abide with us !

Ripples

The Master's greeting to the first company had been in the word " Rejoice ! " (Matt. xxviii. 9, 10.) His greeting to the second was in the phrase, " Peace be unto you ! " And this he said twice over. (John xx. 19, 21.) We should keep in mind the difference between the first company and the second. The first was a small detachment of the general society, and consisted of women only. The second was the general society itself, including all the men ; and all the men had in one moment of panic forsaken their Master. In that shameful moment even John had not been an exception. The women, when Christ met them, had been true, and were only conscious of grief ; the men had not been true ; and, besides their grief, were conscious of deep agitation and burning shame. He knew their thoughts. Like the young Hebrew in their national story, who, years after his brethren had cast him into a pit, then sold him for a slave, met them face to face again, he as their lord, they as his supplicants, but who, that they might not fall back blasted, gently discovered himself to them in the words, " I am Joseph, your brother," to the mention of his name eagerly adding the mention of his relation ; so the Celestial Joseph, in discovering himself to those whom he had so grandly loved, but by whom he had been so basely forsaken, first sent forward by Mary the message, " Go tell my brethren," then followed up the message by personally appearing with these words on his lips—" Peace to you!"—words meant to dispel their fear, to kindle their tenderness, and to still the tempest within them. Brothers in Christ, this message was meant for our one whole family.—*Charles Stanford.*

There are depths in the ocean, I am told, which no tempest ever stirs; they are beyond the reach of all storms, which sweep and agitate the surface of the sea. And there are heights in the blue sky above to which no cloud ever ascends, where no tempest ever rages, where all is perpetual sunshine, and nought exists to disturb the deep serene. Each of these is an emblem of the soul which Jesus visits; to whom he speaks peace, whose fear he dispels, and whose lamp of hope he trims.— *Tweedie.*

In the life of Dr. John Duncan there is a touching passage, which relates how much he suffered from religious melancholy. His mental struggles were often very distressing, casting a shadow over his whole life and work. On one occasion, he went to his college-class in a state of extreme dejection. During the opening prayer, however, the cloud passed away. His eye brightened, his features relaxed, and before beginning his lecture he said, with pathetic sympathy, " Dear young gentlemen, I have just got a glimpse of Jesus."

We are the soldiers of Jesus Christ. Now, that which nerves the soldier's arm, and strengthens his heart, as he goes forth to battle, is not so much the multitude of the army of which he forms a part, as the character of the chief whom he is following. It is related that, in one of the Duke of Wellington's battles, a portion of the army was giving way, under the charge of the enemy, when he rode into the midst of them. A soldier called out in ecstasy, "*There's the Duke—God bless him! I'd rather see his face than a whole brigade;*" and these words, turning all eyes to their chief, so reassured his comrades that they repulsed the foe; they felt, he is beside us who was never defeated yet, and who will not be defeated now. A military friend, with whom I conversed on this subject, said that, though he had never heard the anecdote, he could well conceive it to be true: the presence of the distinguished General, he added, was at any time worth five thousand men.—*Tait on the Hebrews.*

CLXVIII

Luke xxiv. 50 —" And he led them out as far as to Bethany, and he lifted up his hands, and blessed them."

Jesus having spoiled the grave, and sanctified the earth, now purified the air as he passed through it on his way to heaven.

He arose to heaven in a manner worthy of special note.

We will review a few points connected with his ascension.

1. The time he sojourned on earth after his resurrection, namely, forty days, sufficed to prove his identity, to remove doubts, to instruct his disciples, and to give them their commission.

2. The place from which he rose was a mountain, a mount where he aforetime had communed with them. This mount looked down on Bethany, his dearest earthly rest; and was near to Gethsemane, the place of his supreme agony.

3. The witnesses were enough in number to convince the candid, persons who had long been familiar with him, who could not be deceived as to his identity.

   They were persons of character, of simplicity of nature, of ripe years, and of singularly cool temperament.

4. The scene itself was very remarkable.

   So unlike what superstition would have devised.

   So quiet—no chariot of fire and horses of fire.

   So majestic—no angels, nor other agents to lend imaginary splendour; but the Lord's own power and Godhead in sublime simplicity working all.

Our chosen theme at this time shall be the last posture in which our ascending Lord was seen.

I. HIS HANDS WERE UPLIFTED TO BLESS.

1. This blessing was no unusual thing. To stretch out his hands in benediction was his customary attitude. In that attitude he departed, with a benediction still proceeding from his lips.

2. This blessing was with authority. He blessed them while his Father acknowledged him by receiving him to heaven.

3. This blessing was so full that, as it were, he emptied his hands. They saw those dear hands thus unladen of their benedictions.

4. The blessing was for those beneath him, and beyond the sound of his voice : he scattered benedictions upon them all.

5. The blessing was the fit *finis* of his sojourn here: nothing fitter, nothing better, could have been thought of,

II. Those hands were pierced.

This could be seen by them all as they gazed upward.

1. Thus they knew that they were Christ's hands.
2. Thus they saw the price of the blessing. His crucifixion has purchased continual blessing for all his redeemed.
3. Thus they saw the way of the blessing: it comes from those human hands, through those sacrificial wounds.
4. A sight of those hands is in itself a blessing. By that sight we see pardon and eternal life.
5. The entire action is an epitome of the gospel. This is the substance of the matter,—"hands pierced distribute benedictions." Jesus, through suffering and death, has power to bless us out of the highest heaven.

This is the last that was seen of our Lord.

He has not changed his attitude of benediction.

He will not change it till he shall descend in his glory.

III. Those hands sway the sceptre.

His hands are omnipotent. Those very hands, which blessed his disciples, now hold, on their behalf, the sceptre—

1. Of providence: both in small affairs and greater matters.
2. Of the spiritual kingdom: the church and all its work.
3. Of the future judgment, and the eternal reign.

Let us worship him, for he has ascended on high.

Let us rejoice in all the fruit of his ascension, to him, and to us.

Let us continue praising him, and proclaiming his glory.

Glimpses

What spot did Jesus select as the place of his ascension? He selected, not *Bethlehem*, where angel-hosts had chanted his praises ; nor *Tabor*, where celestial beings had hovered around him in homage ; nor *Calvary*, where riven rocks and bursting graves had proclaimed his Deity ; nor the *Temple-court*, in all its sumptuous glory, where, for ages, his own Shekinah had blazed in mystic splendour: but he hallows afresh the name of a lowly village, *Bethany ;* he consecrates a Home of Love.— *Dr. Macduff's " Memories of Bethany."*

The manner of Christ's ascension into heaven may be said to have been an instance of divine simplicity and sublimity combined, which scarcely has a parallel. While in the act of blessing his disciples, he was parted from them, and was carried up, and disappeared behind a cloud.

There was no pomp; nothing could have been more simple. How can the followers of this Lord and Master rely on pomp and ceremony to spread his religion, when he, its Founder, gave no countenance to such appeals to the senses of men? Had some good men been consulted about the manner of the ascension, we can imagine the result.— *N. Adams.*

This is no death-bed scene. "Nothing is here for tears." We are not at the close, but at the beginning of a life. There is no sign of mourning that a great career is over, that the lips of a great Teacher are for ever dumb; no ground for that melancholy question that twice rang in the ears of Elisha, "Knowest thou that the Lord will take away thy master from thy head to day? And he said, Yea, I know it; hold ye your peace." No; the scene before us is one of calm victory—

"All the toil, the sorrow, done;
All the battle fought and won."

The earthly work of the Redeemer is over; the work which that short sojourn on earth was designed to inaugurate is now to begin. We are in the presence of One who said, "All power is given unto me in heaven and in earth"; and again, "Be of good cheer, I have overcome the world." —*Dr. Butler, Head Master of Harrow.*

That wonderful hand of Christ! It was that same hand which had been so quickly stretched out to rescue Peter when sinking in Galilee's waves. It was that same hand which had been held in the sight of the questioning disciples on the third evening after they had seen it laid lifeless in the tomb. It was that same hand which incredulous Thomas must see before he would believe its risen power; it was that same hand which was extended to him not only to see, but to touch the nail-prints in its palm. It was that same hand which the disciples last saw uplifted in a parting blessing when the cloud parted him from them. It was only after ten days that they realized the fulness of blessing which came from that extended, pierced hand of Christ. Peter at Pentecost must have preached with that last sight of it fresh in his memory, when he said, "God hath made that same Jesus, *whom ye have crucified*, both Lord and Christ." That hand, with its nail-prints, knocks at the heart's door for entrance. That hand, with its deep marks of love, beckons on the weary runner in the heavenly way.—*F. B. Pullan.*

CLXIX

John i. 29 —"The next day John seeth Jesus coming unto him, and saith, Behold the Lamb of God, which taketh away the sin of the world."

Places and times become memorable when linked with our Lord ; hence we are told what was done at Bethabara on such a day, and what happened on "the next day."

Let us treasure holy memories with great care—especially memories of Jesus,—times when we saw the Lord.

In the case before us the preacher was a notable man, and his theme more notable still. John the Baptist preaches Jesus.

We have here a model for every minister of Christ.

I. THE TRUE MESSENGER.

1. He is one who sees Jesus for himself. There was a time when John did not know the Christ, but in due time the Holy Spirit pointed him out. Verse 33.

   The true herald of Jesus is like John—

   He is on the look-out for his Lord's appearing.

   He rejoices to preach Jesus as one whom he has himself seen and known, and still hopes to see.

   He preaches him as come, and as coming.

2. He calls upon men to see Jesus. " Behold the Lamb of God."

   This he does plainly and confidently.

   This he does continually : it is his one message. John preached the same sermon "again the next day after" : verse 35.

   This he does earnestly and emphatically. "Behold ! "

3. He leads his own followers to Jesus. John's disciples heard John speak, and followed Jesus : verse 37.

   He had enough force to induce men to be his followers.

   He had enough humility to induce his followers to leave him for Jesus. This is the glory of John the Baptist.

   He had enough grace to make him rejoice that it was so.

   Our speech should make men go beyond ourselves to Christ. " We preach not ourselves, but Christ Jesus the Lord " : 2 Cor. iv. 5.

4. He loses himself in Jesus.

   He sees the necessity of this. "He *must* increase, but I *must* decrease " : John iii. 30.

   He sees the propriety of this : he knows himself to be only the Bridegroom's friend, and not the Bridegroom. John iii. 29.

Blessed is that minister of whom all these point can be asserted.

II. THE TRUE MESSAGE.

John's word was brief, but emphatic.

1. He declared Jesus to be sent and ordained " of God."
2. He declared him to be the one real, divinely-appointed sacrifice for sin,—" the Lamb of God."
3. He declared him to be the only remover of human guilt,—" which taketh away the sin of the world."
4. He declared him to be set forth as the object of faith,—" Behold the Lamb." He exhorted his hearers to look at him with that look which saves.

The end of all ministries and ordinances is to bring men to look to Jesus. Both John, who ran before, and we, who run after, must point in the same direction.

III. THE TRUE RECEPTION OF THAT MESSAGE.

The conduct of John's disciples shows that our true wisdom concerning gospel testimony is—

1. To believe it, and so to acknowledge Jesus as our sin-removing sacrifice.
2. To follow Jesus. See verse 37.
3. To follow Jesus, even if we be alone. These were the vanguard of the vast hosts who have since followed Jesus. They knew not what suffering it might involve, but went first and foremost.
4. To abide with Jesus. See verse 39.
5. To go forth and tell others of Jesus. See verses 40 and 41.

Here, then, is a lesson for those who preach. John's sermon was short, but full of Jesus, and effectual for soul-winning. Imitate him.

Here also is an example for those who have believed.

Here is a gospel for those who hitherto have not known the Saviour.

SPECIALITIES.

In 1857, a day or two before preaching at the Crystal Palace, I went to decide where the platform should be fixed ; and, in order to test the acoustic properties of the building, cried in a loud voice, "Behold the Lamb of God, which taketh away the sin of the world." In one of the galleries, a workman, who knew nothing of what was being done, heard the words, and they came like a message from heaven to his soul. He was smitten with conviction on account of sin, put down his tools, went home, and there, after a season of spiritual struggling, found peace and life by beholding the Lamb of God. Years after, he told this story to one who visited him on his death-bed.—*C. H. S*

Notice, how simple the means, how grand the result! John simply declared, " Behold the Lamb of God." Here is no vehement appeal, no angry rebuke, no feverish, would-be impressive urging ; it is a simple, earnest declaration of God's truth. What else have Christ's servants to do but to set forth the truth, the gospel, the will of God, as revealed in the person and work of Christ ? How much more important to give all our energy and strength to this, than to the attempt of enforcing and applying, threatening and inviting, urging and pressing, in perorations thundering or melting! The truth itself thunders and melts, rouses and whispers, bruises and comforts ; entering into the soul, it brings with it light and power. How calm and objective do Christ's sermons, and those of the apostles, appear ! How powerful by the consciousness which pervades them : this is the truth of God, light from heaven, power from above ! " Behold the Lamb of God."—*Adolph Saphir.*

It is related of John Wesley that, preaching to an audience of courtiers and noblemen, he used the "generation of vipers" text, and flung denunciation right and left. "That sermon should have been preached at Newgate," said a displeased courtier to Wesley on passing out. "No," said the fearless apostle, " my text *there* would have been, ' Behold the Lamb of God, which taketh away the sin of the world.' "

Roger Clark, one of the English martyrs, when at the stake, cried out to the people, " Behold the Lamb of God, which taketh away the sin of the world." How suitable such a cry from a saint about to seal his testimony with his blood !

No *herald* could live long in the wilderness on locusts and wild honey, if he had not to tell of a man or an era nobler than himself, and brighter than his own twilight-hour. John lived more truly on the prophecy he proclaimed than on the honey and locusts.—*Dr. Parker.*

A young telegraph operator was anxious about his soul. After a sleepless night, he went to his duties ; while restless and absorbed in the thought of his being a sinner, he heard the click of his instrument, and, with great astonishment and emotion, spelt out this message :—

" From	To
H——,	J—— B——,
Windermere.	Warkworth.

'Behold the Lamb of God, which taketh away the sin of the world ; in whom we have redemption, through his blood, even the forgiveness of sins.' "

This was sent as an answer to a letter from a young man, who also was seeking peace. It acted as a double blessing, showing to both operator and receiver the way of salvation,

CLXX

John i. 47 —"Jesus saw Nathanael coming to him, and saith of him, Behold an Israelite indeed, in whom is no guile!"

This is a chapter of "beholds." We are first to " Behold the Lamb of God," and then to behold a man of God.

Nathanael was simple, straightforward, honest, "an Israelite indeed."

In this he was not like his great progenitor, Jacob, who was a sup-planter, and not a prince with God, till that memorable night when the angel wrestled with him, and withered his carnal strength. Then, in the weakness of that simplicity which laid hold upon the mighty One, Jacob became Israel. Gen. xxvii. 36 ; xxxii. 28.

A sincere and simple character was not common in our Lord's day.

It is despised by many at this day.

It was greatly appreciated by our Lord, who has the same character in perfection, and is truly called "the holy child Jesus."

This characteristic of guilelessness is—

I. A HAPPY SIGN IN A SEEKER.

We will illustrate this by Nathanael's procedure.

1. He is the sort of man to whom disciples like to speak. "Philip findeth Nathanael ": verse 45.

2. He is outspoken with his difficulties, and therefore his friends see how to meet them. "Can there any good thing come out of Nazareth ?" verse 46.

3. He is ready to apply the proper tests. "Come and see ": verse 46.

4. He is honest in his use of those tests. Our Lord saw that Nathanael was no captious critic, nor idly-curious observer : verse 47.

5. He is open to conviction if fair evidence be supplied. As soon as our Lord proved his omniscience Nathanael believed : verse 48.

6. He is ready to make confession : verse 49.

7. He is prepared to proceed far in the school of Christ. The Lord promised him the sight of greater things because he was prepared to see them : verses 50 and 51.

An Israelite is the man to know "the King of Israel": verse 49.

An Israelite is the man to understand the famous dream of the father of all Israelites : verse 51. Gen. xxviii. 12.

II. A VITAL POINT IN A BELIEVER.

The truly upright man, and he only, can be a Christian.

1. A sense of pardon removes the temptation to guile: we cease to excuse ourselves when pardon is received. See Psalm li.
2. A reception of Christ as "the truth" causes guile to be hated.
3. A truthful assurance of the gospel prevents a hypocritical faith.
4. A complete consecration to the Lord puts an end to a double-minded life, and to all false aims and maxims.
5. A sense of the presence of God makes guile appear absurd.
6. A brave faith in God causes it to appear mean and cowardly.

III. A SURE PRODUCER OF OTHER QUALITIES.
1. It makes a man love his Bible. Nathanael was familiar with the law and the prophets.
2. It makes him pray. He is an Israelite. Gen. xxxii. 28.
3. It leads him to be much alone. "Under the fig-tree": verse 48.
4. It makes him wear his heart in his countenance. "Behold an Israelite indeed."
5. It prepares him to behold the pure and true glories of heaven.

Who among us is renowned for cleverness, craft, shrewdness, and the critical faculty in general?
Let him be afraid of the much-admired quality of cleverness.
The absence of simplicity is by no means a healthy sign.
Let us be true in any case, and may the Lord teach us his truth!

Mosaic

'Twas well Christ spake among plain men. Had the Scribes and the Pharisees heard him, had some men of these times heard him, they would have said that Christ purposed to define a fool. Who is not now a fool that is not false? He is rated as having but small wit that is not of great subtilty and great wiliness? Plainness is weakness, and solid sincerity stolid simplicity. No man is honest but for want of sense. Conscience comes only from a crazed brain. He hath no reach that doth not overreach. Only to disguise is to be wise; and he is the profoundest that is the grandest counterfeit. Christ will have a serpent and a dove coupled together—wisdom and simplicity; and he bids, what God hath joined, that man should not sever. But the world dares uncouple them. Uncouple them? That's little; dares divorce them. In these days doves may not consort with serpents, nor singleness and sapience harbour in one heart. Certainly plain-dealing is a jewel; but the world dubs him a fool that useth it.

Hence it is that, nowadays, men dare not deal uprightly, lest their wit be called in question; they are afraid of honest plainness lest they be held for idiocy. Term one an honest man, you do discredit him. The name of fool is so disgraceful, one will rather be a villain than be called a fool. But here, God's Word, God's Wisdom, defines a true Israelite, by truth and plainness; he is one that hath no guile.—*Richard Clerke.*

"Behold an Israelite indeed, in whom is no guile."—The expression would appear to be so distinct an allusion to the thirty-second Psalm as to amount to a quotation, and to imply that this guilelessness of spirit was not mere amiability, but was the fruit of forgiven sin. "Blessed is he whose transgression is forgiven, whose sin is covered (or atoned). Blessed is the man unto whom the Lord imputeth not iniquity, and in whose spirit there is no guile." Nathanael, if we may follow this clue, was no stranger to the spiritual meaning of atonement; no stranger, therefore, to the consciousness of sin which made its necessity felt. Pressed on the one hand by the sense of guilt, allured on the other by the provision of atonement in the temple sacrifices, he had been forced to earn his first title by wrestling in prayer with God for pardon; and, having prevailed, there had sprung up within the forgiven man the guileless spirit of childlike trustfulness in God, who had thus stooped to his prayer, and granted the benison he sighed for. He is in the happiest state of preparation for the personal knowledge of Christ, and we shall see with what fulness of faith he honours his Master at the first interview, uttering on the threshold of discipleship a confession more advanced than was made at the same point by any other of the twelve.—*C. A. Davis.*

Nathanael was one of these true Israelites; he was in reality, as well as by profession, one of the people of God; and the evidence he gave of this was his freedom from guile. But our Saviour does not say he has no guilt. A man may be freckled, or have spots, and not be painted. A Christian is not sinlessly pure—he has many unallowed and bewailed infirmities, but guile he has not: he is no hypocrite. He does not in religion ascend a stage, to assume a character which does not belong to him. He *is* what he appears to be. There is a correspondence between his professions and actions, his meanings and his words. He is upright in his dealings with himself, in his dealings with his fellow-creatures, and in his dealings with his God. He is all of a piece. He is the same alone as in company; the same in his own house as in the house of God; the same in prosperity as in adversity.—*William Jay.*

The clearer the diamond, the more it sparkles; the plainer the heart is, the more it sparkles in God's eye. What a commendation did Christ give Nathanael—"Behold an Israelite indeed, in whom is no guile"!—*Thomas Watson.*

126

CLXXI

John iv. 6 —"Now Jacob's well was there. Jesus therefore, being wearied with his journey, sat thus on the well: and it was about the sixth hour."

Many things may well remind us of our Lord.

Chiefly may we think of him when we see a well, or a weary peasant resting at noon.

How truly human was Jesus! To him a long walk brought weariness; his weariness needed rest; to rest he "sat thus on the well."

How worn was his humanity! He was more weary than the disciples.

He had a greater mental strain than they.

He had a weariness that they knew not of.

His self-denials were even then remarkable.

He would in all points be made like unto his brethren.

He would not exempt himself from fatigue.

He would not work a miracle for his own refreshment.

He would not refuse to bear heat, thirst, exhaustion.

He has thus made himself able to sympathize with—

The traveller who rests by the roadside.

The labourer who is worn-out with toil.

The sufferer who feels pain in bone and flesh.

The poor man who must rest on a cold stone, and look for refreshment to the public fountain.

The weary mind, oppressed by life's long way, which has no luxurious comfort prepared for it, but finds a measure of repose in the simple arrangements of nature.

Reading this text, let it set a picture before you, and—

I. Let your conscience draw a spiritual picture of your wearied Saviour.

1. He is wearied with our sins. Is. xliii. 24.

2. He is wearied with our formal worship. Is. i. 14.

3. He is wearied with our errings through unbelief. Ps. xcv. 10.

4. He is wearied with our resistance of his Spirit. Is. lxiii. 10.

5. He is wearied with our cavillings and rebellions. Mal. ii. 17.

Perhaps we have specially wearied the Lord, as we read in Amos ii. 13, where singular provocations are mentioned.

That is a grave question asked by the prophet Isaiah, "Will ye weary my God also?" Is. vii. 13.

II. Let your conscience draw a spiritual picture of your waiting Saviour.

1. He waits for comers to the well: he seizes on all occasions to bless, such as affliction, the hearing of the Word, the recurrence of a birthday, or even the simplest event of life. Men have other errands; they come to the well only to draw water, but the Lord meets them with his greater errand.
2. He waits for the most sinful; she that had had five husbands.
3. He waits to enlighten, convince, convert.
4. He waits to accept, and to commission.
5. He waits to begin by one convert the ingathering of a great harvest of souls, as in the case of the Samaritans.

How long he has waited for some of you !
At how many points has he been on the outlook for you!
Is he not waiting for you at this very hour?
Will you not yield to his patient love?

III. Let your penitence draw another picture.

Alter the position of the character.

1. Be yourself weary of your sinful way.
2. Sit down on the well of your Lord's gracious ordinances.
3. Wait and watch till your Saviour comes.
4. Ask him to give you to drink, and, in so doing, give him to drink for this is his best refreshment.
5. Drink yourselves of the living water, and then run to tell others.

Will you not do this at once?
May his Holy Spirit so direct you !

Musings

It was the hour of noon, and weary as he was with the long journey, possibly also with the extreme heat, our Lord sat " thus on the well." The expression in the original is most pathetically picturesque. It implies that the Wayfarer was quite tired out, and in his exhaustion flung his limbs wearily on the seat, anxious, if possible, for complete repose.— *Archdeacon Farrar.*

When hard-working people sit down at mid-day for their few minutes of rest and refreshment, let them recall their Master's noon-day rest at the well. He was tired, like we are, yet his rest was short, and his work scarcely broken. He was tired with seeking for us. Our stubborn hearts brought him all this way from heaven. He has long sought for our love, and hardly finds it. Think on this verse. With whom did Jesus find his portion in this life? Not with the great and luxurious, but with the common people, sharing their toils.—*Practical Reflections on the Gospels. By a Clergyman.*

While we sympathize with the bodily weariness of our Lord, it will be well to remember the soul-weariness which sin must have occasioned him. He hungered to bless men, and they refused the bread of life. He would have gathered them, but they would not be gathered. He must have been specially wearied with the ostentatious hypocrisy of the Pharisees, and the silly legalisms of the Scribes with their tithing of mint and anise. He was often wearied with the dogged unbelief of the Jews, and the provoking want of faith among his own disciples. The sin, the cavilling, the slander, the selfishness, the hardness of heart of those about him, must have worn down his holy soul, and made him every day a Man of sorrows. Yet he never left the well, never refused to give the living water to a thirsting soul, never ceased to entreat men to come to him and drink.—*C. H. S.*

"*Jesus, therefore, being wearied.*"—And in that he himself had suffered, he was the more able and apt to help this poor Samaritan. So the apostle bids us pity those in adversity, as being ourselves in the body, *i.e.,* the body of flesh and frailty, subject to like misery.—*Trapp.*

When wearied, let us still be on the watch to do good. Wearied, and sitting on the well, our Lord is still in the attitude of observation. " I am never too tired to pray," said a minister, who, after a hard day's toil, found his host ready to excuse him from conducting family prayer. When God is blessing the Word, true ministers forget their fatigue, and hold on long into the night with enquirers. Alas ! when the Holy Spirit has nothing to do with a man's heart, the man excuses himself from " making overtime ", as I once heard a professor call it, when he quitted the room the instant the service was over. Another, in describing a minister, said, " Oh, he is so cold ! He is one who thinks it is wrong to be too religious. He cannot endure zeal." Be it ours to show a more excellent way. Holy Brainerd, when he could not preach, because he was on his dying bed, called to him a little Indian boy, and tried to teach him his letters. Let us live soul-saving, and so let us die.—*C.H.S.*

CLXXII

John iv. 11 —"The woman saith unto him, Sir, thou hast nothing to draw with, and the well is deep: from whence then hast thou that living water?"

Our Lord's object was to bring the woman to seek salvation of him.

Our desire is the immediate conversion of all now present.

The Samaritan woman accepted the Saviour upon the first asking.

Many of you have been invited to Jesus many times—will you not at last comply?

Our Lord aimed at her heart by plain teaching and home dealing—we will take the same course with our hearers.

When his interesting emblem failed to reach her, he fell to downright literalism, and unveiled her life. Anything is better than allowing a soul to perish.

I. WE WILL EXPOUND THE PRECEDING TEACHING.

The Lord had said to her, "If thou knewest the gift of God, and who it is that saith to thee, Give me to drink; thou wouldest have asked of him, and he would have given thee living water."

The figure was that of living water in contrast to the water collected in Jacob's well, which was merely the gatherings of the surrounding hills —land-water, not spring-water.

He meant to say that his grace is like water from a springing well.

It is of the best and most refreshing kind.

It is living, and ministers life.

It is powerful, and finds its own way.

It is abiding, and is never dried up.

It is abounding, and free to all comers.

Furthermore, he intimated to the woman that—

1. He had it. There was no need of a bucket to draw with.

2. He had it to give.

3. He would have given it for the asking.

4. He alone could give it. It would be found in no earthly well.

II. WE WILL ANSWER THE QUESTION OF THE TEXT.

In ignorance the woman enquired, "Whence then hast thou that living water?"

We can at this time give a fuller reply than could have been given when our Lord sat on the well.

He has now a boundless power to save, and that power arises—

1. From his divine nature, allied with his perfect humanity.
2. From the purpose and appointment of God.
3. From the anointing of the Holy Ghost.
4. From his redeeming work, which operated for good even before its actual accomplishment, and which is in full operation now.
5. From the power of his intercession at the Father's right hand.
6. From his representative life in glory. Now all power is delivered into his hand. Matt. xxviii. 18.

III. WE WILL DRAW CERTAIN INFERENCES FROM THE ANSWER.

1. Then he is still able to bless. Since he has this living water only from his unchanging self, he therefore has it now as fully as ever.
2. Then he needs nothing from us. He is himself the one sole Fountain, full and all-sufficient for ever.
3. Then we need not fear exhausting his fulness.
4. Then at all times we may come to him, and we need never fear that he will deny us.

DROPS

When we see a great volume of water issuing from a spring, it is natural that we should enquire,—whence does it come? This is one of the mysteries of nature to most people. Job speaks of "the springs of the sea", and hints that none can find them out. But where are the springs of salvation? Whence comes the river, yea, the boundless ocean of divine grace? All fulness is in Jesus; but how came it there? He gives drink to all who come to him; whence has he this inexhaustible supply? Are not these questions worth asking? Must not the reply be instructive to ourselves, and glorifying to our Lord? Come, then, and let us borrow the language of this Samaritan woman, and talk with our Lord.—*C. H. S.*

When I have ridden through London, I have been overwhelmed with the greatness of the supply which must daily be necessary to feed its millions, and have wondered that a famine has not at once set in. But when I have seen the markets and the store-houses, and have thought of the whole earth as eager to obtain a sale for its produce in our vast metropolis, I have rested in content. I see whence the almost illimitable supplies are drawn, and my wonder henceforth is, not that the millions are fed, but that they should be able to consume such immeasurable quantities of food.

Thus, when I behold man's spiritual need, I marvel that it should ever be met ; but when I behold the person and work of the Lord Jesus, my marvel ceases, and a new wonder begins. I wonder rather at the infinity of grace than at the power of sin.—*C. H. S.*

Speaking of Cairo, the author of "Ragged Life in Egypt" says, "Perhaps no cry is more striking, after all, than the short and simple cry of the water-carrier. 'The gift of God' he says, as he goes along with his water-skin on his shoulder. It is impossible to hear this cry without thinking of the Lord's words to the woman of Samaria, 'If thou knewest the gift of God, and who it is that saith to thee, Give me to drink ; thou wouldest have asked of him, and he would have given thee living water?' It is very likely that water, so invaluable, and so often scarce in hot countries, was in those days spoken of, as now, as 'the gift of God', to denote its preciousness ; if so, the expression would be extremely forcible to the woman, and full of meaning."—*The Biblical Treasury.*

How ready are men and women to go to this well and that well to drink water for the help and healing of bodily distempers, and to go many miles, and dispense with all other affairs, that they may be recovered of corporeal diseases : but how few enquire after the water of life, or leave all their secular business for the good and health of their immortal souls !—*Benjamin Keach.*

"*The well is deep,*" the woman said to Jesus ; and so it was. It took two-and-a-half seconds from the time that the pebble was dropped, before we heard the splash in the water below. . . . Turning to the illustration before us,—"*living water,*"—the meaning only dawned upon me when I visited the spot. Jacob's well, deep as it was, and cool as its waters doubtless were, was only an artificial well—a cistern for the collection of rain, and the drainage of the land. . . . In seasons of drought, this well must have been useless—it was a well, or cistern ; not a spring.—*J. W. Bardsley.*

The fountain of living waters is God himself (Jer. ii. 13). "With thee is the fountain of life" (Ps. xxxvi. 9). It is not a mere cistern to hold ; it is a pouring, running, living stream ; nay, rather a fountain that springs up perpetually. We all know that a jet or fountain is produced by a head of water that presses down from a great elevation ; and that, the higher the spring, the loftier and more powerful the jet, which, however, never surpasses the height of its source. Our spiritual life, "our well-spring of life", has its source in heaven : and it is heavenward that it rises, and it is content with no lower level. It came from God, and to God it will return.—*F. A. Malleson.*

CLXXIII

John v. 9 —"On the same day was the Sabbath."

Christ healed men on all sorts of days.

But Sabbaths were high days of grace.

Six special cases of cures wrought on the Sabbath are recorded.

1. The evil spirit cast out.   Luke iv. 31-35.
2. The withered hand restored.   Luke vi. 6-10.
3. The crooked woman made straight.   Luke xiii. 10-17.
4. The man with the dropsy cured.   Luke xiv. 1-6.
5. The impotent man made whole.   John v. 1-9.
6. The blind man's eyes opened.   John ix. 1-14.

As God rested on the Sabbath, and hallowed it; so as God it was rest to Jesus to heal, and thus he hallowed the day.

As man he also rested his heart, exercised a holy ministry, glorified God, and hallowed the day.

I. THESE CURES MEET MANY CASES.

1. Those under Satanic influence.   Luke iv. 31-35.   Many are in this case at this hour.
2. Those conscious of spiritual inability.   Luke vi. 6-10.
3. Those bowed down with great distress, despondency, despair, etc. Luke xiii. 10-17.   This poor woman had been infirm for eighteen years.
4. Those smitten with mortal disease.   Luke xiv. 1-6.   This typifies the deadly character of sin, and represents the case of those upon whom is the dread of the second death.
5. Those altogether paralyzed.   John v. 1-9.   This man had been impotent for thirty-eight years.   Some seem specially unable to feel, or do, or be what they should be.   They are weak and irresolute, and though lying at the healing-pool, others step in before them, and they derive no benefit from the means of grace.
6. Those blind from birth.   John ix. 1-14.   Many are in this condition.   They see no spiritual truth, but abide in total darkness as to all gospel truth.

II. THESE CURES REPRESENT USUAL PROCESSES.

1. A word addressed to the devil.   " Hold thy peace, and come out of him ": Luke iv. 35.   Satan feels the power of the Word of the Lord; but he cares for nothing else.

133

2. A word personal to the sufferer. "Stretch forth thy hand": Luke vi. 10. He was unable, and yet he was commanded; and he obeyed. This is the gospel method.

3. A word accepted as done. "Thou art loosed from thine infirmity": Luke xiii. 12. Faith turns promise into fact, gospel-teaching into actual salvation.

4. Power without a word. Luke xiv. 4.

5. A word arousing and commanding. "Rise, take up thy bed, and walk": John v. 8. Many are saved by being stirred up from long inactivity and lethargy.

6. A word associated with other means. John ix. 6-7. The whole miracle is deeply instructive on this point.

In these varied forms and fashions, Jesus works on the Sabbath.

III. THESE CURES WERE BOTH IN AND OUT OF THE SYNAGOGUE.
   1. There, and misbehaving. Luke iv. 33.
   2. There, and singled out from the crowd. Luke vi. 8.
   3. There, and called to Jesus. Luke xiii. 12.
   4. After the synagogue service. Luke xiv. 1.
   5. Too feeble to get there. John v. 5.
   6. Too poor to be there. John ix. 8.

IV. THESE CURES WERE ALL UNSOUGHT.
   This is one special feature about them all.
   1. The possessed man entreated Christ to leave him alone. Luke iv. 34.
   2. The man with the withered hand did not think of cure. Luke vi. 6.
   3. The infirm woman did not hope for healing. Luke xiii. 11.
   4. The man with the dropsy did not ask for the blessing. Luke xiv. 2.
   5. The infirm man was too paralyzed to seek Christ. John v. 5.
   6. It was an unheard-of thing that the eyes of a man born blind should be opened, and therefore he did not expect it. John ix. 32.

This also is the Sabbath; let us look to the Lord of the Sabbath.
Will he not this day bless those who are seekers?
Will he not bless those whom we bring to him?
Will he not bless those for whom we pray?

SERMON BELLS

On Sunday heaven's gate stands ope;
Blessings are plentiful and rife,
   More plentiful than hope.

George Herbert.

On his death-bed, Brainerd said : "I was born on a Sabbath-day ; I have reason to hope I was new-born on a Sabbath-day ; and I hope 1 shall die on this Sabbath-day."

Was it not meet that the Lord of the Sabbath should specially display his sovereignty upon that day ?   May we not now expect that, on the Lord's-day, the Lord of the day will magnify his own name, and make the day illustrious by his grace ?   The first day of the week was signalized by the giving of the light of nature, and it is most delightful that now it should be a chosen day for bestowing the light of grace.   It is to us the Sabbath ; should not the Lord give rest to wearied hearts upon that day ?   Men call it Sunday : we are happy when the Sun of righteousness then arises with healing in his wings.   Of old the week's work was done, and then the Sabbath dawned ; but now rest leads the way : we begin the week's work with the Sabbath rest, because we first find rest in Jesus, and then labour for him.   Blessed is the Lord's-day when the Lord himself speaks rest in his own finished work, to those who otherwise would have laboured in vain.—*C. H. S.*

Christ came not into the world merely to cast a mantle over us, and hide all our filthy sores from God's avenging eye, with his merits, and righteousness ; but he came especially to be a chirurgeon and physician of souls, to free us from the filth and corruption of them, which are more grievous and burthensome, more noisome to a true Christian, than the guilt of sin itself.—*Cudworth.*

Metaphor : Physicians come not to the sick until they are sent for ; and though they come not far, yet expect to be paid for that, besides their physic.   *Disparity :* Christ came to us, who sent not for him, which made him say, "I am sought of them that asked not for me ; I am found of them that sought me not": Isaiah lxv. 1.   The patients seek not first, come not first, to the Physician ; but the Physician to the patients. "The Son of man is come to seek and to save that which was lost" (Luke xix. 10) ; and, besides, he dearly paid all the charge of his long journey.—*Benjamin Keach.*

CLXXIV

John vii. 11 —"Then the Jews sought him at the feast, and said, Where is he?"

Jesus went to the feast in secret, and the Jews sought him.

From differing motives they enquired for him, but they did enquire.

No man, having once heard of Jesus, can any longer remain indifferent to him: he *must* take some sort of interest in the Lord Jesus.

From many quarters comes the question, "Where is he?"

We will at this time—

I. CONSIDER THE WAYS IN WHICH THE QUESTION HAS BEEN ASKED.

1. Hate, ferociously desiring to slay him, and overthrow his cause. Herod was the type of this school.

2. Infidelity, sneeringly denying his existence, taunting his followers because his cause does not make progress: 2 Peter iii. 4.

3. Timorous fear, sadly doubting his presence, power, and prevalence. "Where is he that trod the sea?" Job xxiii. 8, 9.

4. Penitence, humbly seeking him that she may confess her sin, trust her Lord, and show her gratitude to him. Job xxiii. 3.

5. Love, heartily pining for communion with him, and for an opportunity to serve him. Solomon's Song iii. 3.

6. Fear, bitterly lamenting his absence, and craving his return.

7. Desire, ardently aspiring to meet him in his second advent, and to behold his glory. Rev. xxii. 20.

II. GIVE THE SAINTS' EXPERIMENTAL ANSWER.

1. He is at the mercy-seat when we cry in secret.

2. He is in the Word as we search the sacred page.

3. He is in the assemblies of his people, even with two or three.

4. He is at his table, known in the breaking of bread.

5. He is in the field of service, aiding, sympathizing, guiding, and prospering. In all things glorified before the eyes of faith.

6. He is in the furnace of trial, revealing himself, sanctifying the trial, bearing us through.

7. He is near us, yea, with us, and in us.

III. RETURN THE QUESTION TO YOU.

1. Is he at the bottom of your trust?

2. Is he at the root of your joys?

3. Is he on the throne of your heart?
4. Is he near you by constant converse?
5. Is his presence manifested in your spirit, your words, your actions?
6. Is he before you, the end of your journey, the terminus towards which you are daily hastening?

IV. ASK IT OF THE ANGELS.

They with one voice reply that the Lord Jesus Christ is—
1. In the bosom of the Father
2. In the centre of glory.
3. On the throne of government.
4. In the place of representation.
5. In the almonry of mercy.
6. Within reach of *you*, and of all needy sinners, who will now seek his face.

O come, let us go and find him!
We will hold no feast till he is among us.

ANA

Many years ago, there was a young man in Birmingham whom dissipation and excess had brought into a condition from which he endeavoured to extricate himself by crime. The fear of detection, exposure, and ruin goaded him on to such a pitch of desperation, that he left his father's house resolutely bent on self-destruction. God's good providence led him through Bond Street; and, under some inexplicable impulse, he found himself sitting in the Baptist Chapel almost before he was aware. The minister, a Mr. Edmonds, was reading from the book of Job, occasionally throwing in some shrewd parenthetic remark. Coming to the following passage, the young man's attention was irresistibly arrested : "Behold, I go forward, but he is not there; and backward, but I cannot perceive him; on the left hand, where he doth work, but I cannot behold him : he hideth himself on the right hand, that I cannot see him": Job xxiii. 8, 9. "Job, Job," the preacher cried entreatingly, "why don't you look upward?" These words were as nails fastened in a sure place, and the young man ever thanked God for the belief that he was unconsciously drawn by the Holy Spirit to enter that place, and that the preacher was impelled to the use of those words, to the end that his life might be redeemed from destruction, and crowned with loving-kindness and tender mercy.

"It befell me," says Henry Ward Beecher, "once to visit a friend, and to spend the night with him, in a manufacturing village in New England. I had never been in the place. I supposed that, when I arrived at the station, I should find a hack that could take me directly to the clergyman's residence. But it was an unusual train that I was on, and there were no hacks there; so I had to walk. The distance to the village was three miles; but before I reached it I had walked at least thirteen miles. I got there at a time of night when all sensible people were in bed. I knew nothing about the place, and did not know where to go. I could not see any church, or store, or hotel. I wandered about for nearly half-an-hour, and at the end of that time I knew no better where I was than I did when I began my search. I never felt so helpless as I did then. I realized what it was for a man, in his own country, and speaking his own language, to be utterly lost. I knocked at three or four houses, and received no response. I went to a house where I saw a light, and found the inmates quarrelling. A minister seemed to be the last thing they knew anything about. I began to think I should be obliged to sleep out of doors. But, as I was shooting down a certain street, almost aimless, I saw a light; and on going to the house from which it proceeded, and ringing the bell, I found that it was the very house which I was seeking. I thought a great many profitable things that night. Among the rest, I thought that I was, for all the world, like men that I had seen trying to go about the streets of Jerusalem at night, with nobody to tell them the way, and with no chart of the city, who would turn first to the right, and then to the left, without seeming to have any object except that of finding a place where their souls could put up and rest. It is pitiful to see a man, whose mind is troubled, whose conscience is against him, and who yearns for spiritual rest, going hither and thither, up and down, saying, ' Have ye seen my Lord and Master? Can ye tell me where he tarries, whom my soul delights in?' "

Our glorious Master is always at home, but does not always hold his receptions in the same chamber. One while he will see us in his closet, and anon in his great hall. To-day he meets us in the porch, and to-morrow in the innermost room. In reading the Bible I meet him in his library, in working for him I commune with him in the garden. When full of hope I walk with him on the housetop, at another time I wait for him in the secret places of the stairs. It is well to be in the parlour where he talks in sermons, or in his drawing-room where he converses in holy fellowship; but the best room of the house is that wherein he spreads his table, and makes himself to be our bread and wine. In any case, the one desire of our heart is to find him, and live upon him.

C. H. S.

138

CLXXV.

John vii. 43 —"So there was a division among the people because of him."

Even when Jesus preached so sweetly his meek and loving doctrine there was a division among the people.

Even about himself there was a schism.

We may not, therefore, hope to please everybody, however true may be our teaching, or however peaceful may be our spirit.

We may even dread the unity of death more than the stir of life.

To this day the greatest division in the world is "*because of him.*"

I. THERE WAS A DIVISION AMONG NON-DISCIPLES.

We may view the parties formed in his day as symbolical of those in our own.

1. Some admitted none of his claims.

2. Others admitted a portion, but denied the rest.

3. Certain admitted his claims, but neglected to follow out the legitimate consequences of them.

4. A few became his sincere hearers, going as far with him as they had yet learned of him.

Let us view persons who have thoughts about Jesus with considerable hope. Though they blunder now, they may yet come right. Let us not frighten away the birds by imprudent haste.

Let us pray for those who deny his claims, and resist his kingdom.

Let us aid those who come a little way towards the truth, and are willing to go all the way if they can but find it.

Let us arouse those who neglect holy subjects altogether.

II. THERE WAS A DIVISION OF BELIEVERS FROM NON-BELIEVERS.

This is a great and wide difference, and the more clearly the division is seen the better; for God views it as very deep and all-important.

There is a great division at this present hour—

1. In opinion : especially as to the Lord Jesus.

2. In trust : many rely on self; only the godly on Jesus.

3. In love. Differing pleasures and aims prove that hearts go after differing objects.

4. In obedience, character, and language.

5. In development, growth, tendency.

6. In destiny. The directions of the lines of life point at different places as the end of the journey.

This cleavage divides the dearest friends and relatives.
This is the most real and deep difference in the world.

III. Yet when faith comes, unity is produced.
There is unity among the people because of him.
1. Nationalities are blended. Calvary heals Babel.
Jews and Gentiles are one in Christ.
The near and the far-off as to spiritual things are brought nigh in him, who is the one and only centre of grace and truth.
Believers of all nationalities become one church.
2. Personal peculiarities cease to divide.
Workers for Christ are sure to be blended in one body by their common difficulties.
Position, rank, and wealth give way before the uniting influence of grace.
3. Mental specialities feel the touch of unity.
Saints of varying creeds have an essential union in Christ.
Saints of all the changing ages are alike in him.
Saints of all styles of education are one in Jesus.
Saints in heaven will be many as the waves, but one as the sea.
Ambitions, which else would disintegrate, are overcome, and laid at Jesus' feet.

Let us divide, if there be a division.
Let us closely unite, if there be real union in Christ.

Confirmations

Christ, who is properly the author of peace, is, on account of the wickedness of men, the occasion of discord.—*John Calvin.*

There never lived any one who has so deeply moved the hearts of men as Jesus Christ has done. The greatest monarchs that ever reigned, the greatest warriors that ever fought, the greatest masters in art, or science, or literature, have never affected so many, and that to so great an extent, as Jesus of Nazareth has done. He has changed the course of the world's history, and made its condition almost inconceivably different from what it would have been but for his coming. His teachings are received by the foremost nations of the earth. Millions of men call themselves by his name. He occupies the highest place in the esteem and affection of multitudes. For his sake men have lived as none others were able or willing to live : for his sake they have died as none others could or would have died.

But in proportion to the faith, the veneration, the love with which

140

Christ is regarded by a portion of mankind, are the unbelief, the contempt, and the hatred, which others display towards him. The poles are not more widely sundered than are the sentiments of men respecting Christ. There is nothing about which they are more completely at variance. Do you sing, " How sweet the name of Jesus sounds " ? To this day the Jew curses that name, and the infidel brands it as the name of an impostor. Do you regard Christ as worthy of your warmest love ? There are those who regard him with a passionate hate. Satan himself cannot be more bitterly hostile to Christ than some men are.—*P.*

The union of saints results from union with Christ, as the loadstone not only attracts the particles of iron to itself by the magnetic virtue, but by this virtue it unites them to one another.—*Richard Cecil.*

I have seen a field here, and another there, stand thick with corn. A hedge or two has parted them. At the proper season the reapers entered. Soon the earth was disburdened, and the grain conveyed to its destined place, where, blended together in the barn or in the stack, it could not be known that a hedge once separated this corn from that. Thus it is with the church. Here it grows, as it were, in different fields ; severed, it may be, by various hedges. By-and-by, when the harvest is come, all God's wheat shall be gathered into the garner, without one single mark to distinguish that once they differed in the outward circumstantiality of modes or forms.—*From " Parable, or Divine Poesy."*

Originating amongst the Jews, the Christian religion was regarded at first by great Rome as a mere Jewish sect, and shared alike in the impunity and the contempt with which that people were ever treated by their imperial masters. What did a Claudius or a Vespasian know, or care to know, of this new sect of Christians or Nazarenes, any more than of those other party names of Pharisee, Sadducee, Essene, Libertine, and the like ? . . . Christ was then only " one Christus," and the controversies between his followers and the Jewish priests only one of those paltry squabbles to which that restless people were chronically subject. By-and-by, as the young church became strong, it began to make its existence and its presence felt in the world, and then it stood in its genuine character and distinctive spirit face to face with Rome. Once met, they instinctively recognized each other as its natural and irreconcilable enemy, and straightway a war of deadliest hate began between them, which was from the first one of extermination, and could terminate only by the fall of the one or the other. There was no room in the world for Christ and Cæsar, so one or the other must die.

Islay Burns.

CLXXVI

John viii. 37 —" My word hath no place in you."

Where the Word of Jesus ought at once to be received, it is often rejected. These Jews were Abraham's seed, but they had not Abraham's faith.

Jesus knows where his Word is received, and where it has no place.

He declares that all else is unavailing: it was in vain that they were of the favoured race if they did not admit the Saviour's Word into their hearts.

The practical result appeared in their lives: they sought to kill Jesus.

Let us honestly consider—

I. WHAT PLACE THE WORD SHOULD HAVE IN MEN'S HEARTS.

The Word comes from Jesus, the appointed Messenger of God; it is true, weighty, saving; and, therefore, it must have a place among those who hear it. It ought to obtain and retain—

1. An inside place: in the thoughts, the memory, the conscience, the affections. " Thy Word have I hid in mine heart ": Psalm cxix. 11. See also Jer. xv. 16; Col. iii. 16.

2. A place of honour: it should receive attention, reverence, faith, obedience. John viji. 47; Luke vi. 46; Matt. vii. 24, 25.

3. A place of trust. We ought in all things to rely upon the sure Word of promise, since God will neither lie, nor err, nor change. Is. vii. 9; 1 Sam. xv. 29; Titus i. 2.

4. A place of rule. The Word of Jesus is the law of a Christian.

5. A place of love. It should be prized above our daily food, and defended with our lives. Job. xxiii. 12; Jude 3.

6. A permanent place. It must so transform us as to abide in us.

II. WHY IT HAS NO PLACE IN MANY MEN.

If any man be unconverted, let us help him to a reason applicable to his case.

1. You are too busy, and so you cannot admit it.
There is no room for Jesus in the inn of your life.
Think of it,—" You are too much occupied to be saved " !

2. It does not come as a novelty, and therefore you refuse it.
You are weary of the old, old story.
Are you wearied of bread? of air? of water? of life?

3. Another occupies the place the Word of Jesus should have.
You prefer the word of man, of superstition, of scepticism.
Is this a wise preference?

4. You think Christ's Word too holy, too spiritual.

    This fact should startle you, for it condemns you.

5. It is cold comfort to you, and so you give it no place.

    This shows that your nature is depraved; for the saints rejoice in it.

6. You are too wise, too cultured, too genteel, to yield yourself to the government of Jesus.   John v. 44 ; Rom. i. 22.

7. Is the reason of your rejection of the Word one of these ?

    That you are not in earnest ?

    That you are fond of sin ?

    That you are greedy of evil gain ?

    That you need a change of heart ?

III. WHAT WILL COME OF THE WORD OF CHRIST HAVING NO PLACE IN YOU ?

1. Every past rejection of that Word has involved you in sin.

2. The Word may cease to ask for place in you.

3. You may yourself become hardened, so as to decline even to hear that Word with the outward ear.

4. You may become the violent opponent of that Word, like these Jews.

5. The Word will condemn you at the last great day.   John xii. 48.

Let us therefore reason with you for a while.

Why do you not give place to it ?

All that is asked of you is to give it place.   It will bring with it all that you need.

Open wide the door, and bid it enter !

It is the Word of the Lord Jesus, the Saviour.

It means your highest good, and will greatly bless you.

COMMON-PLACES

Readers of this enlightened, gold-nugget generation can form to themselves no conception of the spirit that then possessed the nobler kingly mind.   VERBUM DEI MANET IN ÆTERNUM was the epigraph and life-motto which John the Steadfast had adopted for himself.   The letters, V.D.M.I.Æ., were engraved on all the furniture of his existence, standards, pictures, plate, on the very sleeves of his lackeys, and I can perceive on his own deep heart first of all.—*Thomas Carlyle.*

> O Book ! Infinite sweetness ! Let my heart
>   Suck every letter, and a honey gain,
>   Precious for any grief in any part ;
> To clear the breast, to mollify all pain.
>
> *George Herbert.*

143

The only reason why so many are against the Bible, is because they know the Bible is against them.—*G. S. Bowes.*

At one time the Malagasy did not know of any book except the Bible. There was a Creole trader, in Antananarivo, who had greatly offended some of the natives. They mobbed his house, they seized his property, and men were seen rushing in all directions, carrying away whatever they had been able to lay their hands upon. One man had got possession of the trader's ledger; and, holding it up aloft, he shouted at the top of his voice, " We have got the big Bible ! We have got the big Bible !" It is to be feared that the trader's ledger is in too many cases his Bible.—*Mr. Cousins, of Madagascar.*

The Bible has been expelled for centuries, by atheistic or sacerdotal hate, from the dwellings of many of the European nations. As a matter of course, the domestic virtues have declined ; the conjugal relation is disparaged ; deception and intrigue have supplanted mutual confidence ; and society has become diseased to its very core. The very best thing we can do—the only thing which will be efficient—to arrest these evils, is to restore to those nations the Word of God; to replace in their houses that Bible of which they have been robbed. Only do for France and Italy, Belgium and Spain, Portugal and Austria, what has been attempted, and to a great extent accomplished, for our country ; put a Bible in every family, and a mightier change will pass over Europe than can be effected by all the diplomacy of her statesmen, or all the revolutions projected by her patriots.—*The Leisure Hour.*

The following anecdote, well told by Mr. Aitken, shows that, in some men, the Word has no place, even in their memories :—" Only a short time ago, a friend of mine was preaching in one of our cathedral churches. As he was going to select for his text a prominent passage in one of the portions for the day, he thought it expedient to enquire of the clerk, ' What did the Canon preach from this morning ? ' The clerk became very pensive, seemed quite disposed to cudgel his brains for the proper answer; but, somehow or other, he really could not think of it just then. All the men of the choir were robing in the adjacent vestry, so he said that he would go and ask them. Accordingly, the question was passed round the choir, and produced the same perplexity. At length the sagacious clerk returned, with the highly-explicit answer, ' It was upon the Christian religion, sir ! ' I think those good people must have needed a reminder as to how we should hear ; don't you ? "

CLXXVII.

John ix. 31 —"Now we know that God heareth not sinners: but if any man be a worshipper of God, and doeth his will, him he heareth."

It is ill to wrench passages of the Bible out of their context, and treat them as infallible Scripture, when they are only the sayings of men.

By acting thus foolishly we could prove that there is no God (Psalm xiv. 1), that God hath forgotten his people (Isaiah xlix. 14), that Christ was a wine-bibber (Matt. xi. 19), and that we ought to worship the devil (Matt. iv. 9).

This will never do. We must enquire who uttered the sentence before we begin to preach from it.

Our text is the saying of a shrewd blind man, who was far from being well instructed. It is to be taken for what it is worth; but by no means to be regarded as Christ's teaching.

The Pharisees evidently admitted the force of it, and were puzzled by it. It was good argument as against *them*.

This remark of the blind man is true or false as we may happen to view it.

I. It is not true in some senses.

We could not say absolutely that God heareth not sinners, for—

1. God does hear men who sin, or else he would hear no one; for there is not a man upon earth that sinneth not. 1 Kings viii. 46.

    Not a saint would be heard; for even saints are sinners.

2. God does sometimes hear and answer unregenerate men.

    To show that he is truly God, and make them own it. Ps. cvi. 44.

    To manifest his great compassion, whereby he even hears the ravens' cry. Ps. cxlvii. 9.

    To lead them to repentance. 1 Kings xxi. 27.

    To leave them without excuse. Exodus x. 16, 17.

    To punish them, as when he sent quails to the murmurers (Numbers xi. 33), and gave Israel a king (1 Sam. xii. 17), in his anger.

3. God does graciously hear sinners when they cry for mercy.

    Not to believe this were to render the gospel no gospel.

    Not to believe this were to deny facts. David, Manasseh, the dying thief, the publican, the prodigal, confirm this testimony.

    Not to believe this were to deny promises. "Let the wicked forsake his way, and the unrighteous man his thoughts: and let him return unto the Lord, and he will have mercy upon him; and to our God, for he will abundantly pardon": Isaiah lv. 7.

145

II. It is true in other senses.

The Lord does *not* hear sinners as he hears his own people.

1. He hears no sinner's prayer apart from the mediation of our Lord Jesus. 1 Tim. ii. 5; Ephesians ii. 18.
2. He will not hear a wicked, formal, heartless prayer. Prov. xv. 29.
3. He will not hear the man who wilfully continues in sin, and abides in unbelief. Jer. xiv. 12; Is. i. 15.
4. He will not hear the hypocrite's mockery of prayer. Job xxvii. 9.
5. He will not hear the unforgiving. Mark xi. 25, 26.
6. He will not hear even his people when sin is wilfully indulged, and entertained in their hearts. Ps. lxvi. 18.
7. He will not hear those who refuse to hear his Word, or to regard his ordinances. Prov. xxviii. 9.
8. He will not hear those who harden their hearts against the monitions of his Spirit, the warnings of his providence, the appeals of his ministers, the strivings of conscience, and so forth.
9. He will not hear those who refuse to be saved by grace, or who trust in their own prayers as the cause of salvation.
10. He will not hear sinners who die impenitent. At the last he will close his ear to them, as to the foolish virgins, who cried, "Lord, Lord, open to us!" Matt. xxv. 11.

One or two things are very clear and sure.

He cannot hear those who never speak to him.

He has never yet given any one of us a flat refusal.

He permits us at this moment to pray, and it will be well for us to do so, and see if he does not hear us.

Observations

Such is the mercy of our God that he will wink at many infirmities in our devotions, and will not reject the prayer of an honest heart because of some weakness in the petitioner. It must be a greater cause than all this that makes God angry at our prayers. In general it is sin. "We know that God heareth not sinners : but if any man be a worshipper of God, and doeth his will, him he heareth." "If I regard iniquity in my heart, the Lord will not hear me." It is our sins that block up the passage of our prayers. It is not the vast distance between heaven and earth, not the thick clouds, not the threefold regions, not the sevenfold orbs, not the firmament of heaven, but only our sins, that hinder the ascent of our prayers. "When ye make many prayers, I will not hear you." Why? "Because your hands are full of blood." God will have none of those petitions that are presented to him with bloody hands. Our prayers are our bills of exchange, and they are allowed in heaven when they come from pious and humble hearts ; but if we be broken in our religion, and bankrupts of grace, God will protest our bills ; he will not be won with our prayers.—*Thomas Adams.*

> My words fly up, my thoughts remain below :
> Words, without thoughts, never to heaven go.
> > *Shakespeare.*

God is "neither hard of hearing, nor hard of giving."

The blood of sheep and the blood of swine are both alike ; yet the blood of swine was not to be offered, because it was the blood of swine : so the prayer of an unregenerate man may be as well framed, both for the petitions and for everything that is required immediately to a prayer, and yet not be accepted, because of the heart and person from whom it comes.—*Samuel Clark.*

It is difficult to illustrate this truth, because, in human life, nothing ever takes place corresponding to what occurs when an impenitent sinner presumes to pray to God. To every government many petitions are presented, but never one by any who are in rebellion against its authority. It is universally recognized, that rebellion against any government of itself cuts off all right of petition to it. So that, for an impenitent sinner to pray to God is one of the most unnatural and monstrous things that can be conceived of.

The fact that God is kind, good, bountiful, does not excuse the presumption of any impenitent sinner in praying to him. *That* only shows how inexcusable is his impenitence. For if God is good, kind, bountiful, why does he continue impenitent and rebellious ?

The fact that he is in great need does not excuse the presumption or lessen the folly of an impenitent sinner in praying to God. It may be that his distress is the punishment of his sin ; and for him in that case to pray to God for deliverance is as if a convicted thief were to petition Her Majesty's Government to release him, on the ground that he found it inconvenient and painful to work the treadmill. Or, it may be that his distresses are the means which God is employing for the very purpose of breaking down his obstinacy and impenitence : by them God is laying siege to his soul. But what rebellious city, besieged by the forces of the lawful government, would venture to ask aid from the government, on the ground that great distress prevailed in it, while all the time its inhabitants had not the slightest intention of surrendering to the government ?—*The Preachers' Monthly.*

CLXXVIII

John x. 9 —"I am the door: by me if any man enter in, he shall be saved, and shall go in and out, and find pasture."

Our Lord sets himself forth very condescendingly.

The most sublime and poetical figures are none too glorious to describe him ; but he chooses homely ones, which the most prosaic minds can apprehend.

A door is a common object. Jesus would have us often think of him.

A door makes a very simple emblem. Jesus would have the lowliest know him, and use him.

A door to a sheepfold is the poorest form of door. Jesus condescends to be anything, so that he may serve and save his people.

I. THE DOOR. In this homely illustration we see—

1. Necessity. Suppose there had been none, we could never have entered in to God, peace, truth, salvation, purity, or heaven.

2. Singularity. There is only one door ; let us not weary ourselves to find another. Salvation is by entrance at that door, and at none other. Acts iv. 12.

3. Personality. The Lord Jesus is himself the door. "I am the door," saith he ; not ceremonies, doctrines, professions, achievements, but the Lord himself, our Sacrifice.

4. Suitability. He is suited to be the communication between man and God, seeing he unites both in his own person, and thus lies open both earthward and heavenward. 1 Tim. ii. 5.

5. Perpetuity. His "I am" is for all times and ages. Matt. xxviii. 20. We can still come to the Father by him. John xiv. 6 ; Heb. vii. 25.

II. THE USERS OF IT.

1. They are not mere observers, or knockers at the door, or sitters down before it, or guards marching to and fro in front of it.
But they *enter in* by faith, love, experience, communion.

2. They are not certain persons who have special qualifications, such as those of race, rank, education, office, or wealth. Not lords and ladies are spoken of ; but "*any man*."

3. They are persons who have the one qualification : they do "*enter in*." The person is " any man," but the essential distinction is entrance.

This is intended to exclude —

> Character previously acquired as a fitness for entrance.
> Feeling, either of grief or joy, as a preparation for admission.
> Action, otherwise than that of entering in, as a term of reception.

A door may be marked PRIVATE, and then few will enter.

A door which is conspicuously marked as THE DOOR is evidently meant to be used. The remarkable advertisement of " I am the door," and the special promises appended to it, are the most liberal invitation imaginable.

Come then, ye who long to enter into life !

III.. THE PRIVILEGES OF THESE USERS.

> They belong to all who enter : no exception is made.

1. Salvation. "He shall be saved." At once, for ever, altogether.

2. Liberty. He "shall go in and out." This is no prison-door, but a door for a flock whose Shepherd gives freedom.

3. Access. " Shall go in " : for pleading, hiding, fellowship, instruction, enjoyment.

4. Egress. " He shall go out " : for service, progress, etc.

5. Nourishment. " And find pasture." Our spiritual food is found through Christ, in Christ, and around Christ.

Let us enter : a door is easy of access ; we shall not have to climb over some lofty wall.

Let us enter : it is a door for sheep, who have no wisdom.

Let us enter : the door is Jesus ; we need not fear to draw nigh to him, for he is meek and lowly in heart.

KNOCKERS

The work of the Reformation was thus described by Stern, a German statesman : " Thank heaven, Dr. Luther has made the entrance into heaven somewhat shorter, by dismissing a crowd of door-keepers, chamberlains, and masters of ceremony."

In olden times, cathedrals were regarded as places of sanctuary, where criminals and others might take refuge. Over the north porch of Durham Cathedral was a room, where two doorkeepers kept watch alternately, to admit any who at any time, either by day or by night, knocked at the gate, and claimed the protection of St. Cuthbert. Whoever comes to the door of our house of refuge, and at whatever time, finds ready admittance.

It is said that the ancient city of Troy had but one way of entrance. In whatever direction the traveller went, he would find no way to go into the city but the one which was legally appointed, and the only one which was used by those who went in and out. There is only one right way to the favour of God, to the family of God, to the presence of God in prayer, and, finally, to the city of God in eternity, and that one way is Christ. " I am the way," he declares, "and no man cometh unto the Father but by me."—*John Bate.*

We cannot go abroad or return home without passing through an emblem of our Lord. So near as he is in the type, so near let him be in reality.

The sheep enters the fold at first by the door, and it remains in the fold because the door shuts it in. When the flock go forward, they proceed by way of the door; and when they return to their united rest, it is by the same passage. Take away the door from the fold, and the enemy would enter, or the flock would stray. A sheep-fold without a door would in effect be no fold at all.—*C. H. S.*

There are not half-a-dozen ways out of our sin and misery—not a choice of ways over the steep hills and desolate waste-places of this mortal life, so that by any of them we may reach heaven at last, but only one way.

But, if this is the only way, it is likewise a perfectly secure way. *Via unica, via certa*, is a Latin proverb in which this truth is stated very forcibly.—*Dean Howson.*

Since Jesus glories that he is the door, let us not hesitate to use him in that capacity. Let us hasten to enter in by him into peace, life, rest, holiness. When we see it written up in large characters, THIS IS THE WAY, we do not fear that we shall trespass if we follow it. What is a way for, but to be followed ? What is a door for, but to be passed through ? Say that a door-way is never passed, and you have said that it is useless. Why not brick it up ? It would be no honour to the Lord Jesus for sinners to be so in awe of him as never to come to God by him; but he delights in being evermore our way of access.—*C. H. S.*

CLXXIX.

John x. 22, 23 —" And it was at Jerusalem the feast of the dedication, and it was winter.

" And Jesus walked in the temple in Solomon's porch."

The presence of Jesus brings into prominence—
The place : " at Jerusalem, in the temple."
The exact part of it : " Solomon's porch."
The time—the season- –the exact date: " it was winter."
The proceedings : " it was the feast of the dedication."

The main feature in all history, and in all the events of a private life, is the presence or absence of Jesus.

At the time mentioned, the Lord Jesus walked manifestly among the people.

We greatly desire his spiritual presence now.

I. WILL HE BE HERE? Will he be in our assembly?

The place may be a very Jerusalem ; but will he be there?
Our meeting-place may be a temple ; but will he be there?
It may be a high day ; but will the Lord be with us?
It may be cold and wintry ; but what of that if he be there?
Our one eager enquiry is about his presence, and we feel sure that
he will come, for—

1. We have invited him, and he will not refuse his friends.

2. We are prepared for him. We are waiting to welcome him.

3. We have great need of him, and he is full of compassion.

4. We have some of his brethren here among us, and these bring him
with them : indeed, he is in them.

5. We have those here whom he is seeking. He seeks lost sheep, and
such are here.

6. He has promised to come. Matt. xviii. 20.

7. Some declare that they have already seen him. Why should not
others of us enjoy the same privilege?

II. WILL HE STAY? He will—

1. If we prize his company, and feel that we cannot live without it
We must by earnest prayer constrain him to abide with us.
Luke xxiv. 29.

2. If we love his truth, and delight to make it known.

3. If we obey his will, and walk in sincerity and holiness.

4. If we are diligent in his service and worship.

151

5. If we are united in love to him, to one another, and to poor sinners.

6. If we are humbly reverent, and sit at his feet in lowly confession. The proud he will never favour.

7. If we are jealously watchful.

III. WHAT WILL HE DO IF HE COMES ?

1. He will walk among us, and observe what we are doing, even as he noticed those who went to the temple at Jerusalem.

2. He will grieve over the spiritual condition of many, even as he mourned over the ruin of Jerusalem.

3. He will wait to give audience to any who desire to speak with him.

4. He will teach by his servant ; and his Word, whether received or rejected, will be with great authority and power.

5. He will this day explain to us the temple itself, by being himself the Key to it.

   Think of Jesus, who is the temple of God (Rev. xxi. 22), in the temple, and then understand, by the light of his presence,—
   The temple.   Heb. ix. 11 ; Rev. xv. 5.
   The altar.   Heb. xiii. 10; Rev. viii. 3.
   The Sacrifice.   Heb. ix. 28 ; 1 Cor. v. 7.
   The shewbread.   Heb. ix. 2.
   The veil.   Heb. x. 20.
   The ark and mercy-seat.   Heb. ix. 4, 5 ; Rev. x. 19.
   The Priest.   Heb. x. 12.

6. He will to his own people reveal his love, as once the Lord's light shone above the mercy-seat.

7. He will take us where he always walks, but where there is no winter: to the New Jerusalem, to the temple, to a more beautiful building than Solomon's Porch.   Rev. xxi. 10, 11.

EXPOSITORY

What is here called " Solomon's Porch ", was, strictly speaking, not a porch at all in the English sense of the word, but one of the large open colonnades that surrounded the courts. . . The whole length of the four sides of the outer court was three quarters of a mile.   The eastern side was "Solomon's Porch."   It was a vast gallery of columns in double rows.   Each column, thirty-five feet high, consisted of one piece of white marble.   The roof above was in panels of cedar-wood.   The view, through the columns, eastward and outward, ranged across the valley over the Mount of Olives.   The inward view was into the court itself, which was planted with trees, and where, at festival times, there were crowds of people.

There is much solemnity in contemplating Jesus as he "walked" among the pillars of this famous colonnade ; and it is interesting to compare this passage of the life of Jesus with a much earlier one recorded by the same Evangelist. We read, in the first chapter of John's Gospel, that Jesus was "walking"—in solitude—by the banks of the Jordan, while John the Baptist and two of his disciples looked on. Then, perhaps, the Lord was meditating on his great mission, on the beginning of his work, and on the calling of the first disciples which speedily followed in that place. Now, perhaps, he was meditating on the accomplishment of his work, on the destruction of Jerusalem and the Jewish temple, and on the doom of the Jewish people. The impression upon the mind is very serious when we think of Jesus, on either of these occasions, as walking in silence, either by the banks of the famous historical river, or in this colonnade of the temple, which, in another way, is equally famous in the sacred annals.—*Dean Howson's " Thoughts for Saints' Days."*

The Mohammedans have a saying, that, whenever two persons meet, there is always a third. The proverb refers to the presence of God.—*Professor Hoge.*

As the sun is as ready to pour its radiance upon the daisy on a village common as upon the oaks in Windsor Park, so is Christ as willing to visit the heart of the poorest and feeblest as well as the richest and noblest of earth.—*Handbook of Illustration.*

When Christ saith, " I will be with you," you may add what you will—to protect you, to direct you, to comfort you, to carry on the work of grace in you, and in the end to crown you with immortality and glory. All this and more is included in this precious promise.— *John Trapp.*

CLXXX

John xiv. 28 —"Ye have heard how I said unto you, I go away, and come again unto you. If ye loved me, ye would rejoice, because I said, I go unto the Father: for my Father is greater than I."

Jesus' love makes him use the disciples' love to himself as a comfort for themselves when they are distressed about his going away.

He appeals to the warmest feeling in their hearts in order to raise their spirits.

It is well when grace has put within us principles which are springs of consolation.

O blessed Master, thou speakest ever with a view to our joy!

From our text let us learn—

I. THAT WE SHOULD TRY TO SEE THINGS IN CHRIST'S LIGHT.

    1. He sees the whole of things. He says not only, "I go away," but also, "I come again unto you."

    2. He sees through things. He does not say, "I die," but he looks beyond, and says, "I go unto the Father."

    3. He sees the true bearing of things. The events which were about to happen were in themselves sad, but they would lead to happy results. "If ye loved me, ye would rejoice."

To see facts in his light we must dwell with him, live in him, grow like him, and especially love him more and more.

II. THAT OUR LOVE SHOULD GO FORTH TOWARDS HIS PERSON. "If ye loved *me*." All about him is amiable; but he himself is altogether lovely. Solomon's Song v. 16.

    1. He is the source of all the benefits he bestows.

    2. Loving him, we have him, and so his benefits.

    3. Loving him, we prize his benefits the more.

    4. Loving him, we sympathize in all that he does.

    5. Loving him, we love his people for his sake.

    6. Loving him, our love endures all sorts of rebuffs for his sake.

    7. Loving him, the Father loves us. John xiv. 23.

    8. Loving him, we are married to him. Love is the sure and true marriage-bond whereby the soul is united to Christ.

Love to a person is the most real of emotions.

Love to a person is the most influential of motives.

Love to a person is, in this case, the most natural and satisfying of affections.

III. THAT OUR SORROW OUGHT NOT TO PUT OUR LOVE IN QUESTION.
Yet, in the case of the disciples, our Lord justly said, "*If* ye loved me." He might sorrowfully say the same to us—

1. When we lament inordinately the loss of creatures.

2. When we repine at his will, because of our severe afflictions.

3. When we mistrust his wisdom, because we are sore hampered and see no way of escape.

4. When we fear to die, and thus display an unwillingness to be with our Lord. Surely, if we loved him, we should rejoice to be with him.

5. When we complain concerning those who have been taken from us to be with him. Ought we not to rejoice that Jesus in them sees of the travail of his soul, and has his prayer answered, " Father, I will that they also, whom thou hast given me, be with me where I am " ? John xvii. 24.

IV. THAT OUR LOVE SHOULD MAKE US REJOICE AT OUR LORD'S EXALTATION, THOUGH IT BE OUR PERSONAL LOSS.

1. It was apparently the disciples' loss for their Lord to go to the Father ; and we may think certain dispensations to be our loss—
When we are tried by soul-desertion, while Christ is magnified in our esteem.
When we are afflicted, and he is glorified, by our sorrows.
When we are eclipsed, and in the result the gospel is spread.
When we are deprived of privileges for the good of others.
When we sink lower and lower in our own esteem, but the kingdom of God comes with power.

2. It was greatly to our Lord's gain to go to his Father.
Thus he left the field of suffering for ever.
Thus he reassumed the glory which he had laid aside.
Thus he received the glory awarded by the Father.
Thus he became enthroned for his church and cause.

It will be well for us to look more to our love than to our joy, and to expect our joy through our love.

It will be well for us to know that smallness of love may dim the understanding, and that growth in it may make us both wiser and happier.

In all things our Lord must be first. Yes, even in those most spiritual delights, about which it may seem allowable to have strong personal desires.

Observe that Christ does not say, " My Father *was* greater than I," in reference to his pre-existent glory ; nor, " My father *will be* greater than I," in reference to the glory which he was to resume after his exaltation ; but he uses a style of expression which shows that he refers to the *present* time—to the time of his humiliation in the flesh. The apostles had been expressing regret at the announcement of his immediate departure, and this passage contains a soft rebuke of the selfishness of their feelings. We may paraphrase it thus : " If ye really loved me on my own account —if the regard and affection you profess to entertain were purely disinterested in its nature—so far from evincing sorrow at the prospect of my departure, you would rejoice that I shall leave this state of temporary degradation ; that I shall cease to be the Man of Sorrows, and acquainted with grief ; that I shall resume that original and essential glory which I enjoyed with the Father from eternity. As long as I continue in my present state of humiliation, my Father is greater in glory than I ; but when the days of my flesh shall terminate, I shall then be glorified with the Father's own self, with that glory which I had with him before the world was created." This is obviously the correct paraphrase of the passage ; no other interpretation of the words, "For my Father is greater than I," could justify, or attach any force to, the interesting appeal which the Saviour makes to the love and affection of his disciples.—*Dean Bagot.*

Dr. John Duncan, having heard a sermon on the kingdom of heaven, in which the blessings of the new covenant were compared to a market, in which a man could buy everything needed for eternal life, met his friend, Dr. Moody Stuart, at the close of the service, and said to him, " Dear friend, when I heard of the good things that were offered in the market, I said to myself, I will marry the merchant, and they will all be mine."—*The Christian.*

The author of a biographical sketch of the late Rev. W. Robinson, of Cambridge, says, " In one of my last conversations with him, I was referring to the sadness of seeing our good men die ; and he turned to me with the well-known blaze in his eye, and emphasis of his voice, saying, ' I think it glorious.' "

A saint cares not how ill it goes with him so it goes well with Jesus Christ ; he saith, as Mephibosheth to David, " Yea, let him take all, forasmuch as my lord the king is come again in peace unto his own house " : 2 Sam. xix. 30. So it may go well with God's name, Moses cares not though his be blotted out of the book of life ; and, said John the Baptist, " He must increase, but I must decrease ; this my joy, therefore, is fulfilled."—*Ralph Venning.*

CLXXXI

John xiv. 31 —"Arise, let us go hence."

We cannot be long in one stay. A voice ever sounds in our ear, "Arise, let us go hence."

Even when we have conversed on the sweetest themes, or have enjoyed the holiest ordinances, we have not yet come to our eternal abode; still are we on the march, and the trumpet soundeth. "Arise, let us go hence."

Our Lord was under marching-orders, and he knew it: for him there was no stay upon this earth.

Hear how he calls himself, and all his own, to move on, though bloody sweat and bloody death be in the way.

I. OUR MASTER'S WATCHWORD. "Arise, let us go hence."

By this stirring word—

1. He expressed his desire to obey the Father. "As the Father gave me commandment, even so I do. Arise, let us go hence."

   He was not hindered by expected suffering.

   He did not start back, though in that suffering there would be the special element of his Father's forsaking him.

   He did not hesitate though death was in near prospect.

   He was eager to do the will of the Father, and make all heaven and earth know how entirely he yielded himself to the Father.

2. He indicated his readiness to meet the arch-enemy. "The prince of this world cometh. Arise, let us go hence."

   He was prepared for the test. He "hath nothing in me."

   He was eager to overthrow his dominion.

3. He revealed his practical activity. All through the chapter observe our Lord's energy. He is ever on the move. "I go. I will come again. I will do it. I will pray. Arise, let us go hence."

   He prefers action to the most sacred rites, and so leaves the Supper-table with this word on his lips.

   He prefers action to the sweetest converse. "I will not talk much with you. Arise, let us go hence."

4. He manifested his all-consuming love to us.

   He was straitened till he had accomplished our redemption.

   He could not rest in the company of his best-beloved till their ransom was paid.

   He would not sit at God's right hand till he had felt the shame of the cross, and the bitterness of death. Heb. xii. 2.

II. Our own motto. " Arise, let us go hence."

Ever onward, ever forward, we must go.   Exodus xiv. 15.

1. Out of the world when first called by grace.   2 Cor. vi. 17.
    How clear the call !   How prompt should be our obedience !
    Jesus is without the camp, we go forth unto him.   Heb. xiii. 13.
    We must arouse ourselves to make the separation.   " *Arise*, let
    us go hence."

2. Out of forbidden associations, if, as believers, we find ourselves
    like Lot in Sodom.   " Escape for thy life ": Gen. xix. 17.

3. Out of present attainments when growing in grace.   Phil. iii. 13, 14.

4. Out of all rejoicing in self.   There we must never stop for a single
    instant.   Self-satisfaction should startle us.

5. To work, anywhere for Jesus.   We should go away from Christian
    company and home comforts, to win souls.   Mark xvi. 15.

6. To defend the faith where it is most assailed.   We should be
    prepared to quit our quiet, to contend with the foe.   Jude 3.

7. To suffer when the Lord lays affliction upon us.   2 Cor. xii. 9.

8. To die when the voice from above calls us home.   2 Tim. iv. 6.

O sinner, where would you go if suddenly summoned ?

O saint, what better could happen to you than to arise and go hence ?

TRUMPET CALLS

It was well said once by a remarkable man, and the words are worth
remembering,—" Bear in mind that you are just then beginning to go
wrong when you are a little pleased with yourself because you are going
right."   Let us watch against this as a snare of Satan, and endeavour
ever to maintain the apostolic attitude: " In lowliness of mind let each
esteem other better than himself."   And let me caution you not to
make the mistake of supposing that this self-complacency can be
effectually guarded against by a mere use of the recognized theological
expressions duly ascribing all the merit and all the praise to God.
These are too often merely the garments of spiritual pride, and by no
means must they be mistaken for true humility.—*W. H. M. H. Aitken.*

I heard a friend of mine, not long ago, relate an incident, which I will
venture to repeat, as well as I remember it.   He was having an earnest conversation, upon the necessity of full consecration, with a lady who professed
to know Christ as her Saviour, but shrank from yielding herself fully to him.
At last she said, with more outspoken honesty, I am afraid, than many who
mean exactly the same thing display, "I don't want to give myself right
over to Christ ; for, if I were to do so, who knows what he might do with
me ?   For aught I know, he might send me out to China."   Years had

passed away when my friend received a most deeply interesting letter from this very lady, telling of how her long conflict with God had come to an end, and what happiness and peace she now felt in the complete surrender of herself to her Lord; and referring to her former conversation she said, "And now I am my own no longer, I have made myself over to God without reserve, and he *is* sending me to China."—*W. H. M. H. Aitken.*

Pressed on all sides by the enemy, the Austrian General Melas sent a messenger to Suwarrow, asking whither he should "retire." Suwarrow wrote with a pencil, "*Forward.*"

That pencil wrote a word immortal—a word which, in the memory and admiration of mankind, shall outlive a thousand boastful records on stoned marble—a word which no lapse of ages can erase.

The zealous are impatient of any hindrances. As Edmund Burke said to the electors of Bristol, "Applaud us when we run; console us when we fall; cheer us when we recover; but let us pass on—for God's sake, let us pass on!"

History tells us that, when the great Roman Catholic missionary—the apostle of the east—was lying on his dying bed, among the barbarous people whom he loved so well, his passing spirit was busy about his work, and even in the article of death, while the glazing eye saw no more clearly, and the ashen lips had begun to stiffen into eternal silence, visions of further conquests flashed before him, and his last word was "*Amplius,*"—onward. Brethren, let this be our motto, and our cry, "Onward." Until the last wandering sheep, far out upon the bleak mountain-side, hears Christ's voice, and is gathered into his fold.—*A. H. Baynes.*

We must be careful not to get out of the sound of the Master's voice. It is for us to watch and wait for his orders.

When adjutant of my regiment there were always orderlies on duty at the orderly-room. In a garrison town, such as Dublin, I always had two. Their place was just outside the orderly-room door, within sound of my voice. They were watching and waiting for orders; they took letters, messages, etc. They were not always carrying messages, but they could not go away without my leave, and it was their duty to be always ready. They were doing their duty while watching and waiting, as much as when actually carrying a letter or message. So with the servant of Christ— "Blessed is the man that heareth me, watching daily . . . waiting at the posts of my doors."

A lady, who had been maid of honour to the Queen, said that it used to be her great delight to try and place herself near the Queen, that she might have the opportunity of doing any little service for her sovereign.— *From "Communion and Conflict," by Captain Dawson.*

CLXXXII

John xix. 14 —"**He saith unto the Jews, Behold your King!**"

Pilate spake far more than he understood, and therefore we shall not confine ourselves to his meaning.

Everything concerning our Lord was more than ever full of meaning just then; the saying of Caiaphas, the fleeing of the disciples, the dividing of his garments, the soldier piercing his side, &c.

It was to the Jews that Jesus was brought forth, and by them he was rejected; yet was he distinctly declared to be their King.

The same is repeated at this day among those favoured with special privileges; but whether they accept him or not, he is assuredly in some sense or other their King.

To the summons of the text the answer was mockery.

We would with deepest reverence draw near, and behold our King.

I. BEHOLD HIM PREPARING HIS THRONE.

   1. He lays the foundation of it in his suffering nature.

   2. He makes it a throne of grace by his atoning griefs.

   3. He prepares access to it through his ability to have compassion on those who come to him, by partaking in all their sorrows.

   4. He canopies and glorifies it by the shame to which he willingly and unreservedly yields himself.

Believe in the perpetuity of a throne thus founded.

II. BEHOLD HIM CLAIMING OUR HOMAGE.

He claims and wins our adoration—

   1. By the right of supreme love.

   2. By the right of complete purchase.

   3. By the right of grateful consecration, which we heartily accord to him under a sense of loving gratitude.

Glory in rendering homage thus made due.

III. BEHOLD HIM SUBDUING HIS DOMINIONS.

   1. Jews and Gentiles are won to obedience by beholding his sufferings for them.

   2. This brings in his own elect everywhere.

   3. This restores backsliders. They look to him whom they have wounded, and return to their allegiance.

   4. This holds all his true servants captive: they glory in yielding their all to him who was thus put to shame for them.

5. This subdues all things unto him. By his cross and passion he reigns in heaven, earth, and hell.

Bow low before the sceptre of his Cross.

IV. BEHOLD HIM SETTING FORTH THE PATTERN OF HIS KINGDOM.

He stands there the Prophet and the Type of his own dominion.

1. It is no earthly kingdom : the difference is palpable to all.
2. It is associated with shame and suffering, both on the part of the King and of his loyal subjects.
3. It is based on his love and self-sacrifice : this is his right of sovereignty, this his force of arms, this the source of his revenue.
4. It is made resplendent by his woes : these are the insignia and ornaments of his court; his glory even in heaven.

Glory only in the cross.

V. BEHOLD HIM PROVING THE CERTAINTY OF HIS KINGDOM.

1. Is he King there in his shame ? Then, assuredly, he is King now that he has risen from the dead, and gone into the glory.
2. Is he King amid shame and pain ? Then he is able to help us if we are in like case.
3. Is he King while paying the price of our redemption ? Then, certainly, he is King now that it is paid, and he has become the author of eternal salvation.
4. Is he King at Pilate's bar ? Then truly he will be so when Pilate stands at his bar to be judged.

Come hither, saints, and pay your accustomed worship !
Come hither, sinners, and adore for the first time !

GLIMPSES

It is far worse to despise a Saviour in his robes than to crucify him in his rags. An affront is more criminal to a prince upon his throne than when he is disguised as a subject, and masked in the clothes of his servant. Christ is entered into glory after his sufferings ; all who are his enemies must enter into misery after their prosperity: and whosoever will not be ruled by his golden sceptre shall be crushed by his rod.— *Stephen Charnock.*

Did Pilate hope to melt the Jewish heart to a sort of scornful pity ? Did he think that they would turn away from so wretched an object, and be ashamed of having accused *him* of treason ? Perhaps so. But he failed. The sorrows of Jesus do not of themselves overcome the hate of man; but this fact proves how desperately hardened his heart has become.

Given the Holy Spirit, there is nothing more likely to win men to Jesus than beholding him in his sorrows. Behold, O man, and see what thy sin has done, what thy Redeemer has borne, and what he claims of thee! Behold him not as another's, but as thine! Behold him not only as thy Friend, thy Saviour, but thy King! Behold him, and at once fall at his feet, and own thyself his loving subject!— *C. H. S.*

"*Behold your King.*"—This is neither an impossible nor a delusive command. The eye that looks away up to Jesus *will* behold him now: and what shall we behold? The vision is all of beauty, and glory, and coronation *now*. The sorrow and the marred visage are past; and even when we behold him as the Lamb of God, it is the Lamb "in the midst of the throne" *now*.

O daughters of Zion, who gaze by faith upon Jesus our King, what do you see? Oh the music of the answers!—"We see Jesus crowned with glory and honour!" "Fairer than the children of men." "Beautiful and glorious!" "How great is his beauty!" "His countenance is as Lebanon, excellent as the cedars," and "as the sun shineth in his strength!" "Yea, he is altogether lovely!"—*Frances Ridley Havergal.*

CLXXXIII

John xx. 15 —" Jesus saith unto her, Woman, why weepest thou ? Whom seekest thou ? "

Woman has had many reasons for weeping since the fall.

Jesus went to his death amid weeping women, and on his rising he met a little company of them.

The first words of a risen Saviour are to a weeping woman.

He who was born of woman has come to dry up woman's tears.

Observe the wise method followed by the divine Consoler.

Magdalene is to state the reason of her weeping. " Why weepest thou ? " Often sorrow vanishes when it is defined. It is wise to chase away mystery and understand the real cause of grief.

He helps her also by coming nearer to her grief in the second question : " Whom seekest thou ? " She was seeking *him*.

He was himself the answer to his own enquiries.

In all cases Jesus is the most suitable Comforter and comfort.

Let us put this question, " Why weepest thou ? " in two ways.

I. IS IT NATURAL SORROW ?

1. Art thou bereaved ? The risen Saviour comforts thee ; for—
   He assures thee of the resurrection of the departed.
   He is with thee, thy living Helper.
   He sympathizes with thee, for he once lost his friend Lazarus ; yea, he himself has died.

2. Are thy beloved ones sick ? Sorrow not impatiently ; for—
   He lives to hear prayer for healing.
   He waits to bless them if they are dying.

3. Art thou thyself sick ? Be not impatient ; for—
   Jesus lives to moderate thy pains.
   Jesus lives to sustain thy heart under suffering.
   Jesus lives to give life to thy body, as he has done to thy soul.

4. Art thou poor ? Do not murmur, for—
   He lives, and is rich.
   He would have thee find thine all in himself.
   He will never leave thee nor forsake thee.

5. Art thou of a sorrowful spirit ? Do not despond, but—
   See where *his* sorrows have brought *him*.
   See how he came to the sorrowful, and how he cometh still.
   See what he does in his consoling ministry, and imitate him by cheering others. Thus thou shalt thyself be comforted.

II. Is it spiritual sorrow?

1. *Distinguish.* See whether it be good or ill.   " Why weepest thou?"

Is it selfish sorrow ?   Be ashamed of it.

Is it rebellious?   Repent of it.

Is it ignorant?   Learn of Jesus, and so escape it.

Is it hopeless?   Believe in God and hope ever.

Is it gracious ?   Then thank him for it.

2. *Declare.* Tell Jesus all about it.   " Why weepest thou?"

Is it sorrow for others?   He weeps with thee.

Are loved ones abiding in sin ?

Is the church cold and dead ?

Is it the sorrow of a seeking saint ?   He meets thee.

Dost thou miss his presence ?

Hast thou grieved his Holy Spirit?

Canst thou not attain to holiness ?

Canst thou not serve him as much as thou desirest ?

Do thy prayers appear to fail ?

Does thine old nature rebel ?

Is it the sorrow of one in doubt?   He will strengthen thee.

Come to Jesus as a sinner.

Is it the sorrow of a seeking sinner ?   He will receive thee.

Dost thou weep because of past sin ?

Dost thou fear because of thine evil nature?

Art thou unable to understand the gospel ?

Dost thou weep lest thou grow hardened again ?

Dost thou mourn because thou canst not mourn ?

He is before thee : believe in him, and weeping will end.

He accepts thee : in him thou hast all thou art seeking for.

Consolatory Thoughts

A Hindoo woman said to a missionary, " Surely your Bible was written by a woman." " Why?" " Because it says so many kind things for women. Our pundits never refer to us but in reproach."

" *Woman, why weepest thou ?* "   God and his angels take notice of every tear of our devotion. The sudden wonder hath not dried her eyes, nor charmed her tongue : she freely confesseth the cause of her grief to be the missing of her Saviour : " They have taken away my Lord, and I know not where they have laid him." Alas ! good Mary, how dost thou lose thy tears ? Of whom dost thou complain but of thy best Friend ? Who hath removed thy Lord but himself? Who but his own Deity hath taken away his human body out of the region of death ? Neither is he now laid any more ; he stands by thee, whose removal thou complainest of. Thus many a tender and humble soul afflicts itself with the want of that Saviour whom it hath, and feeleth not.—*Bishop Hall.*

She turns away from the angels, like a Rachel who will not be comforted. But there is comfort in store for her, sorrow as she may. We have an example given us here of how only the Lord himself can suffice to comfort spirits like that of Mary Magdalene. The Lord sees the heart, and none shall weep for him in vain ; but even the angels, gracious though their sympathy be, must leave the task of comforting the deepest sorrow to the Lord.—*Rudolf Stier.*

The first words that ever Christ spake after his resurrection to them he appeared to, were, " Woman, why weepest thou ? " It is a good question after Christ's resurrection. What cause of weeping remains now that Christ is risen ? Our sins are forgiven, because he, our Head and Surety, hath suffered death for us ; and if Christ be risen again, why weep we ? If we be broken-hearted, humbled sinners, that have interest in his death and resurrection, we have no cause to grieve.— *Richard Sibbes.*

" Good men weep easily," says the Greek poet ; and the better any are, the more inclined to weeping, especially under affliction. As you may see in David, whose tears, instead of gems, were the ornaments of his bed ; in Jonathan, Job, Ezra, Daniel, etc. " How," says one, "shall God wipe away my tears in heaven if I shed none on earth ? And how shall I reap in joy if I sow not in tears ? I was born with tears, and I shall die with tears ; and why then should I live without them in this valley of tears ? "—*Thomas Brooks.*

Be not troubled, my soul. God has for thee something better than thy imaginings. It is with thee as with the women of Galilee. They sought only a dead form, and they found a living Lord. Thou also hast been too eager for the earthly form of thy hope's fulfilment. Has he promised that all things shall work together for thy good, and yet denied thee the comforts of the world ? What then ? Is his promise void ? May it not be that thou hast found thy promise in the very region where it seems to have failed thee, in the privations and sorrows of life ? What matter though thou hast lost the form, if thou hast found the sepulchre vacant ? The loss is a gain, and the vacancy is fulness of joy. There are losses which mean nothing less than resurrection. I rise more by the discovery of my wants than by the discovery of my possessions . . . O fragrance of the broken ointment box ! O light of resurrection ! reached from human emptiness, I am enriched by the gain of thee.

Dr. George Matheson.

CLXXXIV

John xx. 17 —" Jesus saith unto her, Touch me not; for I am not yet ascended to my Father: but go to my brethren, and say unto them, I ascend unto my Father, and your Father; and to my God, and your God."

The lesson is to a soul brought into the conscious presence of the Lord.

Oh, to be in that condition !

Mary Magdalene had wept because of her Lord's absence, and longed to find him; and now she has her desire: he stands before her.

Oh, that we knew where we might find him ! Job xxiii. 3.

Her conduct in holding him by the feet was natural, and yet it was forbidden by a higher wisdom than that of mortal men.

I. THE CAUTION. " Touch me not."

1. We may blunder even in our closest fellowship, and may need a prohibition. We have never greater need of caution than in our nearest approaches to God. Courtiers must be most careful in the throne-room.

2. We may carnalize the spiritual.
   This has ever been a tendency with even the best of the saints; and it has misled many in whom affection has been stronger than intellect.

3. We may seek most passionately what is by no means essential.
   The assurance of sense, by touch or otherwise : when the assurance of faith is far better, and quite sufficient.
   The detaining of one who has no intention of going.

4. We may crave what were better further on.
   When we are raised to eternal glory we shall be able to enjoy what now we must not ask.

5. We may be selfish in our enjoyments.
   Staying to contemplate alone by ourselves, when we ought rather to bless others by publishing the blessed news. 2 Kings vii. 9.

II. THE MISSION. " Go to my brethren."

She would have preferred to stay, but Jesus bids her go.

1. This was better for her. Contemplation alone may degenerate into the sentimental, the sensuous, the impracticable.

2. This was better for them. They heard the best of news from the most trustworthy of informants.

3. This was unquestioningly done by this holy woman.

What she had seen she declared.

What she had heard she told.

Women are said to be communicative; and so there was wisdom in the choice.

Women are affectionate, and so persuasive; and therefore fit to bear such a tender message as we have now to consider.

III. THE TITLE. "My brethren."

Our Lord, of design, chose this title to comfort his sorrowing ones. They had so acted as almost to cease to be his followers, disciples, or friends; but brotherhood is an abiding relationship. They were—

1. His brethren, though he was about to ascend to his throne.

He was still a man, though no more to suffer and die.

He still represented them as their risen Head.

He was still one with them in all his objects and prospects.

2. His brethren, though they had forsaken him in his shame.

Relationship abiding, for brotherhood cannot be broken.

Relationship owned more than ever; since their sense of guilt made them afraid. He was a true Joseph to them. Gen. xlv. 4.

Relationship dwelt upon, that they might be reassured.

Never let us omit the tender sweetnesses of the gospel, its courtesies, benedictions, and love-words, such as the "My brethren" of the text before us. If we leave out these precious words we shall mar the Master's message of grace.

IV. THE TIDINGS. "I ascend unto my Father, and your Father."

This message was meant to arouse and comfort them.

1. By the news of his departure they are to be aroused.

2. By the news of his ascension they are to be confirmed.

3. By his ascension to the common Father they are to be comforted with the prospect of coming there themselves. He is not going into an unknown country, but to his home and theirs. John xiv. 2.

4. By his ascent to God they are to be struck with solemn awe, and brought the more reverently to look for his presence among them.

> See how practical our Lord is, and how much he values the usefulness of his servants.
>
> Have *we* not somewhat to tell?
>
> Whether man or woman, tell the Lord's brethren what the Lord hath told to *thee*.

It is this that men will labour after, and have laboured for, even from the beginning of the world,—to be too much addicted to the things of sight and sense. They will worship Christ, but they must have a picture before them. They will adore Christ, but they must bring his body down to a piece of bread. They must have a presence, and so, instead or raising their hearts to God and Christ in a heavenly manner, they pull down God and Christ to them. This the pride and base earthliness of man will do. And therefore saith Christ, "Touch me not" in that manner; it is not with me now as it was before. We must take heed of mean and base conceits of Christ. What saith Paul in 2 Cor. v. 16? "Henceforth know we no man after the flesh: yea, though we have known Christ after the flesh, yet now henceforth know we him no more." Christ after the flesh was of such a tribe and of such a stature, and had such gifts and qualities. What is that to me? Christ is now Lord of lords and King of kings. He is glorious in heaven, and so I conceive of him.—*Richard Sibbes.*

"*Touch me not.*"—By which we are to understand, not that the Lord would have objected to this token of her affection, for we find that soon after the Lord made Thomas put his hand into his side (verse 25); but this was not the moment for Mary to be so employed. The Lord had a message to send by her to his disciples. It was time that they, as well as herself, should receive the joyful tidings of his resurrection; therefore he would first send her to them.—*Dr. Hawker.*

To whom then dost thou send her? "*Go to my brethren.*" Blessed Jesu! who are these? Were they not thy followers? Yea, were they not thy forsakers? Yet still thou stylest them thy brethren. O admirable humanity! O infinite mercy! How dost thou raise their titles with thyself? At first they were thy servants, and then thy disciples; a little before thy death they were thy friends; now, after thy resurrection, they were thy brethren. Thou that wert exalted infinitely higher from mortal to immortal, descendest so much lower to call them brethren who were before friends, disciples, servants.—*Bishop Hall.*

While the going up of Elias may be compared to the flight of a bird which none can follow, the ascension of Christ is, as it were, a bridge between heaven and earth, laid down for all who are drawn to him by his earthly existence.—*Baumgarten.*

CLXXXV

John xx. 27 —"Then saith he to Thomas, Reach hither thy finger, and behold my hands; and reach hither thy hand, and thrust it into my side: and be not faithless, but believing."

How struck must Thomas have been when his Lord addressed to him the very words which he had himself used! (See verse 25.) Jesus knows how to send the word home to us.

In the church of to-day we have many a Thomas,—slow, suspicious, critical, full of doubts, yet true-hearted.

Thomas set his Lord a test, and thus tried his patience.

The Lord accepted the test, and so proved his condescension.

The proof sufficed for Thomas, and thus showed the Lord's wisdom.

Peradventure, certain among us would desire tests of some such sort.

To those we would earnestly say,—

I. CRAVE NO SIGNS.

After the full proofs which Christ gave to his apostles, we need no more, and to look for further signs and evidences would be wrong. Yet some are demanding miracles, faith healings, visions, voices, impressions, transports, depressions, etc.

1. It is dishonouring to your Lord.

2. It is unreasonable, when the truth bears its own evidence.

3. It is presumptuous. How dare we stipulate for proof more than sufficient, or demand evidence of a sort which pleases our prejudices!

4. It is damaging to ourselves. Faith must be weak while we demand for it such proofs; and in this weakness lies incalculable mischief.

5. It is dangerous. We may readily be driven either into infidelity or superstition, if we give way to this craving for signs.

Picture what Thomas could and would have become under the influence of his unbelief, had not his Lord interposed.

II. YET TURN TO CHRIST'S WOUNDS. Let these stand to you instead of signs and wonders.

Behold in these wounds—

1. The seals of his death. He did actually and truly die. How could he outlive that wound in his side?

2. The identification of his person as actually risen.

3. The tokens of his love. He has graven us upon the palms of his hands.

4. The ensigns of his conflict, of which he is not ashamed, for he displays them.

5. The memorials of his passion, by which he is manifested in glory as the Lamb that was slain. Rev. v. 6.

This should more than suffice you ; but should doubt still linger—

III. USE SUCH EVIDENCES AS YOU POSSESS.

1. The sacred narrative of our Lord's life and death, if carefully studied, exhibits a singular self-evidencing power.

2. The regenerating and purifying result of faith in the great Lord is a further piece of evidence. "By their fruits ye shall know them": Matt. vii. 20.

3. The solace which faith yields in sorrow is good proof.

4. The strength it gives in the hour of temptation is further help.

5. The ardour of mind and elevation of aim, which faith in Jesus creates, are other experimental arguments.

6. The visitations of the Holy Spirit, in quickening the heart, reviving the spirit, and guiding the mind, are additional proofs. Thus the Holy Ghost bears witness to our Lord.

7. The actual enjoyment of fellowship with the Lord Jesus himself is the master-key of the whole controversy. "We have known and believed": 1 John iv. 16.

Does this seem an idle tale to you ?

Should you not see cause for fear, if it be so ?

Seek now to view those wounds believingly, that you may live.

NOTES

For all thy rankling doubts so sore,
  Love thou thy Saviour still
Him for thy Lord and God adore.
  And ever do his will.
Though vexing thoughts may seem to last,
Let not thy soul be quite o'ercast ;
Soon will he show thee all his wounds, and say,
"Long have I known thy name—know thou my face alway."

Keble.

We learn here how prone we are to establish improper criteria of truth. How often do we judge of things exclusively by our experience, our reason, our senses ! But what can be more foolish than this? To how small a distance do these powers extend? How many things are certainly true, the truth of which falls not within the compass of either! How many things can a man relate, which appear impossible to a child! Tell the inhabitants of the sultry climes, that, at a certain season of the year, water, which he has only seen in a fluid state, becomes solid, and hard enough to walk upon—and it will seem to him an idle tale: he has witnessed no such thing, and reasoning from what he knows, deems it incredible. If Thomas had constantly judged according to the rule he professed, how little could he have believed at all! . . . To believe no more than we can comprehend, or reduce to some of our modes of knowledge, is not to honour the authority of God at all; yea, it is a reflection upon his wisdom, and upon his veracity: upon his wisdom—as if he could tell us no more than we know; and upon his veracity—as if he were not to be trusted if he could.— *William Jay.*

Skilful swimmers are not afraid to go above their depth, whereas young learners feel for the ground, and are loth to go far from the bank-side. Strong faith fears not when God carries the creature beyond the depth of his reason. "We know not what to do," said good Jehoshaphat, "but our eyes are upon thee": 2 Chron. xx. As if he had said, "We are in a sea of trouble beyond our own help, or any thought how we can wind out of these straits, but our eyes are upon thee. We dare not give up our case for desperate so long as there is strength in thine arm, tenderness in thy bowels, and truth in thy promise." Whereas weak faith, that is groping for some footing for reason to stand on, is taken up with how to reconcile the promise to the creature's understanding.— *William Gurnall.*

CLXXXVI

John xx. 29 —"Jesus saith unto him, Thomas, because thou hast seen me, thou hast believed: blessed are they that have not seen, and yet have believed."

Those who saw and believed not, were far from being blessed.

Those who saw him, and believed, were undoubtedly blessed.

Those who have not seen, and yet have believed, are *emphatically* blessed.

There remains the superlative degree of blessedness in seeing Jesus face to face without need of believing in the same sense as now.

But for the present this is *our* blessedness, this is our place in the gospel history,—we have not seen, and yet have believed. What a comfort that so high a degree of blessedness is open to us !

I. Do not let us diminish this blessedness.

   1. Let us not diminish it by wishing to see.

      By pining for some imaginary voice, or vision, or revelation.

      By craving marvellous providences, and singular dispensations.

      By hungering for despairs or transports.

      By perpetually demanding arguments, and logical demonstrations.

      By clamouring for conspicuous success in connection with the preaching of the word, and the missionary operations of the church.

      By being anxious to believe with the majority. Truth has usually been with the minority.

   2. Let us not diminish it by failing to believe.

      Believe practically, so as to act upon our faith.

      Believe intensely, so as to laugh at contradictions.

      Believe livingly, so as to be simple as a child.

      Believe continually, so as to be evenly confident.

      Believe personally, so as to be assured alone, even if all others give the lie to the doctrines of the Lord.

      Believe thoroughly, so as to find the rest of faith.

II. Do not let us think this blessedness unattainable.

   1. This blessedness is linked for ever with the faith which our Lord accepts : in fact, it is the appointed reward of it.

   2. God deserves such faith of us. He is so true that his unsupported word is quite enough for faith to build upon. Can we only believe him as far as we can see him ?

3. Thousands of saints have rendered, and are rendering, such faith, and are enjoying such blessedness at this moment. We are bound to have fellowship with them in like precious faith.

4. Hitherto our own experience has warranted such faith. Has it not?

5. Those of us who are now enjoying the blessed peace of faith can speak with great confidence upon the matter.

Why, then, are so many cast down? Why will they not believe?

III. Do NOT LET ANY OF US MISS IT.

The faith which our Lord described is exceedingly precious, and we ought to seek after it, for—

1. It is the only true and saving faith. Faith which demands sight is not faith at all, and cannot save the soul.

2. It is in itself most acceptable with God. Nothing is acceptable without it (Heb. xi. 6). It is the evidence of the acceptance of the man and his works.

3. It is a proof of grace within: of a spiritual mind, a renewed nature, a reconciled heart, a new-born spirit.

4. It is the root-principle of a glorious character.

5. It is exceedingly useful to others : in comforting the despondent, in impressing unbelievers, in cheering seekers, etc.

6. It enriches its possessor to the utmost, giving power in prayer, strength of mind, decision of character, firmness under temptation, boldness in enterprise, joy of soul, realization of heaven, etc.

Know *you* this faith?

Blessedness lies that way. Seek it !

CONTRIBUTIONS.

But why specially blessed? Because the Holy Spirit hath wrought this faith in their hearts. They are blessed in having a believing heart; they are blessed in the instrument of their belief; blessed in having an evidence that they are passed from death unto life : "whom, having not seen, ye love." It is more blessed to believe than to see, because it puts more honour upon God's word. It is more blessed, because it presents us with a more invariable object. He that can trust an unseen Saviour may trust him in all circumstances : shut him up in a dungeon, separate from all sight and light, it matters not; for he has always a heart to believe unto righteousness, and his soul rests upon a rock that shall never be moved. The same faith that takes hold of an unseen, risen Saviour, takes hold of every other truth in the gospel.—*Richard Cecil.*

"With men," says Bishop Hall, "it is a good rule to try first, and then to trust; with God it is contrary. I will first trust him, as most wise, omnipotent, merciful, and try him afterwards."

By constant sight, the effect of objects seen grows less; by constant faith, the effect of objects believed in grows greater. The probable reason of this is that personal observation does not admit of the influence of the imagination in impressing the fact; while unseen objects, realized by faith, have the auxiliary aid of the imagination, not to exaggerate them, but to clothe them with living colours, and impress them upon the heart. Whether this be the reason or not, the fact is true that, the more frequently we see, the less we feel the power of an object; while the more frequently we dwell upon an object by faith, the more we feel its power.—*J. B. Walker.*

Faith makes invisible things visible, absent things present, things that are very far off to be very near unto the soul.—*Thomas Brooks.*

The region of unbelief is black with God's frown, and filled with plagues and wrath; but the region of faith is as the floor of heaven for brightness. Christ's righteousness shelters it, the graces of the Spirit beautify it, and the eternal smile of God comforts and glorifies it.—*Dr. Hoge.*

It would grieve an indulgent father to see his own child come into court, and there bear witness against him and charge him of some untruth in his words, more than if a stranger should do it; because the testimony of a child, though, when it is *for* the vindication of a parent, it may lose some credit in the opinion of those that hear it, upon the suspicion of partiality, yet, when *against* a parent, it seems to carry some more probability of truth than what another that is a stranger says against him; because the band of natural affection with which the child is bound to his parent is so sacred that it will not be easily suspected. He cannot be supposed to offer violence to it, except upon the more inviolable necessity of bearing witness to the truth.

O think of this, Christian, again and again—by thy unbelief thou bearest false witness against God! And if thou, a child of God, speakest no better of thy heavenly Father, and presentest him with no fairer character to the world, it will be no wonder if it be confirmed in its hard thoughts of God, even to final impenitency and unbelief, when it shall see how little credit he finds with thee, for all thy great profession of love towards him and near relationship to him.— *William Gurnall.*

CLXXXVII

Acts ii. 24.—"Whom God hath raised up, having loosed the pains of death: because it was not possible that he should be holden of it."

Our Lord felt the pains of death truly and really.

His body was in very deed dead, yet there was no corruption.

It was not needful: it could have borne no relation to our redemption.

It would not have been seemly.

It was not demanded by the law of nature; for he was sinless, and sin is the worm which causes corruption.

But from the pains of death his body was loosed by resurrection.

I. IT WAS NOT POSSIBLE THAT THE BANDS OF DEATH SHOULD HOLD OUR LORD.

He derived his superiority to the bondage of death—

1. From the command of the Father that he should have power to take his life again : John x. 18.

2. From the dignity of his human person.
As in union with Godhead.
As being in itself absolutely perfect.

3. From the completion of his propitiation.
The debt was discharged: he must be freed.

4. From the plan and purpose of grace which involved the life of the Head as well as that of the members. John xiv. 19.

5. From the perpetuity of his offices.
"Priest for ever after the order of Melchizedec": Heb. vi. 20.
King—"Thy throne, O God, is for ever and ever": Ps. xlv. 6.
Shepherd—"brought again from the dead": Heb. xiii. 20.

6. From the nature of things, since without it we should have—
No assurance of our resurrection. 1 Cor. xv. 17.
No certainty of justification. Rom. iv. 25.
No representative possession of heaven. Heb. ix. 24.
No crowning of man with glory and honour, and exaltation of him over the works of God's hands.

II. IT IS NOT POSSIBLE THAT ANY OTHER BANDS SHOULD HOLD HIS KINGDOM.

1. The firm establishment of error shall not prevent the victory of truth. The colossal systems of Greek philosophy and Roman priestcraft have passed away; and so shall other evil powers.

2. The scholarship of his foes shall not resist his wisdom. He baffled the wise in his life on earth ; much more will he do it by his Holy Spirit. 1 Cor. i. 20.

3 The ignorance of mankind shall not darken his light. " The poor have the gospel preached to them " : Matt. xi. 5. Degraded races receive the truth. Matt. iv. 16.

4. The power, wealth, fashion, and prestige of falsehood shall not crush his kingdom. Acts iv. 26.

5. The evil influence of the world upon the church shall not quench the divine flame. John xvi. 33.

6. The rampant power of unbelief shall not destroy his dominion. Though at this hour it seems to bind the church in the bands of death, those fetters shall melt away. Matt. xvi. 18.

III. IT IS NOT POSSIBLE TO HOLD IN BONDAGE ANYTHING THAT IS HIS.

1. The poor struggling sinner shall escape the bonds of his guilt, his depravity, his doubts, Satan, and the world. Ps. cxxiv. 7.

2. The bondaged child of God shall not be held captive by tribulation, temptation, or depression. Ps. xxxiv. 19. Ps. cxvi. 7.

3. The bodies of his saints shall not be held in the grave. 1 Cor. xv. 23 ; 1 Peter i. 3-5.

4. The groaning creation shall yet burst into the glorious liberty of the children of God. Rom. viii. 21.

Here is a true Easter hymn for all who are in Christ.
The Lord is risen indeed, and the happiest consequences must follow.
Let us rise in his rising, and walk at large in his loosing.

FREE THOUGHTS

Christ being imprisoned for our debt, was thrown into the bands of death ; but, divine justice being satisfied, it was not possible that he should be detained there, either by right or by force, for he had life in himself and in his own power, and had conquered the prince of death.—*Matthew Henry.*

The Emperor Theodosius, having on a great occasion opened all the prisons, and released his prisoners, is reported to have said, " And now, would to God I could open all the tombs, and give life to the dead !" But there is no limit to the mighty power and royal grace of Jesus. He opens the prisons of justice, and the prisons of death with equal and infinite ease : he redeems not the soul only, but the body.—*Dr. Stanford,*

CLXXXVIII

Acts ii. 37 —"Now when they heard this, they were pricked in their heart."

Peter's sermon was not a fine display of eloquence ;
Neither was it a very pathetic plea ;
Nor a loud but empty cry of " Believe, believe ! "
It was simple, a plain statement, and a soberly earnest argument.
Its power lay in the truthfulness of the speaker, his appeal to Scripture,
the concurrence of his witnessing brethren, and his own evident faith.
Above all, in the Holy Spirit who accompanied the word.

I. SAVING IMPRESSION IS A PRICK IN THE HEART.

To be cut to the heart is deadly (Acts v. 33) : to be pricked in the heart is saving.

1. All true religion must be of the heart.
    Without this—
        Ceremonies are useless. Is. i. 13.
        Orthodoxy of head is in vain. Jer. vii. 4.
        Profession and a constrained morality fail. 2 Tim. iii. 5.
        Loud zeal, excited and sustained by mere passion, is useless.
2. Impressions which do not prick the heart may even be evil.
    They may excite to wrath and opposition.
    They may lead to sheer hypocrisy.
    They may create and foster a spurious hope.
3. Even when such superficial impressions are good, they are transient ;
    and when they have passed away, they have often hardened
    those who have felt them for a season.
4. They will certainly be inoperative. As they have not touched the
    heart, they will not affect the life.
    They will not lead to confession and enquiry, nor
                    to repentance and change of life.
            to glad reception of the word, nor
            to obedience and steadfastness.
    Heart-work is the only real work.

II. WHAT TRUTHS PRODUCE SUCH A PRICK ?

1. The truth of the gospel has often, by the power of the Holy Ghost,
    produced an indelible wound in minds sceptical and opposed.
2. A sense of some one specially startling sin has frequently aroused
    the conscience. 2 Sam. xii. 7.

3. Instruction in the nature of the law, and the consequent heinousness of sin, has been blessed to that end. Rom. vii. 13.

4. The infinite wickedness of sin, as against the very being of God, is also a wounding thought. Ps. li. 4.

5. The exactness, severity, and terror of the judgment, and the consequent punishment of sin, are stirring thoughts. Acts xvi. 25-30.

6. The great goodness of God has led many to see the cruel wantonness of sin against him. Rom. ii. 4.

7. The death of Christ as a Substitute has often been the means of revealing the greatness of the sin which needed such an atonement, and of showing the true tendency of sin in having slain One so good and kind. Zech. xii. 10.

8. The abundant grace and love revealed in the gospel, and received by us are sharp arrows to wound the heart.

III. WHAT HAND MAKES THESE PAINFUL PRICKS?

1. The same hand which wrote the piercing truths also applies them

2. He is well acquainted with our hearts, and so can reach them.

3. He is the Quickener, the Comforter, the Spirit helping our infirmities, showing to us the things of Jesus : his fruit is love, joy, peace, etc. We need not utterly despair when wounded by such a tender Friend.

4. He is a Spirit to be sought unto, who acts in answer to his people's prayers. We turn for healing to him who pricks.

IV HOW CAN THESE PRICKS BE HEALED?

1. Only One who is divine can heal a wounded heart.

2. The only medicine is the blood of his heart.

3. The only hand to apply it is that which was pierced.

4. The only fee required is gladly to receive him.

Let us ask the question, "Men and brethren, what shall we do ? " Let us then obey the gospel, and believe in the Lord Jesus.

POINTED PASSAGES

Conversion is a work of *argument*, for the judgment is gained by the truth. It is a work of *conviction*, for the awakened are pricked in their hearts. It is a work of *enquiry*, for they ask, "What must we do to be saved ?" And, lastly, it is a work of *comfort*, for its subjects have received remission of sins, and the gift of the Holy Ghost.—*Joseph Sutcliffe.*

Peter, standing up, said : " We heard from him whom we know that

God has raised from the dead the promise of the Holy Ghost. He hath shed forth this; therefore let Jerusalem know assuredly that God hath made him Lord." I call that Peter's colossal "therefore." It is the strongest word in the first oration delivered in the defence of Christianity. The Holy Spirit was promised; he has been poured out; therefore, let those who receive him know that the power behind natural law—our Lord, who was, and is, and is to come—is now breathing upon the centuries as he breathed upon us symbolically. He hath shed forth this; therefore, let all men know assuredly that God hath made him Lord. When they who were assembled at Jerusalem at that time heard this "*therefore,*" they were pricked in the heart.—*Joseph Cook.*

Heart-work must be God's work. Only the great heart-Maker can be the great heart-Breaker.—*Richard Baxter.*

The Comforter came to convince the world. The Comforter! Does it seem a strange name to any of you, my brethren, for him who came on such an errand? Does it seem to you that, in convincing you of your sins, instead of comforting you, he must needs cover you with shame and confusion, and make you sink to the ground in unutterable anguish and dismay? No, dear brethren, it is not so. Those among you whom the Spirit has indeed convinced of sin, will avouch that it is not. They will avouch that, in convincing them of sin, he has proved that he is indeed the Comforter. If the conviction and consciousness of sin arises from any other source, then indeed it is enough to crush us with shame, and to harrow us with unimaginable fears. But when it comes from the Spirit of God, it comes with healing and comfort on its wings. Remember what the sin is, of which he convinces us—that we believe not in Christ. All other conviction of sin would be without hope; here the hope accompanies the conviction, and is one with it. If we have a deep and lively feeling of the sin of not believing in Christ, we must feel at the same time that Christ came to take away this along with all other sins.—*J. C. Hare.*

When a man is wounded with a barbed arrow, the agonies he suffers will cause him to toss about in pain; but the harder he strives to release the weapon from his flesh, the more does it become entangled in his sinews, the wound becomes enlarged, and the torture is increased. When, by the power of the Holy Spirit, a man is wounded on account of sin, and the arrows of the Most High tear his soul, he frequently tries to pluck them out with his own hand, but finds that the misery becomes worse, and the inflaming wounds at last cause faintness and despair. Only the Good Physician knows how to relieve the pain without tearing and festering the spirit.—*Handbook of Illustration.*

Acts iv. 14 —"And beholding the man which was healed standing with them, they could say nothing against it."

The rulers and elders were opposed to Peter and John.

It is no new thing for the gospel to be opposed.

Nor a strange thing for the great, the official, the powerful, and the influential to be foremost in such opposition.

The opposition of ungodly men is—

Natural, seeing that the heart of man is depraved.

Endurable, since our Lord and his apostles suffered it.

Harmless, if we commit the case to God.

Overruled for good by divine grace and wise providence.

The best and perhaps the only way to silence opposition is by exhibiting the blessed results which follow from the gospel.

Those who would say *anything* if they could, can say *nothing* of what they would, when they see before their eyes the cures wrought by the word of the Lord Jesus. "The man that was healed" is our best apologist. Better than Paley's "Evidences," or Butler's "Analogy," is the proof given by results.

I. THE GOSPEL IS VINDICATED BY ITS RESULTS.

1. On a broad scale in nations. England, the islands of the Pacific, Jamaica, Madagascar, etc.

2. In individual conversions from open sin. Some of the worst of men have become clear instances of the purifying power of the gospel.

3. In restoring to hope the comfortless and despairing. Very marvellous is its efficacy in the direction of healing mental maladies.

4. In elevating saints above selfish aims and designs, and inducing heroic consecrations. The biographies of gracious men and women are demonstrations of the divine power of the Word.

5. In sustaining character under fierce temptation. Wonderful is the preserving salt of grace amid surrounding putrefaction.

6. In holy and happy death-beds. These are plentiful throughout history, among all ranks ; and they never fail to convince the candid.

Many another catalogue of results might be made.

Many a man is unable to be an infidel because of what he has seen in his mother, wife, or child.

II. Gospel-works and workers must look for like vindication.

Nowadays men ask for results : the tree must bear fruit, or the cry is, "Cut it down." We do not shrink from this test.

1. The minister must find in his converts a proof of his call, and a defence of his doctrines, methods, peculiarities, etc.
2. A society, college, or institution must stand or fall by its fruits.
3. The individual professor must abide the same test.
4. The church in any place, and the church on the largest scale, must be tried by similar methods.
5. Even our Lord himself loses or gains honour among men according as his followers behave themselves.

III. The gospel and its workers deserve vindication at our hands.

Those who are healed should boldly stand with Peter and John, as witnesses and fellow-workers.

This suggests a series of practical questions :—

1. Has it produced blessed results in us?
2. Have we come forward to stand with the preachers of it in evidence that it has wrought our cure? Are we continually witnessing to the truth and value of the Gospel of Christ?
3. Does the influence of the gospel upon us so continue and increase unto holiness of life as to be a credit to its influence?
4. Are there not points in our character which harm the repute of the gospel? Should not these be amended at once?
5. Could we not henceforth so live as more effectually to silence the opponents of the Word?

Let the Church plainly see that her converts are her best defence : they are, in fact, her reason for existence.

Let converts see the reason why they should come forward and declare their faith, and unite with the people of God.

Cases in Point

In the course of one of his journeys, preaching the word, Mr. Wesley went to Epworth. Having offered to assist the curate on the following day (Sunday), and his offer being refused, he took his stand upon his father's tombstone in the evening, and preached to the largest congregation Epworth had ever witnessed. This he did night after night. He preached also during his stay of eight days at several of the surrounding villages, where societies had been formed and a great work wrought among the people, and some of them had suffered for it. "Their angry neighbours," says Wesley, " had carried a whole waggon-load of these new heretics before a magistrate. But when he asked wnat they had done, there was a deep silence ; for it was a point their conductors had forgotten. At length one said, 'They pretended to be better than other people, and prayed from morning to night'; and another said, 'They have *convarted* my wife. Till she went among them she had such a tongue ! and now she is as quiet as a lamb !' 'Take them back, take them back,' replied the justice, and 'let them convert all the scolds in the town.'"—*Tyerman's Life of Wesley.*

Lord Peterborough, more famed for his wit than for his religion, when he had lodged with Fenelon, the Archbishop of Canterbury, was so charmed with his piety and beautiful character, that he said to him at parting, " If I stay here any longer I shall become a Christian in spite of myself." —*G. S. Bowes.*

A person who had expressed doubts whether the negroes received any real advantage by hearing the gospel, was asked whether he did not think one, named Jack, was better for the preaching. He replied, " Why, I must confess that he was a drunkard, a liar, and a thief; but certainly now he is a sober boy, and I can trust him with anything ; and since he has talked about religion I have tried to make him drunk, but failed in the attempt."—*Arvine.*

Certain gentlemen waited upon Rev. Matthew **Wilks to** complain of the eccentricities of his discourses. Wilks heard them through, and then produced a long list of names. "There," said the quaint divine, " all those precious souls profess to have found salvation through what you are pleased to call my whims and oddities. Can you produce a similar list from all the sober brethren you have been so much extolling?" This was conclusive : they withdrew in silence.

The behaviour of some professors has often given the wicked an opportunity to reproach religion. Lactantius reports, that the heathen were wont to say, " The Master could not be good, when his disciples were so bad." The malice of sinners is such that they will reproach the rectitude of the law, for the obliquity of their lives who swerve from it. Oh that your pure life did but hang a padlock upon their impure lips !—*William Secker.*

CXC

Acts xlii. 13 —"And at the second time Joseph was made known to his brethren."

There is a plain parallel between Joseph and Jesus, his brethren and ourselves.

Certain classes of real seekers do not at once find peace: they go to Jesus after a fashion, and return from him as they went.

Our fear is that they may grow indifferent or despairing.

Our hope is that they will go again, and before long discover the great secret, and find food for their souls.

To this end we would follow the track of Joseph's story, and use it as an allegory for the benefit of the seeker.

I. THERE IS A SOMETHING WHICH YOU DO NOT KNOW.

The sons of Israel did not know Joseph. Like them—

1. You have no idea of who and what Jesus is. Power and pity blend in him. He is far more than he seems.

2. You view him only as great, lordly, unapproachable; a great and stern governor and tax-master.

3. You do not know that he is your brother, one with you in nature, relationship, and love.

4. You cannot conceive how he loves; he yearns to make himself known; his heart is swollen big with compassion.

5. You cannot guess what he will do for you: all that he is and has shall be at your disposal.

Picture the Israelitish shepherds in the presence of the exalted Egyptian prince, as he stands veiled in mystery, girded with power, and surrounded with honour. Little could they imagine that this was Joseph their brother.

II. THERE IS A REASON WHY AT YOUR FIRST GOING YOU HAVE NOT LEARNED THIS.

Joseph was not made known to his brethren on their first journey: nor have you yet found out Jesus, so as to know his love.

1. You have not looked for him. The sons of Jacob went to Egypt for corn, not for a brother. You are looking for comfort, etc., not for the Saviour.

2. You have not yet felt your sin against Jesus, and he would bring you to repentance, even as Joseph brought his brethren to confess their great wrong.

3. You have not yet gone with your whole force. As the brothers left Benjamin at home, so have you left some faculty or capacity dormant, or chill, in your seeking for grace.

4. You will have a larger blessing through the delay ; and the Lord Jesus will in the most seasonable hour reveal himself, as Joseph did. Till then he refrains.

III. THERE IS GREAT HOPE IN YOUR GOING AGAIN TO HIM.

Joseph's brethren made a great discovery *the second time;* you are in similar circumstances to them. Go a second time ; for—

1. You must go or perish. There was corn only in Egypt, and there is salvation only in Christ.

2. Others have gone and speeded. All nations went to Egypt, and none were refused. Has Jesus cast out one ?

3. You have lingered too long already, even as did Israel's sons.

4. A welcome awaits you. Joseph longed to see his brethren, and Jesus longs to see you.

IV. THERE ARE FORECASTS OF WHAT WILL HAPPEN IF YOU GO.

The story lends itself to prophecy. As the sons of Israel fared with Joseph, so shall you fare with Jesus.

1. You will tremble in his presence.

2. He will bid you draw near.

3. He will comfort you by revealing himself to you.

4. He will bless and enrich you and send you home rejoicing, to fetch all your family to him.

5. He will rule all the world for your sake, and you shall be with him, and be nourished by him.

Let us hasten to go to our Saviour the second time.
Surely this is the season, for the Holy Ghost saith "to-day."

LINE UPON LINE

You take it hard, that you are not answered, and that Christ's door is not opened at your first knock. David must knock often : " O my God, I cry by day, and thou hearest not, and in the night season I am not silent": Psa. xxii. 2. The Lord's Church must also wait: "And when I cry and shout, he shutteth out my prayer " : Lam. iii. 8. Sweet Jesus, the heir of all, prayed with tears and strong cries, once, " O my Father "; again, "O my Father "; and the third time, " O my Father", ere he was heard. Wait on : die praying : faint not.

It is good to have the heart stored with sweet principles concerning Christ and his love, so as to rest in hope though the Lord heareth not at the first. He is Christ, and therefore he will answer a sinner's cry ere long. It is but Christ's outside that is unkind.—*Samuel Rutherford.*

A man who had long been seeking religion in a half-hearted way, one day lost his pocket-book. He said to his wife: "I know it is in the barn; I had it after I went there, and before I left it was gone. I am going back to find it; and find it I will, if I have to move every straw." Such seeking soon secured the prize, and enabled his wife so clearly to illustrate the way to seek Jesus, that the man soon found him also, and rejoiced in a full salvation.

The last time I preached upon the matter of decision in religion was in old Farwell Hall. I had been for five nights preaching upon the life of Christ. I took him from the cradle, and followed him up to the judgment hall, and on that occasion I consider I made as great a blunder as ever I made in my life. If I could recall my act I would give this right hand. It was upon that memorable night in October, and the Court House bell was sounding an alarm of fire, but I paid no attention to it. We were accustomed to hear the fire bell often, and it didn't disturb us much when it sounded. I finished the sermon upon "What shall I do with Jesus?" And I said to the audience, "Now, I want you to take the question with you and think over it, and next Sunday I want you to come back and tell me what you are going to do with it." What a mistake! It seems now as if Satan was in my mind when I said this. Since then I have never dared to give an audience a week to think of their salvation. If they were lost they might rise up in judgment against me. "Now is the accepted time." We went down-stairs to the other meeting, and I remember when Mr. Sankey was singing, and how his voice rang when he came to that pleading verse :—

> "To-day the Saviour calls ;
> For refuge fly.
> The storm of justice falls,
> And death is nigh."

After our meeting, on the way home, seeing the glare of flames, I said to my companion, "This means ruin to Chicago." About one o'clock, Farwell Hall went, soon the church in which I had preached went down, and everything was scattered. I never saw that audience again. My friends, we don't know what may happen to-morrow; but there is one thing I do know, and that is, if you take the gift of God, even Christ Jesus, you are saved. What are you going to do with him to-night? Will you decide now?—*D. L. Moody.*

CXCI

Acts vii. 58 —"The witnesses laid down their clothes at a young man's feet, whose name was Saul."

The Holy Spirit records Stephen's martyrdom, but does not enter into details of his sufferings and death, as uninspired recorders would have been so apt to do.

The object of the Holy Ghost is not to indulge curiosity nor to harrow the feelings, but to instruct and move to imitation.

He tells us of the martyr's posture,—" He kneeled down"; his prayer, —" Lord, lay not this sin to their charge"; and his composure,—" he fell asleep."

Upon each of these points volumes might be written.

Our attention is now called to the incident of Saul's being present. This supplies us with—

I. A SUGGESTED CONTRAST. Stephen and Saul.

These were both highly earnest, fearless men.

Yet at this time they were wide as the poles asunder.

1. Stephen spiritual; giving in his address great prominence to the spiritual nature of religion, and the comparative insignificance of its externals. See verses 48-50.

Saul superstitious, worshipping form and ritual, full of reverence for the temple and the priests, and so forth.

2. Stephen, a humble believer in the Lord Jesus, saved by faith alone. Saul, a self-righteous Pharisee, as proud as he could live.

3. Stephen, defending and vindicating the gospel of Jesus. Saul, giving his countenance, his vote, his assistance in the persecution of the servant of the Lord Christ.

Enquire if a Saul is now present. Call him forth by name.

Have you been a *consenting* party to the persecution of good men?

Have you thus copied this young man Saul?

You do not object to making Christian men the theme of ridicule.

You smile when you hear such ridicule.

By your indecision in religion you aid and abet the adversary.

In these ways the witnesses lay down their clothes at your feet, and you are their accomplice.

Oh, that grace may yet convert you!

II. A SINGULAR INTRODUCTION TO TRUE RELIGION.

Many have been brought to God by means somewhat similar.

The young man, whose name was Saul, met with the religion of Jesus in the person of Stephen, and thus he saw it with the following surroundings :—

1. The vision of a shining face.
2. The hearing of a noble discourse.
3. The sight of a triumphant death.

These did not convert Saul, but they made it harder for him to be unconverted, and were, no doubt, in after days thought of by him.

Let us so introduce religion to men, that the memory of its introduction may be worth their retaining.

III. A REMARKABLE INSTANCE OF THE LORD'S CARE FOR HIS CHURCH.

The apostolical succession was preserved in the church.

1. Stephen's death was a terrible blow to the cause; but at that moment his successor was close at hand.
2. That successor was in the ranks of the enemy.
3. That successor was far greater than the martyr, Stephen, himself.

There is no fear for the church : her greatest champions, though as yet concealed among her enemies, will be called in due time.

The death of her best advocates may assist in the conversion of others.

IV. A GRACIOUS MEMORIAL OF REPENTED SIN.

Did not Paul give Luke this information concerning himself? and cause it to be recorded in the Acts of the Apostles?

It was well for Paul to remember his sin before conversion.

It will be well for us to remember ours.

1. To create and renew feelings of humility.
2. To inflame love and zeal.
3. To deepen our love to the doctrines of sovereign grace.
4. To make us hopeful and zealous for others.

Let dying Stephen be cheered by the hope of young Saul's salvation.

Let wicked young Saul repent of his wrong to Stephen.

OBSERVANDA

A Spanish painter, in a picture of Stephen conducted to the place of execution, has represented Saul as walking by the martyr's side with melancholy calmness. He consents to his death from a sincere, though mistaken, conviction of duty : and the expression of his countenance is strongly contrasted with the rage of the baffled Jewish doctors and the ferocity of the crowd who flock to the scene of bloodshed. Literally considered, such a representation is scarcely consistent either with Saul's conduct immediately afterwards, or with his own expressions concerning himself at the later periods of his life. But the picture, though historically incorrect, is poetically true. The painter has worked according to the true idea of his art in throwing upon the persecutor's countenance the shadow of his coming repentance. We cannot dissociate the martyrdom of Stephen from the conversion of Paul. The spectacle of so much constancy, so much faith, so much love, could not be lost. It is hardly too much to say with Augustine, that " the church owes Paul to the prayer of Stephen."—*Conybeare and Howson.*

Here first comes in view an individual destined to be the most extraordinary character in the church of God. Had a prophet stood near on this occasion, and said, " Ah ! Saul, you will by-and-by be stoned for the same profession, and die a martyr in the same cause"; he would have been filled with surprise and indignation, and have exclaimed, " What, is thy servant a dog, that he should do this thing?" —*William Jay.*

As soon as Satan heard of the conversion of Saul, he ordered the devils into deep mourning.—*John Ryland, Senior.*

Among the leaders of the great revival of the eighteenth century were Captain Scott and Captain Toriel Joss, the former a captain of dragoons, the latter a sea-captain. Both became famous preachers. Whitefield said of them, " God, who sitteth upon the flood, can bring a shark from the ocean, and a lion from the forest, to show forth his praise."

The following lines by *William Hone,* author of the " Every-day Book," were written to describe his own experience—

> The proudest heart that ever beat
>   Hath been subdued in me ;
> The wildest will that ever rose
> To scorn thy cause, and aid thy foes,
>   Is quell'd, my God, by thee.
>
> Thy will, and not my will, be done ;
>   My heart be ever thine ;
> Confessing thee, the mighty Word,
> My Saviour Christ, my God, my Lord,
>   Thy cross shall be my sign.

Might they not have been written by the young man, " whose name was Saul "?

CXCII

Acts xiii. 26 —"**To you is the word of this salvation sent.**"

Paul and Barnabas first preached the gospel to the seed of Abraham.
These Jews contradicted and blasphemed, and therefore, in verse 46,
the servants of the Lord boldly exclaimed, "We turn to the
Gentiles." A blessed turning this for you and for me !

Herein is a warning to ourselves, lest we refuse the gospel, and find it
taken from us, and sent to others.

At this moment, to our hearers we earnestly say, " To you is the word
of this salvation sent."

Let us then consider—

I. WHAT IS THE WORD OF THIS SALVATION ?

1. It is the testimony that Jesus is the promised Saviour. Verse **23.**

2. The word which promises forgiveness to all who exhibit repentance
   of sin, and faith in the Lord Jesus. Verses 38, 39.

3. In a word, it is the proclamation of perfect salvation, through the
   risen Saviour. Verses 32, 33.

It is comparable to a *word* for conciseness and simplicity.

It is a word, as being spoken by God, and as being his present utterance even at this moment.

It is a word; for it reveals Him who is truly " the Word."

It is a word *of salvation ;* for it declares, describes, presents, and
presses home salvation.

It is a word *sent,* for the Gospel dispensation is a mission of mercy
from God, the Gospel is a message, Jesus is the Messiah, and the Holy
Ghost himself is *sent* to work salvation among men.

II. IN WHAT MANNER IS THE GOSPEL SENT TO YOU ?

1. In the general commission, which ordains that it be preached to
   every creature.

2. In the fact that the gospel is preached in our land, the Bible is in
   every house, and the word is proclaimed in our streets.

3. In the providence which has brought you this day to hear the
   word. Very specially may you be sent to the preacher, the
   preacher sent to you, and the special message be sent through
   the preacher to you.

4. In the peculiar adaptation of it to your case, character, and
   necessity. A medicine which suits your disease is evidently
   meant for you.

5. In the power which has attended it, while you have been hearing it, though you may have resisted that power.

It would be a sad thing if we had to single out even one, and say,—"This word is *not* sent to you"; but we are under no such painful necessity.

III. IN WHAT POSITION DOES IT PLACE YOU?

In a position—

1. Of singular favour. Prophets and kings died without hearing what you hear. Matt. xiii. 16.

2. Of notable indebtedness to martyrs and men of God, in past ages, and in these days; for these have lived and died to bring you the gospel.

3. Of great hopefulness; for we trust you will accept it and live.

4. Of serious responsibility; for if you neglect it, how will you escape? Heb. ii. 3.

It puts it out of your power to remain unaffected by the gospel.

It must either save you, or increase your condemnation.

IV. IN WHAT MANNER WILL YOU TREAT THIS WORD?

1. Will you decidedly and honestly refuse it? This would be a terrible determination; but the very idea of so doing might startle you into a better mind.

2. Will you basely and foolishly delay your reply? This is a very dangerous course, and many perish in it.

3. Will you play the hypocrite, and pretend to receive it, while in your heart you reject it?

4. Will you act the part of the temporary convert?

5. Will you not rather accept the word of salvation with delight?

Suppose the gospel should be taken from you by your removal to a place where it is not preached, or by the death of the minister whom you so greatly esteem. It would be just. It may happen. It has happened to others. Refuse the heavenly message no longer, lest your day of grace should end in an eternity of woe.

PERSONALITIES

A minister having to preach in the city gaol, was accompanied by a young man of fine mind and cultivated manners, but who was not a Christian. As the minister looked at the audience, he preached to them Jesus with so much earnestness as deeply to impress his companion. On their return home, the young man said, " The men to whom you preached to-day must have been moved by the utterance of such truth. Such preaching cannot fail to influence." "My dear young friend," answered the minister, "were *you* influenced? Were you impelled by the words you heard to-day to choose God as your portion?" "You were not preaching to me, but to your convicts," was quickly answered. "You mistake. I was preaching to you as much as to them. You need the same Saviour as they. For all there is but one way of salvation. Just as much for you as for these poor prisoners was the message of this afternoon. Will you heed it?" The word so faithfully spoken was blessed of God.

Jesus said, "Preach the gospel to every creature." I can imagine Peter was asking him: "What, Lord! shall we offer salvation to the men who crucified you?" And I can imagine Jesus answering him: "Yes, Peter, I want you to preach my gospel to everybody, beginning at Jerusalem. Proclaim salvation to the men who crucified me. Peter, I'd like you to find that man who put the crown of thorns on my head. Tell him, if he'll take salvation as a gift he shall have a crown of glory from me, and there shan't be a thorn in it. Look up that Roman soldier who thrust that spear into my side, to my very heart, and tell him that there's a nearer way to my heart than that. My heart is full of love for his soul. Proclaim salvation to him."—*D. L. Moody.*

To whom is it that the God of salvation sent "the word of salvation"? He sent it to all sinners that hear it. It is a word that suits the case of sinners; and therefore is it sent to them. If it be enquired, for what *purpose* is it sent to sinners? . . . . . It is sent as a word of *pardon* to the condemned sinner. Hence may every condemned sinner take hold of it, saying, This word is sent to me. It is sent as a word of *peace* to the rebellious sinner. It is sent as a word of *life* to the dead. It is a word of *liberty* to the captives, of *healing* for the diseased, of *cleansing* to the polluted. It is a word of *direction* to the bewildered, and of *refreshment* to the weary. It is sent as a *comforting* word to the disconsolate; and as a *drawing* word and a *strengthening* word to the soul destitute of strength. It is sent, in short, as a *word of salvation*, and *all sorts* of salvation and redemption to the lost soul, saying, "Christ came to seek and to save that which was lost."—*Condensed from Ralph Erskine.*

CXCIII

𝕬cts xix. 18—20 —" 𝕬nd many that believed came, and confessed, and shewed their deeds.

"𝕸any of them also which used curious arts brought their books together, and burned them before all men : and they counted the price of them, and found it fifty thousand pieces of silver.

" So mightily grew the word of God and prevailed."

This last verse is a despatch from the seat of war announcing a glorious victory for the royal arms.

Past triumphs of the gospel may be used as encouragements.

We, too, shall see the Word of God grow and prevail ; for—

> The gospel is the same as ever.
> The human race is unchanged at heart.
> The sins to be overcome are the same.
> The Holy Spirit is just as mighty to convince and renew.

The trophies of victory may be expected to be the same.

Men, magic, books, and the love of money shall all be subdued.

Let us turn aside to see—

I. THE WORD OF GOD PLANTED.

Planted it was, or it could not have grown.

The work proceeded in the following fashion—

1. Certain disciples were further enlightened, aroused, and led to seek a higher degree of grace. This was an admirable beginning, and revivals thus commenced are usually lasting.

2. These became obedient to an ordinance which had been overlooked (verse 5), and also received the Holy Ghost, of whom they had heard nothing : two great helps to revival.

3. A bold ministry proclaimed and defended the truth.

4. Opposition was aroused. This is always a needful sign. God is not at work long without the devil working also.

5. Deceitful counterfeiting commenced, and was speedily ended in the most remarkable manner.

6. Paul preached, pleaded, made the gospel to sound forth, and on departing could say, "I am pure from the blood of all men."

Read this and the following chapter, and see how three years were well spent in planting the church at Ephesus.

II. The word of God growing.

"So mightily grew the word of God." The measure of it was seen—

1. In a church formed with many suitable elders.
2. In a neighbourhood fully aware of the presence of the gospel among them ; for it touched them practically ; so much so, that important trades were affected.
3. In a people converted, and openly confessing their conversion.
4. In a general respect paid to the faith. Even those who did not obey it, yet yielded it homage and owned its power.

Here we see Paul's work and God's work. Paul laboured diligently in planting, and God made it to grow : yet it was all of God.

Is the word of God growing among us ? If not, why not ?

It is a living seed, and should grow.

It is a living seed, and will grow unless we hinder it.

III. The word of God prevailing.

Growth arouses opposition ; but where the word grows with inward vitality it prevails over outward opposition.

The particular proof of prevalence here given is the burning of magical books.

1. Paul does not appear to have dwelt continually upon the evil habit of using magical arts ; but gospel light showed the guilt of witchcraft, and providence cast contempt on it.
2. The sin being exposed, it was confessed by those who had been guilty of it, and by those who had commenced its study.
3. Being confessed, it was renounced altogether, and, though there was no command to that effect, yet in a voluntary zeal of indignation the books were burned. This was right because—

If sold, they would do harm.

They were so detestable that they deserved burning.

Their public burning lighted up a testimony.
4. Their destruction involved expense, which was willingly incurred, and that expense gave weight to the testimony.

No other proof of power in our ministry will equal that which is seen in its practical effect upon our hearers' lives.

Will you who attend our preaching see to it that you purge yourselves from all filthiness of the flesh and of the spirit ?

SPARKS,

It's a blessed time in a soul, it's a blessed time in a family, it's a blessed time in a congregation, it's a blessed time in a country—when the word of God grows mightily and prevails . . . . . It's a blessed time when open sinners are seen leaving their sins and seeking the Saviour; when men are seen giving up their unholy gains; when tavern-keepers take down their signs and burn them—when they give up their licenses; and it's a blessed time when card-players throw away their cards and take the Bible instead.   It's a blessed time when the lovers of gaudy dress take their gaudy dresses and destroy them.—*Robert Murray M'Cheyne.*

The gospel, like a plant of great vigour, will grow almost among stones.   Thus have I seen it to grow among hypocrites, formalists, and worldlings; and I have seen it laying hold of one, and another, and, indeed, of many, however untoward the surrounding soil.   "So mightily grew the word of God and prevailed."

When the leaven of the gospel begins to work, there will be no need of a train of arguments to prove how inexpedient, how utterly unworthy it is for a Christian to turn aside after the vain amusements and trifling books used by the world : "Ephraim shall say, What have I to do any more with idols?"   What have I to do with black arts, or dealing with a lie ?   Those who first trusted in Christ were willing to forsake all and follow him.   The grace of the gospel produces a new taste—it alters everything about us,—our friends, our pursuits, our books, &c.— *Richard Cecil.*

Agesilaus, when he saw the usurer's bonds and bills blazing in the fire, said, " I never saw a better or a brighter fire in all my life !" and it were heartily to be wished that all scandalous, blasphemous, and seditious books and pamphlets were on the fire, too.—*John Spencer.*

Yes, God blessed the self-denial, and gave them compensation—and a compensation, too, remarkably appropriate.   They who burned books, obtained books.   They burned books for Christ, and they received books from him.   Have you never heard of Paul's Epistle to the Ephesians ? Do you recollect no such letter as one from the Saviour " to the Angel of the church at Ephesus"?—*T. R. Stevenson.*

The Earl of Rochester, of whom it has been said that he was " a great wit, a great scholar, a great poet, a great sinner, and a great penitent," left a strict charge to the person in whose custody his papers were, to burn all his profane and lewd writings, as being only fit to promote vice and immorality, by which he had so highly offended God, and shamed and blasphemed the holy religion into which he had been baptized.

CXCIV

Acts xxvi. 14 —" Saul, Saul, why persecutest thou me? it is hard for thee to kick against the pricks."

Jesus even out of heaven speaks in parables, according to his wont.
To Paul he briefly utters the parable of the rebellious ox.

Note the tenderness of the appeal: it is not, " Thou art harming me by thy persecutions," but, " Thou art wounding thyself." He saith not, "it is hard for *me*," but "hard for *thee*."

May the Lord thus speak in pity to those who are now resisting his grace, and thus save them from wounding themselves.

Listen attentively to the simple comparison, and observe—

I. THE OX. A fallen man deserves no higher type.

    1. You are acting like a brute beast, in ignorance and passion. You are unspiritual, thoughtless, unreasonable.

    2. Yet God values you more than a man does an ox.

    3. Therefore he feeds you, and does not slay you.

    4. You are useless without guidance, and yet you are unwilling to submit to your Master's hand.

    5. If you were but obedient you might be useful, and might find content in your service.

    6. You have no escape from the choice of either to obey or to die, and it is useless to be stubborn.

II. THE OX-GOAD. You have driven the Lord to treat you as the husbandman treats a stubborn ox.

    1. The Lord has tried you with gentle means, a word, a pull of the rein, etc. : by parental love, by tender admonitions of friends and teachers, and by the gentle promptings of his Spirit.

    2. Now he uses the more severe means—
        Of solemn threatening by his law.
        Of terrors of conscience, and dread of judgment.
        Of loss of relatives, children, friends.
        Of sickness, and varied afflictions.
        Of approaching death, with a dark future beyond it.

    3. You are feeling some of these pricks, and cannot deny that they are sharp. Take heed lest worse things come upon you.

III. THE KICKS AGAINST THE GOAD. These are given in various ways by those who are resolved to continue in sin.

    1. There are early childish rebellions against restraint.

2. There are sneers at the gospel, at ministers, at holy things.

3. There are wilful sins against conscience and light.

4. There are revilings and persecutions against God's people.

5. There are questionings, infidelities, and blasphemies.

IV. THE HARDNESS OF ALL THIS TO THE OX. It hurts itself against the goad, and s .ffers far more than the driver designs.

1. In the present. You are unhappy : you are full of unrest and alarm, you are increasing your chastisement, and fretting your heart.

2. In the best possible future. You will feel bitter regrets, have desperate habits to overcome, and much evil to undo. All this if you do at last repent and obey.

3. In the more probable future. You are preparing for yourself increased hardness of heart, despair, and destruction.

Oh, that you would know that no possible good can come of kicking against God, who grieves over your infatuations !

Yield to the discipline of your God.

He pities you now, and begs you to consider your ways.

It is Jesus who speaks ; be not so brutish as to refuse him that speaks from heaven.

You may yet, like Saul of Tarsus, become grandly useful, and plough many a field for the Lord Jesus.

STRIKING THOUGHTS

Did not Lord Byron feel the sharpness of the goad when he exclaimed, concerning the gospel, " The worst of it is, I believe it " ?

You have heard of the sword-fish. It is a very curious creature, with a long and bony beak, or sword, projecting in front of its head. It is also very fierce, attacking other fishes that come in its way, and trying to pierce them with its sword. The fish has sometimes been known to dart at a ship in full sail, with such violence as to pierce the solid timbers. But what has happened ? The silly fish has been killed outright by the force of its own blow. The ship sails on just as before, and the angry sword-fish falls a victim to its own rage. But how shall we describe the folly of those who, like Saul of Tarsus, oppose the cause of Christ ? They cannot succeed : like the sword-fish, they only work their own destruction.—*Illustrative Teaching*.

Dr. John Hall, in one of his sermons, compared the attacks of infidelity upon Christianity to a serpent gnawing at a file. As he kept on gnawing, he was greatly encouraged by the sight of the growing pile of chips ; till feeling pain, and seeing blood, he found that he had been wearing his own teeth away against the file, but the file was unharmed.

> Oh cursèd, cursèd Sin ! Traitor to God,
> And ruiner of man! Mother of Woe,
> And Death, and Hell !
>
> *Pollok.*

Cowper describes Voltaire as—
> " An infidel in health, but what when sick ?
> Oh—then a text would touch him at the quick."

Men complain of their circumstances, and cry, " *This* is hard—hard as for the bird of plumage to beat against the wires of its cage." Nay, harder far than that. It is hard for loss of time, for loss of temper, for loss of strength, for loss of trusting, loving obedience ; and because *no* good can come of it, no success can be gained in the vain, Utopian, and worse than foolish struggle. Let every man struggle to improve *himself,* and he will not fail to improve his lot also. But let him never " kick " against his earthly lot ; for so, if hurt at all, he hurts himself the more. He " kicks against the pricks."—*Pulpit Commentary.*

The Spirit of God can make use of any agency to bring sinners to repentance and faith in the Redeemer. Commenting once upon the words, " The ox knoweth his owner, and the ass his master's crib ; but Israel doth not know, my people doth not consider," the speaker sought to impress upon his people how strangely guilty the human heart is, despising the goodness of God, and forgetting his very existence. Three or four days after, a farmer, who had been present, was giving provender to his cattle, when one of his oxen, evidently grateful for his care, fell to licking his bare arm. Instantly, with this simple incident, the Holy Spirit flashed conviction on the farmer's mind. He burst into tears, and exclaimed, " Yes, it is all true. How wonderful is God's word ! This poor dumb brute is really more grateful to me than I am to God, and yet I am in debt to him for everything. What a sinner I am !" The lesson had found its way to his heart, and wrought there effectually to lead him to Christ.

CXCV

Acts xxviii. 2 —"And the barbarous people shewed us no little kindness: for they kindled a fire, and received us every one, because of the present rain, and because of the cold."

Here was an early Shipwrecked Mariners' Society.

Among rough people there is much of genuine kindness.

Let not people of a gentler mould, greater education, and larger possessions, come behind them in deeds of kindness.

Their kindness was thoroughly practical. We have too much of "Be ye warmed," and too little kindling of fires.

There may be spiritual as well as physical cold, and for this last the kindling of a fire is needed.

This is our present subject.

I. THAT WE ARE VERY APT TO BE COLD.

1. The world is a cold country for gracious men.

2. By reason of our inbred sin, we are cold subjects, and far too apt to be lukewarm, or frozen.

3. Cold seasons also come, when all around lies bound in frost. Ministers, churches, saints, are too often cold as ice.

4. Cold corners are here and there, where the sun seldom shines. Some good men live in such cold harbours.

5. Chilling influences are now abroad. Modern thought, worldliness, depression in trade, depreciation of prayer, etc.

If we yield to the power of cold, we become first uncomfortable, next inactive, and then ready to die.

II. THAT THERE ARE MEANS OF WARMTH.

1. The Word of God is as a fire. Heard or read, it tends to warm the heart.

2. Private, social, and family prayer. This is as coals of juniper.

3. Meditation and communion with Jesus. "While I was musing the fire burned": Ps. xxxix. 3. "Did not our heart burn within us, while he talked with us by the way?" Luke xxiv. 32.

4. Fellowship with other Christians. Malachi iii. 16.

5. Doing good to others. Job prayed for his friends, and then his captivity was turned. Job. xlii. 10.

6. Returning to first love and doing first works, would bring back old warmth. Rev. ii. 4, 5.

Let us get to these fires ourselves, lest we be frost-bitten and benumbed.

III. That we should kindle fires for others.

We need the fire of revival, seeing so many are washed upon our shores in dying circumstances.

Concerning a true revival, let it be remembered that it both resembles the fire in the text, and differs from it.

1. It must be lighted under difficulties,—"because of the present rain." The sticks are wet, the hearth is flooded, the atmosphere is damp. It is not easy to make a fire in such circumstances; and yet it must be done.

2. The fire we need cannot, however, be kindled by barbarians: the flame must come from above.

3. Once get the flame, the fire begins with littles. Small sticks are good for kindling.

4. It is well to nourish the flame by going down on your knees, and breathing upon it by warm and hearty supplications.

5. It must be fed with fuel. Think of the great Paul picking up a bundle of sticks. Let each one bring his share.

6. This fire must be kindled for "every one." We must not be content till all the shivering ones are comforted.

7. The fire will be of great service, and yet it may warm into life more than one viper. Thank God, the fire which revived the creature into venomous life will also destroy it.

What can we each do towards this fire? Can we not each one either kindle or feed the fire? Bring a stick.

Let no one damp the flame.

Let us pray.

KINDLING

How to maintain spiritual warmth. Philip Henry's advice to his daughter was: "If you would keep warm in this cold season (January, 1692), take these four directions : 1. Get into the sun. Under his blessed beams there are warmth and comfort. 2. Go near the fire. ' Is not my word like a fire?' How many cheering passages are there ! 3. Keep in motion and action—stirring up the grace and gift of God that is in you. 4. Seek Christian communion. ' How can one be warm alone?' "—*Feathers for Arrows.*

"Ane stick 'll never burn ! Put more wood on the fire, laddie ; ane stick 'll never burn!" my old Scotch grandfather used to say to his boys. Sometimes, when the fire in the heart burns low, and love to the Saviour grows faint; it would grow warm and bright again, if it could only touch another stick. . . . . What we need, next to earnest prayer to God and communion with Christ, is communion with each other. "Where two or three are gathered together," the heart burns; love kindles to a fervent heat. Friends, let us frequent the society of those who are fellow-pilgrims with us to Canaan's happy land. "Ane stick 'll never burn," as a great generous pile will be sure to.—*Anon.*

I will tell you a story, which I have from very good hands, of two very eminent men, both for learning and piety, in the beginning of the last century, one of them a great prelate (indeed, a primate), and the other a Churchman of great note. These two eminent men often met together to consult upon the interests of learning and the affairs of the church; and when they had despatched that business, they seldom parted from one another without such an encounter as this: "Come, good doctor," saith the bishop, "let us talk now a little of Jesus Christ"; or, on the other side, said the doctor, "Come, my Lord, let me hear your Grace talk of the goodness of God with your wonted eloquence; let us warm one another's hearts with heaven, that we may better bear this cold world." Here is now an example of holy conference without a preface and yet without exception; a precedent easy to imitate wherever there is a like spirit of piety. A few such men would put profaneness out of countenance, and turn the tide of conversation.—*Goodman.*

> See how great a flame aspires,
> Kindled by a spark of grace!
> Jesus' love the nations fires,
> Sets the kingdoms in a blaze:
> To bring fire on earth he came,
> Kindled in some hearts it is:
> Oh that all might catch the flame,
> All partake the glorious bliss!
>
> *C. Wesley.*